Cuba's Aborted Reform

Published in cooperation with the Cuban Research Institute
at Florida International University

Florida A&M University, Tallahassee
Florida Atlantic University, Boca Raton
Florida Gulf Coast University, Ft. Myers
Florida International University, Miami
Florida State University, Tallahassee
University of Central Florida, Orlando
University of Florida, Gainesville
University of North Florida, Jacksonville
University of South Florida, Tampa
University of West Florida, Pensacola

Para Joaquín M. Pérez-Fobler, con un saludo cordial

Carmelo

Washington DC May 1, 2006

Cuba's Aborted Reform

Socioeconomic Effects, International
Comparisons, and Transition Policies

Carmelo Mesa-Lago and Jorge F. Pérez-López

Para Joaquín — con muchos afectos —

Jorge

5/1/06

University Press of Florida

Gainesville · Tallahassee · Tampa · Boca Raton
Pensacola · Orlando · Miami · Jacksonville · Ft. Myers

10 09 08 07 06 05   6 5 4 3 2 1

Library of Congress Cataloging-in-Publication Data
Mesa-Lago, Carmelo, 1934–
Cuba's aborted reform: socioeconomic effects, international
comparisons, and transition policies/Carmelo Mesa-Lago
and Jorge F. Pérez-López.
p. cm.
Includes bibliographical references and index.
ISBN 0-8130-2868-X (alk. paper)
1. Cuba—Economic conditions—1959–1990. 2. Cuba—Economic
conditions—1990– 3. Cuba—Economic policy. 4. Cuba—Social
conditions—1959–. I. Pérez-López, Jorge F. II. Title.
HC 152.5.M467 2005
330.97291'064—dc22
2005042308

The University Press of Florida is the scholarly publishing agency
for the State University System of Florida, comprising Florida A&M
University, Florida Atlantic University, Florida Gulf Coast University,
Florida International University, Florida State University, University
of Central Florida, University of Florida, University of North Florida,
University of South Florida, and University of West Florida.

University Press of Florida
15 Northwest 15th Street
Gainesville, FL 32611-2079
http://www.upf.com

To my grandsons, Tomás and Matías
  CML

To Dan, Andrew, Tom, Anya, and Tonya
  JFPL

Contents

Tables

Preface

On January 1, 2005, Maximum Leader Fidel Castro started his 47th year in power. Now more than 78 years of age, Castro remains fully in control of the island's polity and military, despite rumors about his health and a fall in mid-October 2004 at a public event that resulted in a broken arm and badly shattered knee.

Fifteen years after the breakup of the socialist economic community and thirteen since the dissolution of the Soviet Union, the Cuban economy continues to struggle in an unending economic crisis, euphemistically referred to as the Special Period in Time of Peace (El Período Especial en Tiempo de Paz). Modest economic growth since the mid-1990s has not been sufficient to off-set the sharp drop in gross domestic product (GDP) and in standard of living that the population endured from 1989 to 1993.

With the economy in a free fall, between 1993 and 1996 the Cuban government put in place a number of measures that strengthened the role of the private sector in the economy. Among these pro-market reforms were the legalization of the use of foreign currencies, the promotion of foreign direct investment, the expansion of self-employment, the breakup of state farms and their conversion into cooperatives, and the establishment of private agricultural markets. These measures, undertaken reluctantly by the Cuban leadership, were sufficient to stop the contraction of GDP and bring about modest economic growth. Only two significant policy initiatives were taken in 1997–98, both of an administrative nature, a revamping of the banking system and promotion of a new enterprise management system, the *sistema de perfeccionamiento empresarial*.

Concerned that reforms that strengthened the private sector weakened their political control, the Cuban leadership not only aborted the modest market-oriented reforms of 1993–96, which had led to a partial socioeconomic recovery, but in 2003–4 took steps to reverse them, recentralizing the economy, eliminating the limited spaces opened to private economic activity, exerting increased control over hard currency transactions, and stepping up repressive measures on peaceful dissidents, civil rights activists, and other groups of citizens. As of 2005, Cuba has yet to return to the economic levels of the late 1980s.

While the economy remains in crisis, social inequities expand. The vaunted education and public health systems have been weakened by reductions in expenditures and an inability to import necessary products and services. Many social services have not recovered the level of access and quality that they had achieved prior to the economic crisis triggered by the collapse of the socialist camp. The unequal access of the population to foreign remittances has exacerbated social differences and widened the consumption gap between those who have access to foreign currencies and those who do not.

This book focuses on Cuban socioeconomic policies and performance since the collapse of the Soviet Union and the socialist countries. To put the recent period in context, we present an overview of socioeconomic policies and performance in the revolutionary period, and then analyze in detail the economic and social deterioration and incomplete recovery since 1990, compare Cuba's socioeconomic performance with that of other countries in Latin America and in the former Soviet camp, summarize the views of noted Cuban economists living on the island regarding the economic situation and policies necessary to break out of the crisis, and propose some socioeconomic policies that Cuban leaders might wish to put in place under two scenarios: a continuation of the socialist system or a change in political system.

In chapter 1 we examine Cuba's economic and social policies during the revolutionary period, 1959 to the present, focusing on ideological-economic cycles that have dominated Cuban policymaking. These cycles, driven by ideological tendencies of the leadership, alternatively shifted economic policies toward the market (pragmatist) or away from the market (idealist). Economic outcomes diverged significantly, deteriorating during idealist cycles and improving during pragmatist ones. We believe that the core reason why the leadership limited, slowed down, and eventually reversed pro-market policies and launched anti-market cycles—actions certain to bring about adverse economic performance—is the fear of losing political control as a result of decentralization of economic policymaking, expansion of the market and the private sector, and the subsequent surge in economic behavior independent of the state. Political logic, therefore, has trumped economic logic, even though the result has been the deterioration of economic conditions and standard of living. That Cuba aborted incipient economic reforms and has been entrenched in an idealist cycle since 1997—strengthened in 2003–4—does not augur well for the economic and social well-being of the Cuban population in the new century.

The disruption and eventual breaking of trade and economic relations with the former socialist community in the early 1990s propelled Cuba into a severe economic crisis, the Special Period in Time of Peace. In chapter 2 we examine Cuba's economic and social performance from 1990 through 2004, comparing the overall period with 1989 (the year before the crisis) and 1993 (the trough of the crisis). We examine the performance of selected macroeconomic, external-sector, physical output, and labor market and social security indicators. In addition, we compare the government's economic and social goals for 1998–2003 with actual performance, discuss the feasibility of 2004 goals, and summarize prominent Cuban economists' views on the current economic situation. Finally, we analyze in considerable detail the slowdown in economic growth that has occurred since 2001 and conclude that, although external factors contributed to it, its root cause has been politically motivated paralysis of essential structural reforms.

In chapter 3 we turn to social welfare, with an emphasis on how Cuba has performed in terms of delivery of social services and equality during the Special Period. This task is made particularly challenging by the dearth of statistical information on key variables such as income and wealth distribution, real wages, racial discrimination, distribution of remittances, and so on. We rely on the scarce figures available; proxy variables; and qualitative evaluations based on public documents, surveys, articles by experts published in Cuba and abroad, and interviews conducted by Mesa-Lago of recent émigrés and visitors from the island to document the deterioration in social welfare and growing socioeconomic disparities in Cuba from 1993 to 2004.

Chapters 4 and 5 provide an international comparative dimension to our analysis. In chapter 4, we analyze how Cuba's socioeconomic performance has been measured by a very prominent international comparative economic development yardstick, the Human Development Index (HDI), compiled and published annually by the United Nations Development Programme. We conclude that Cuba's relatively strong performance with respect to the HDI is the result of faulty data and methodological quirks that tend to prop up Cuba's HDI index rankings in spite of strong evidence from other sources—including official Cuban data—that contradicts such high rankings.

In chapter 5 we take a closer look at Cuba's economic and social development model, and its performance. We compare these with the models and performance of Chile and Costa Rica over the last 50 years. The choice of

these countries is deliberate, in order to contrast Cuba's socialist development model and authoritarian, single-party political system with the situa-
tions of two other countries in the region that have followed different paths:
for Chile, a neoliberal economic model and authoritarian military regime
that turned to democratic pluralism in 1990, and for Costa Rica, a mixed
economic model and pluralist political system.

The comparisons indicate that through 2000, Chile was the best performer with respect to economic growth. It was the worst with respect to
social development during the military dictatorship, but rose to second and
even tied Costa Rica for first place at certain times during democratic governments. Costa Rica was first with respect to social development and second
with respect to economic growth. Meanwhile, Cuba ranked at the bottom in
terms of economic growth and fell from first to middle or last place in social
development after 1990. Both the Chilean and Costa Rican models are highly
viable in the mid-term, although their future success could be enhanced by a
variety of policy actions. The Cuban model is the least viable of the three;
improving it would require a broad program of reforms, discussed in the
concluding chapter.

Finally, in chapter 6 we discuss conceptually the set of reforms that Cuba
must tackle to improve the challenging socioeconomic situation it currently
faces. First, we review some of the reform experiences of countries of central
and eastern Europe, the Baltic States, and the Commonwealth of Independent States (CIS, an association of former Soviet Union countries), identifying
transition strategies, results, and key variables that influenced these transition processes. We then examine Cuban economists' suggestions regarding
necessary changes *within* Cuba's socialist system and conclude that deeper
and more comprehensive measures that move Cuba faster toward a market
economy are necessary. We end this chapter with a discussion of reform measures that Cuba should take in order to overcome the ongoing economic crisis
under two transition scenarios: (1) under the continuation of the current
political system, although presuming a willingness to return to the moderate
reform path followed from 1993 to 1996; and (2) assuming a change in
political system and faster transition toward a market economy.

To the maximum extent possible, we have based our analysis on quantita-
tive, objective information in order to avoid the controversies that usually
accompany studies of Cuba. Working with official economic and social statistics is a hazardous task, however. Information on the methods that Cuban
statistical agencies use in compiling data is very sparse or lacking altogether;
definitions of statistical series are not always clear and change often; at certain times Cuba has used statistical methodologies that differ from those used
by most of the rest of the world; and there is always a concern that the

statistics could be manipulated or distorted to serve political ends. Our documented opinion based on many years of work with Cuban statistics is that the quantity and quality of Cuban economic and social statistics improved during the 1980s and again in the second half of the 1990s, when Cuba shifted the methodology for computing its national accounts from the system used by the socialist nations to the one used by nearly all other nations in the world. This step made it technically possible to compare Cuban measures of aggregate output (such as gross domestic product, GDP) with those of other countries.

We are however concerned about recent developments suggesting that some manipulation of key statistical series may be occurring. First, as we discuss in chapter 2, in 2001 Cuba changed its price basis for calculating macroeconomic indicators, particularly GDP, to a 1997 base. This is a routine procedure. Statistical offices periodically rebase their statistical series, and Cuba had been relying on statistics based on 1981 prices for more than 20 years. Normally, the current-price data should not be affected, but in 2001 Cuban officials published a new GDP series at constant prices going back to 1996 that differs by an average of 60% from the previous current price series for the years 1996–2001. As this discrepancy cannot be attributed to the change in price basis, some underlying methodological changes must have been made. Cuba's statistical yearbook for 2001 (ONE 2002) mentions in passing that the new GDP series provides better coverage of sectors such as financial services and insurance, housing services, tourism, and self-employment, but there is no precise information on the changes or on adjustments made to earlier data.

Second, it is clear that Cuban statisticians, perhaps pressured by government leaders, are manipulating macroeconomic statistics to make Cuba's dire economic situation seem less so in comparison with other nations. Thus, in 2002 and 2003 Fidel Castro criticized the conventional methodology used to estimate GDP by the United Nations and virtually all countries in the world. In his report to the National Assembly at the close of 2003, Minister of Economics and Planning José Luis Rodríguez not only reported a very high growth rate (2.6% compared to the planned rate of growth of 1.5%) based on the "conventional" GDP methodology, but also disclosed an even higher rate of growth (3.8%) based on a "new methodology" that adjusts the GDP data to account for the free services that the Cuban population receives. The methodology for this calculation has not been made public. More ominously, Rodríguez stated that Cuban statisticians are undertaking further adjustments to GDP statistics to take into account the purchasing power parity of the peso and that upward adjustments in growth rates can be anticipated. If analyzing Cuban economic performance was challenging with GDP computed following the conventional method, it will be more so in the future when and if these additional methodological changes are implemented.

Third, the obvious manipulation of unemployment statistics renders them useless as an indicator of labor market tightness. A lingering concern about Cuban unemployment statistics has been that they paint an erroneous picture of the labor market because they fail to account for the severe underemployment in the state sector. As we discuss in chapter 2, independent estimates suggest that underemployment may have been in the range of one-third of the labor force in the mid-1990s. But the more recent sharp declines in open unemployment rates—to 2.3% in 2003—are inconsistent with the overall economic situation and result from counting as employed persons who are working part-time in urban agriculture and former sugar industry workers who are undergoing reeducation and retraining, as well as keeping out of the labor force school dropouts who are enrolled in remedial programs.

Fourth, as we discuss in chapter 3, the behavior of higher education enrollment statistics in the 2002 statistical yearbook suggests statistical manipulation. Without explanation, higher education enrollment series for the academic years 1996/97 to 2000/1 reported in that source were changed, increasing in some disciplines by as much as three times and raising the overall higher education enrollment figures from 10% to 14% over the same period.

And fifth, official morbidity data are suspect because of the sudden disappearance in 2002 of contagious diseases that had peaked in the midst of the crisis, such as hepatitis, despite the persistence and aggravation of the deterioration in the nation's water and sewage infrastructure. In addition, venereal diseases (gonorrhea and syphilis) significantly decreased in the early 2000s according to official data, despite growing prostitution and scarcity of prophylactics and antibiotics. Furthermore, the series on maternal mortality published since 1959 was changed in 2000, with the new series excluding certain causes of mortality, thus resulting in figures 8 to 11 percentage points lower than the old series.

Acknowledgments

The authors gratefully acknowledge the authorization granted to reproduce in this volume materials from the following works by Carmelo Mesa-Lago: "Cuba in the Human Development Index in the 1990s," *Cuba in Transition* 11 (Washington D.C.: ASCE, 2002); *Growing Economic and Social Disparities in Cuba: Impact and Recommendations for Change* and *The Slowdown in the Cuban Economy in 2001–2003: External Causes or Domestic Malaise?* (Coral Gables: University of Miami, Institute for Cuban and Cuban-American Studies, Cuba Transition Project, 2002, 2003); *La economía y el bienestar social en Cuba a comienzos del siglo XXI* (Madrid: Editorial Colibrí, 2003); and "Economic and Ideological Cycles in Cuba: Policy and Performance, 1959–2002," in *The Cuban Economy*, edited by Archibald Ritter (Pittsburgh: University of Pittsburgh Press, 2004). For this book we have integrated all these materials, updated them to early 2005, and added new sections, tables, statistics, analysis, and bibliographical sources.

Valuable comments on previous versions of some chapters in the book were made by Claes Brundenius, Sergio Díaz-Briquets, Jorge Domínguez, Damián Fernández, Kristin Kleinjans, Manuel Madrid-Aris, Manuel Pastor Jr., Marifeli Pérez-Stable, Omar Everleny Pérez Villanueva, and the New York Office of the UN Human Development Report. Important materials or information were supplied by, among others, Uva de Aragón, Fabio Bertranou, Damián Fernández, Jesús García, Rex García, Guillermo Grenier, Thomas Manz, Reiner Radermacher, and Julia Valderrama. We take responsibility for what is said herein.

Abbreviations

ACP	Asian, Caribbean, and Pacific countries that benefit from economic associations with the European Union
ANPP	Asamblea Nacional del Poder Popular (National Asssembly of People's Power)
BCC	Banco Central de Cuba (Cuban Central Bank)
CACM	Central American Common Market
CADECA	Casa de Cambio (hard-currency exchange agency)
CD	certificate of deposit
CEE	Comité Estatal de Estadísticas (State Statistical Committee)
CIEM	Centro de Investigaciones de la Economía Mundial (Research Center on the World Economy)
CIS	Commonwealth of Independent States
CMEA	Council for Mutual Economic Assistance
CPI	consumer price index
CTC	Central de Trabajadores de Cuba (Cuban Workers Central)
EBRD	European Bank for Reconstruction and Development
ECLAC	Economic Commission for Latin America and the Caribbean
EU	European Union
GDP	gross domestic product
GDP p/c PPP US$	gross domestic product per capita, at purchasing-power parity exchange rate in U.S. dollars

GSP	global social product
HDI	Human Development Index
ICCAS	Institute for Cuban and Cuban-American Studies
IDB	Inter-American Development Bank
IFI	international financial institutions
ILO	International Labor Organization
IMF	International Monetary Fund
ISI	import substitution industrialization
MPS	material product system
NHS	Sistema Nacional de Salud (National Health System)
OAS	Organization of American States
ONE	Oficina Nacional de Estadísticas (National Statistical Office)
PCC	Partido Comunista de Cuba (Cuban Communist Party)
PDVSA	Petróleos de Venezuela (Venezuela's state oil corporation)
PPP	purchasing-power parity
S.A.	sociedad anónima (a limited liability quasi-private company)
SNA	system of national accounts
TRD	tienda de recaudación de divisas (a hard-currency shop)
UBPC	Unidad Básica de Producción Cooperativa (agricultural production cooperative)
UNDP	United Nations Development Programme
UNESCO	United Nations Educational, Scientific, and Cultural Organization
UNHDRO	United Nations Human Development Report Office
VAT	value-added tax

1

Half a Century of Economic and Social Policies in Socialist Cuba, 1959–2004

In this chapter we review Cuban economic and social policies since the Cuban Revolution, from 1959 to 2004. The chapter is divided into two sections. The first describes the nature of ideological-economic cycles and uses this technique to analyze Cuba's economic history for the period 1959–90. The second part does the same for 1991–2004, a time span during which Cuba suffered its most severe economic crisis since the start of the revolution. This crisis prompted the government to launch a series of market-oriented reforms in the early 1990s, but the reform process has been paralyzed since 1996 and was significantly reversed in 2003–4.

Ideological-Economic Cycles and Cuba's Economic Policies

A socialist economic system was introduced in the island in 1961 and continues today, albeit substantially transformed and without some key elements. During this period, Cuban economic policies have shifted five or six times, following a "vicious cycle" tendency. These cycles, driven by ideological tendencies of the leadership, have alternately shifted economic policies toward or away from the market, and economic outcomes have diverged significantly. For the lack of better terms, in a previous work Mesa-Lago (2000) labeled shifts away from the market as *idealist* policies, and movements toward the market as *pragmatist*.

Features of the Cycles

During idealist cycles, the leadership set unrealistic targets that eventually failed; for example, to reach within four years the highest industrial production per capita in the hemisphere, to accomplish a harvest of 10 million tons of sugar and stable annual production at twice that level thereafter, to create a "New Man" free from selfishness, and to attain self-sufficiency in food production. The economic failures raised the threat (real or perceived) of regime instability and prompted the political leadership to shift toward the market in order to maintain its control. Pragmatist cycles resulted in moderate economic growth and some improvements in living standards but also generated adverse social effects, such as higher socioeconomic inequality and unemployment. Once the political leadership felt that the regime regained stability through a pragmatist cycle, it launched an idealist cycle.

Economic logic suggests that because pragmatist cycles bring about overall positive economic outcomes, such policies should be fostered and strengthened. Yet this has not been the case, as movement toward the market entails delegation of economic power, decentralization in decision making, and emergence of independent economic agents that bring about a loss of government control. Political logic (maintaining political power) runs counter to economic logic and explains the return to idealist policies. Furthermore, moves toward the market increase inequality and unemployment and give rise to other effects unacceptable to the leadership, at least until the 1990s.

Most policy cycles in Cuba have lasted from five to seven years, creating instability and hindering long-term economic performance because no policy has been in effect for a sufficiently long time to allow full implementation, maturation, and reaping of results. During early pragmatist cycles, market reforms were introduced in a very cautious and timid manner. Their implementation became bolder—and more difficult to reverse—in more recent pragmatist cycles. In contrast, idealist cycles have become less radical over time and more difficult to reinstate.

President, Commander in Chief, and Maximum Leader Fidel Castro Ruz has played a crucial role in the generation of policy cycles. Despite some degree of political and economic institutionalization in Cuba over the last 46 years, Castro still wields considerable political power and makes the most important policy decisions. His long-standing proclivities for centralized decision making, collectivization of the means of production, egalitarianism, and mass mobilization predispose him against market-oriented policies. But he has not hesitated to adopt pragmatist stances when he has understood that they were necessary to preserve the regime and his power.

External factors, positive or negative, have also contributed to launching, sustaining, or terminating cycles. For example, the termination of Soviet aid was critical in shifting policies toward the market at the start of the 1990s. And the Cuban leadership's fear—real or imagined—that domestic political instability would open the door to U.S. intervention has played a key role in the launching of idealist cycles over the years.

Cycles, Policies, and Effects

During the 46 years of revolutionary government (1959–2004), we have identified six policy cycles: (1) 1959–66, although not easy to classify, was an idealist, away-from-the-market cycle that can be divided into three subcycles: market erosion, orthodox Soviet central planning, and debate over socialist models; (2) 1966–70 was a very strong idealist cycle corresponding to the adoption and radicalization by Castro of the Guevarist model; (3) 1971–85 was a pragmatist cycle characterized by the adoption of the Soviet model of timid (pre-Gorbachev) economic reform; (4)1986–90 was another idealist cycle, the so-called Rectification process; (5) 1991–96 saw the pragmatist and market-oriented Special Period in Time of Peace; and (6) 1997 to the present has been a weakly idealist cycle characterized by slowdown, eventual paralysis, and reversal of market-oriented reforms.

For each of the policy cycles, in the top panel of table 1 we examine changes in a set of eleven policies: (1) collectivization; (2) centralized decision making; (3) state budget; (4) foreign investment; (5) allocation of goods through rationing (rather than prices); (6) agricultural free markets; (7) self-employment; (8) voluntary (unpaid) work and labor mobilization; (9) egalitarianism; (10) moral rather than material incentives; and (11) free social services. Some of these policies are typically associated with idealist cycles (that is, a move away from the market), for instance, a rise in the degree of collectivization and of centralized decision making, an increase in voluntary work and mobilization, allocation of goods through rationing rather than market forces, and more extensive egalitarianism, moral incentives, and free social services. Other policies are associated with pragmatist cycles (that is, a move toward the market), such as creation and extensive use of agricultural free markets, self-employment, opening to foreign investment, decentralization in decision making, use of the state budget to control fiscal balance, reliance on markets rather than rationing to allocate goods, material incentives, and charging for some public services. The direction of changes in those policies is denoted with the following signs: ↑ for increase; ↓ for decrease; and ↔ for no change. In addition, "B" denotes the point in time when a policy begins to be implemented, "P" when its implementation reaches a peak, "E" when it ends, and "R" when it is reestablished.

We assume that Castro's views and decisions are the key domestic determinant of economic policy changes. There has been a debate in the literature

Table 1. Cuban Economic Cycles, Policies, External Factors, and Effects, 1959–2004

Cycles	1959–66	1966–70	1971–85	1986–90	1991–93/ 1994–96	1997–2004
Policies						
Collectivization	↑	↑	↔↓	↑P	↓	↔
Centralized decision making	↑	↑	↓	↑	↓	↑
State budget	↔	↓E	R↑	↓	↑P	↔
Foreign investment	↓	↓E	↑a	↓	↑P	↔↓
Rationing rather than prices	B↑	↑P	↓	↑	↓	↓
Agricultural free markets	↔	↓E	R↑	↓E	R	↔↓
Self-employment	↔	↓E	R↑	↓E	R↑	↓
Voluntary work and labor mobilization	B↑	↑	↓	↑	↓	↔
Egalitarianism	↑	↑P	↓	↑	↓	↓
Moral rather than material incentives	↔	↑P	↓	↑	↓	↓
Free social services	↑	↑P	↓	↑	↓	↔
External Factors						
Soviet economic aid	B↑	↑	↑P	↔	↓E	↔
U.S. embargo	B	↔	↑↓	↓	↓	↑↓
Other	↓	↔	↑	↓	↑	↓
Effects						
Economic growth	↑↓↑	↓	↑P	↓	↓↑	↓↑↓
Monetary liquidity	↑	↑	↓↔	↑	↑↓	↑P
Fiscal deficit	↔	?	↓	↑	↑P↓	↑
Merchandise trade deficit	↑	↑	↔↑	↑	↓↑	↑P
Open unemployment	↑↓	↓	↑	↑	↑P	↓

Sources: Mesa-Lago 2000; chapters 2 and 3 in this volume.
Notes: ↑ Increase; ↓ Decrease; ↔ No change; B Beginning; E End; P Peak; R Reestablished.
a. Authorized subject to strict restrictions.

about whether the political changes that occurred in Cuba during the 1990s transformed the nature of the Cuban political system and the role of Castro. Pérez-Stable (1999) has argued that Cuban cycles cannot be explained by the normal tension between central planning and the market alone, but also involve a tension between political institutionalization and "mobilizational authoritarianism." She adds that Castro's control over how Cuba is governed, as well as his charismatic leadership and revolutionary ideology, has prevented the developmental logic from regularizing state socialism and implementing comprehensive market reforms. And she concludes that "although reluctantly open to partial economic reforms, the government adamantly resists significant changes in the political system" (Pérez-Stable 1999: 63–82). Suchlicki (2001–2: 131) argues that there has been "more continuity than change" in Cuba's political system in the 1990s and that Castro has not signaled a willingness to make any significant concessions on political matters. In contrast, Domínguez (1997) argues that there has been a transition in the political system from totalitarianism to an incipient authoritarian system. Meanwhile, Mujal-León and Busby posit that Cuba's current political regime is "charismatic and early post-totalitarian" but with significant differences from the typical post-totalitarian regime: "The first and most significant difference is the continuing presence of Fidel Castro who, as the charismatic founder of the revolutionary regime, retains broad power and influence. No one within the elite questions his role or his decisions" (Mujal-León and Busby 2001–2: 113). González (2002: 5–7) also characterizes Cuba's current regime as "post-totalitarian." He adds that Castro remains the "Great Helmsman," with a charismatic presence that helps legitimize and give direction to his regime. González compares him with China's Mao Zedong, the "Lord of Misrule," noting that Castro has gone so far as to extol the virtues of Cuba's totalitarianism. In April 2003, the small political spaces that were open on the island were virtually shut down with the arrest and conviction of 75 peaceful human-rights activists and independent professionals (see the end of this chapter).

Notwithstanding the different interpretations of the nature of the Cuban regime and the significance of political changes during the 1990s, all of the scholars cited agree that Castro continues to be the determining factor in the key decisions that affect the nation. Castro still holds the key political positions in the nation: chief of state, president of the Council of State, president of the Council of Ministers and its executive committee, first secretary of the Cuban Communist Party (Partido Comunista de Cuba, PCC) and head of its Political Bureau, and commander in chief of the armed forces. As president of the Council of State he nominates the president of the Supreme Court, and that institution is subordinated to the Council of State. The only institution he does not preside over is the National Assembly of People's Power (Asamblea Nacional del Poder Popular, ANPP), but that institution has very little power and meets only twice annually for two or three days at a time; for the rest of the year the Council of State governs and legislates by decree. Finally, based on his position as chief of state, the Cuban constitution empowers Castro to declare a state of emergency and to modify the exercise of rights and obligations enshrined in that document.

There are remarkable similarities between Cuba under Castro and China under Mao with regard to economic policymaking. In both cases, a powerful revolutionary leader shaped the economic policy cycles. It was only after Mao's death that market-oriented reform in China was consolidated, broadened, and deepened to create a "market socialism" model. Cuba's modest market-oriented reforms of 1993 to 1996 fall far short of Chinese reforms in terms of breadth and depth. Time and time again in the 1990s and the 2000s, Castro has rejected implementing Chinese- or Vietnamese-style reforms in Cuba and has continued to reserve for himself the power to make the crucial policy decisions. It can be argued that his power to fully reverse the market-oriented policies of the 1990s and to launch a new idealist cycle has been considerably eroded because of the lack of alternatives and the drying up of external sources of economic support. However, the paralysis of reforms since 1996 and reversal of some market-oriented reforms, particularly since 2003, suggest that he is still able to affect the speed of change.

The main external factors (positive and negative) that may have influenced Cuban economic policy cycles are presented in the middle panel of table 1. The two most important foreign actors vis-à-vis Cuba since the 1960s have been the former USSR and the United States. Beginning in 1960, the USSR played a very positive role for the Cuban economy through foreign aid, price subsidies for Cuban exports, steady supplies of fuels, and technical assistance, particularly after 1968 when Castro supported the Soviet invasion of Czechoslovakia. Soviet assistance peaked in the mid-1980s and decreased in the second half of the 1980s as Gorbachev pursued economic restructuring at home (*perestroika*) and in Soviet international economic relations; in the 1990s, Soviet assistance vanished with the dissolution of the USSR. The role of the United States has been a negative factor for Cuba since 1961, when a broad trade embargo was established. Since then, policy changes have resulted in the relative softening or tightening of the embargo. For example, the embargo was relaxed during the Ford (1974–77), Carter (1977–81), and Clinton (1993–2001) administrations, creating a more favorable external environment for Cuba, and tightened during the Reagan (1981–89), George H. W. Bush (1989–93), Clinton (the Helms-Burton Act was enacted in March 1996), and George W. Bush (2001–present) Administrations. The role of other external factors is recognized in table 1 as well, for example the worsening of the external economic environment for Cuba in the early 1960s with the multilateralization of the U.S. trade embargo under the auspices of the Organization of American States (OAS), the relative improvement in the 1970s from the loosening of the OAS embargo coupled with Cuba's ability to borrow in international markets, the tightening of international credit in the second half of the 1980s because of Cuba's first debt crisis, the improvement in the early 1990s associated with the opening of the Cuban economy to foreign investment, and a more adverse external economic environment since the late 1990s as foreign investment slowed down and Cuba endured a second debt crisis.

The bottom panel of table 1 presents outcomes of the policies listed in the upper panel, influenced by the external factors in the middle panel of the table, with respect to five macroeconomic variables: economic growth, monetary liquidity (excess money in circulation, or monetary overhang), fiscal deficit, merchandise trade deficit, and open unemployment (based on official statistical series compiled in Mesa-Lago 2000 and in chapters 2 and 3 of this book). The effect of policies on income distribution and poverty incidence cannot be measured throughout the revolutionary period because Cuba has never published official statistics on these two indicators. There are some estimates, however, based on studies done by domestic and foreign experts, as well as scattered data, that allow us to assess inequality and poverty, particularly for 1995–2002 (see chapter 3). The same symbols that we used to denote changes in policies are used for denoting changes in effects. Where more than one symbol is used, this indicates variation in the outcome during that cycle; for example, in the three sub-periods within the 1959–66 cycle, economic growth first speeded up, then slowed down, then speeded up again.

Cycles, Policies, Contributing Factors, and Effects, 1959–90

In this section we describe policies during the 1959–90 period, analyze domestic and external factors that may have influenced the start and end of each cycle, and evaluate economic and social effects. We provide a similar treatment of the two most recent cycles, covering the 1990s through the present, in a separate section in order to permit a more thorough discussion.

Market Erosion, Soviet Orthodox Model, and Socialist Debate, 1959–66

This cycle is divided into three subcycles. During the first subcycle (elimination of capitalism and erosion of the market, 1959–60) Cuba underwent rapid collectivization of the means of production and by the end of 1960 virtually eliminated the market. The vacuum created thereby was filled, in the next subcycle, by the establishment of a Stalinist-type command economy (orthodox Soviet central planning model, 1961–63), supported by economic assistance from the USSR. The imposition of the U.S. embargo (1961), and its multilateralization under the auspices of the OAS (1964), coupled with Castro's public declaration (1961) that Cuba's revolution was socialist, resulted in Cuba's isolation within the Western Hemisphere and facilitated the establishment of the Soviet model. There were significant continuities in these two subcycles: steady collectivization of the means of production, elimination of foreign investment (through nationalization of foreign properties), centralization of decision making, introduction and expansion of commodity rationing with a consequent reduction in the role of markets in determining resource allocation, increasing egalitarianism, and provision of free social services. The development strategy pursued by Cuba during these two subcycles emphasized rapid industrialization and agricultural diversification. (Recall that in 1963, then–minister of industries Guevara predicted that by 1965, Cuba would lead Latin America in industrial output per capita.)

The Soviet central planning model was unsuited to Cuba, which had an economy heavily centered on production of one agricultural commodity (sugar), lacked previous experience with central planning, and lacked the statistical base to support central planning. To compound the problem, collectivization cut across all sectors of the economy and proceeded at lightning speed, while the planning mechanism was introduced haphazardly. The industrialization strategy set overly ambitious short-term targets. and was predicated on imports of capital goods and raw materials that did not materialize. The agricultural diversification plan failed to meet production targets for new crops, although it did result in the reduction of land devoted to sugarcane cultivation, with a consequent decrease in sugar production and exports and a worsening of the merchandise trade deficit.

The double failure—of central planning and of the industrialization/agricultural diversification strategy—led to the third subcycle (socialist debate and experimentation with alternative models, 1964–66), during which two groups within the ruling elite espousing different ideological views about socialist development proposed competing policy prescriptions and strongly advocated for their views. On one side, Guevara and his followers, partly influenced by Mao's ideas, advocated an idealist, anti-market approach: forging an unselfish "New Man," using moral incentives to stimulate hard work, relying more extensively on voluntary work and labor mobilization, promoting further collectivization, espousing egalitarianism, and providing universal and free social services. On the other side was a pro-Soviet, pragmatist faction led by economist Carlos Rafael Rodríguez, one of the founders of the PCC in 1925. Influenced by Libermanism in vogue in the USSR at the time, this group favored limited market-oriented policies: application of selected market-oriented economic tools, reliance on material incentives, some decentralization of decision making, and a halt in collectivization, egalitarianism, and the expansion of free social services. To keep both factions in check, Castro split control over economic ministries between them: Guevara and his followers controlled two-thirds of economic ministries, while the pro-

Soviet group controlled a third. This division of power and influence makes it difficult to characterize the subcycle but, in general, the tendency was for economic policy to move away from the market.

This first cycle lasted 7½ years, consisting of three subcycles that lasted roughly two, three, and 2½ years, respectively. The briefness of the subcycles meant that policies were not in place long enough to have significant results. Assessing policy effects is particularly challenging because very few statistics are available for 1959–60 and with the adoption of the Soviet economic model in 1962, Cuba changed its national accounts methodology, so that it is technically impossible to compare the new statistics with those available for earlier periods. Generally speaking, economic outcomes were mixed: Economic growth first increased, then declined, and partly recovered; monetary liquidity and the merchandise trade deficit expanded throughout the entire cycle; the fiscal deficit apparently remained roughly unchanged (although reliable statistics are not available); and open unemployment initially increased and then decreased.

Adoption and Radicalization of the Guevarist Model, 1966–70

Although Castro did not intervene directly in the debate on the socialist development model, by the end of 1965 the leaders of the two contending factions had disappeared from the spotlight: Guevara had left the island to lead a guerrilla movement in South America and Rodríguez had resigned as director of the National Institute of Agrarian Reform. In mid-1966, Castro publicly embraced several policies associated with Guevara's model, which began to be implemented during this cycle, although shaped by Castro into a more radical form. For example, during this cycle Cuba virtually eliminated the central plan and the national budget (both essential to Guevara's model), further centralized decision making (increasingly under Castro's control in the absence of a central plan and a budget), and considerably expanded the use of moral incentives. Not only did Castro diverge from the Soviet orthodox model, but he boasted that Cuba had surpassed the USSR in building socialism and communism. He also fomented guerrilla warfare in Latin America, relying on the doctrine of the guerrilla *foco* and undermining the traditional, pro-Soviet communist parties in the region. Despite Castro's challenge, the USSR continued to provide economic assistance and maintained trade relations with Cuba, but Soviet leaders ran out of patience in 1967 and slowed oil shipments to the island. Castro responded with a very visible trial and eventual jail sentences against a group of prominent pro-Soviet government and PCC officials (the so-called *microfacción*), who were found guilty of disloyalty and sectarianism, fueling already tense relations with the USSR. In 1968, however, Castro publicly threw his support behind the Soviet invasion of Czechoslovakia (arguing that the "Prague Spring" was a counterrevolutionary, pro-capitalist movement). This support, offered at a time when the USSR faced intense criticism from the international community, earned Cuba improved relations with the USSR and the resumption of Soviet oil deliveries and aid.

In 1965, the development strategy shifted in orientation from inward (import-substitution industrialization) to outward (export promotion), centering on a sugar plan for 1965–70 with a target of 10 million tons of sugar by 1970. The most severe deviations from the market during the entire revolutionary period occurred during this cycle, under the guise of a "Revolutionary Offensive," launched in 1968, consisting of the following policies: further collectivization through the elimination of peasant free markets and family plots within state farms; nationalization of 58,000 small businesses; severe restrictions on self-employment, including criminal penalties for engaging in such activities; increased centralization in economic decision making and replacement of the central plan with ad hoc sectoral plans (for example, for sugar, for cattle) spurred by Castro; continuation of the policy of operating without a national budget; very extensive use of voluntary work and labor mobilizations aimed primarily at the sugar harvest but also at creating a socialist "New Man"; and greater emphasis on egalitarianism, through such means as narrowing of salary differentials across occupations, increasing reliance on moral rather than material incentives, and expanding free social services (including public telephones, burials, and admission to sports and cultural events).

This idealist cycle lasted only 4½ years. It is difficult to measure economic performance because of the deliberate decision by the government to reduce statistical data collection and publication. Enrollment in economic training and education was also cut back. Fragmentary information suggests however that most economic outcomes were negative: Economic growth slowed down and the economy either stagnated or contracted in 1970. (Sugar production in 1970 was 15% below the 10–million-ton target and the single-purpose concentration on sugar production harmed the rest of the economy.) Monetary liquidity reached a record high and excess money in circulation made the currency virtually worthless, prompting labor absenteeism to jump to 25% of the labor force (casting serious doubts on the effectiveness of moral incentives and delivering a coup de grâce to the myth of the socialist "New Man"). There was a significant increase in the merchandise trade deficit; open unemployment declined to a record low at the expense of a substantial increase in underemployment and declining labor productivity; and income distribution probably became the most equitable of any time during the revolutionary period, as suggested by some foreign estimates.

Soviet Model (Pre-Gorbachev) of Limited Economic Reform, 1971–85

The double failure in 1970 of the sugar plan and the creation of a socialist "New Man," combined with a severe economic slowdown, gave rise to a dangerous situation (Richard Nixon was president of the United States) and prompted a timid policy shift toward the market starting in 1971. The failure of the guerrilla movement in South America supported by Cuba and the death of Guevara in 1967, combined with Castro's support of the Soviet invasion of Czechoslovakia in 1968, opened the way for reconciliation with the USSR. Soviet soft credits, technical assistance, trade, and non-repayable price subsidies to the island peaked during this cycle. Thus, the USSR purchased Cuban sugar and nickel at prices much higher than those prevailing in the world market, and the USSR sold oil to Cuba at prices below world market prices. Moreover, in 1972 Cuba became a full member of the Council for Mutual Economic Assistance (CMEA), the economic organization that grouped the USSR and the socialist countries of eastern Europe. Thereby Cuba gained enhanced trade relations with the socialist bloc and access to additional credits and technical assistance. These positive developments contributed decisively to the start of this cycle and to its long duration (15 years).

Under President Ford (1974–77), the United States engaged in secret negotiations to improve relations with Cuba, and the OAS lifted its multilateral sanctions in 1975, leaving each member country to determine whether to reestablish diplomatic and economic relations with Cuba. Then Cuba's involvement in the factional war in Angola after the Portuguese withdrawal stymied a potential rapprochement between Cuba and the United States under Ford. The Carter administration (1977–81) in its first years in office worked to relax tensions between the two nations, and the United States and Cuba agreed to establish interests sections (a level lower than embassies) in each other's territory. However, Cuba's continued presence in Angola and intervention in the war between Somalia and Ethiopia, as well as the flight to the United States in 1980 of more than 125,000 Cubans on small boats from the port of Mariel, aided and abetted by Castro's government, led to new tensions and halted the process that might have led to relaxation of the trade embargo. During the Reagan presidency in the 1980s, tensions between the United States and Cuba escalated, with Cuba creating "territorial militias" to defend the nation against a supposed invasion from the United States. An offsetting factor during this cycle was the granting of credits to Cuba by western countries and financial institutions.

During this pragmatist cycle, the Cuban leadership virtually reversed all of its previous idealist policies in a limited move toward the market. Although the process of gradual reduction of private farms and expansion of state-controlled agricultural cooperatives continued, some measures contrary to collectivization were taken: reintroduction of peasant free markets, of family plots in state farms, and of self-employment; allowing private farmers to hire helpers; permission for individuals to build private homes and to swap existing dwellings; and enactment of a law allowing foreign investment (although with so many restrictions that it did not have much effect). At the same time, central planning was reintroduced and reinforced, albeit with some built-in flexibilities (such as increasing the power of state enterprise administrators), and the state budget was reinstated as the main instrument of financial control in a command economy. Castro labeled the previous emphasis on egalitarianism, moral incentives, voluntary work, and labor mobilizations as "idealistic errors." The pendulum swung to the other extreme with the implementation of the following policies: reinstating material incentives and lauding the positive role of wage differentials on productivity; severely curtailing voluntary work and acknowledging its inefficiency; establishing official "parallel markets" for certain consumer products in which prices were determined by demand and supply; and charging for some public utilities and other services that were formerly free.

A process of political institutionalization also took place during this cycle; for example, Cuba's first socialist constitution was promulgated in 1976, the National Assembly of People's Power was created, and the PCC underwent restructuring. But the new planning technocracy faced serious resistance from the "old guard," which feared that further movement toward the market would threaten the survival of the regime. As we will discuss later, at the end of this cycle, Castro denounced some of the measures (such as the farmers' free markets, self-employment) as being inconsistent with Cuban socialism. Other measures (such as workers' profit sharing, self-financing of state enterprises) were never fully implemented.

The development strategy pursued during this cycle was more rational and balanced than in previous cycles. The emphasis on outward orientation was maintained, with a focus on increasing sugar production and exports. Mechanization of the sugar harvest (cutting and loading sugarcane) permitted increases in sugar production without re-creating the severe dislocations that occurred during the 1970 harvest. Technical and financial assistance from the USSR underwrote the expansion of nickel production and exports. Tourism became an important source of foreign exchange. Finally, export capability expanded for citrus, fish, and shellfish.

The long length of this cycle—15 years, the longest under the revolutionary government—coupled with the gradual improvement in the quantity and quality of Cuban economic statistics, made it possible to assess the effects of the policies implemented during this period. Economic growth achieved its highest rates under the revolutionary government (particularly in 1971–75, when international sugar prices reached record highs); monetary liquidity decreased dramatically until 1980; the fiscal deficit remained within manageable levels (the state budget was reintroduced in 1978); and the merchandise trade deficit remained stable or even shrank because of generous Soviet subsidies. For the first time since the 1960s, however, there were pockets of unemployment that arose from the emphasis on increasing labor productivity, a reduction in the demand for labor, and the entry into the labor force of a "baby boom" conceived during the period immediately following the revolutionary victory (1959–65). It is likely that inequality rose during this cycle, but statistical information to support this hypothesis is not available.

The Rectification Process, 1986–90

The economic recovery during the previous pragmatist cycle led to a marked improvement in living conditions on the island. Despite these accomplishments, domestic and external forces worked against the continuation and deepening of the limited market-oriented policies implemented during 1971–85. Castro and the old guard resented the growing power of the planning technocracy, the elimination of some institutions dear to them (such as voluntary labor), the growing inequality, and the rise of a wealthy capitalist class composed of private farmers, middlemen who benefited from the peasant free markets, some self-employed individuals, and individuals involved in private home construction and in home swaps. Although these sectors were very tiny, Castro criticized them in 1982, accused them of greed and corruption, and proposed imposing taxes to reduce their income, ominous signals of an upcoming policy shift.

In the external arena, Gorbachev rose to power in the USSR in 1985 and launched *perestroika* and *glasnost*, two policies that generated pressure within the USSR to force Cuba to make better use of the Soviet aid it was receiving and to balance merchandise trade with the island (the bilateral trade was severely unbalanced, with Cuba accumulating huge annual trade deficits). In subsequent years, the USSR reduced price subsidies and froze credits and trade flows. To compound the situation, due to the heavy burden of the debt service in hard currency, in 1986 Cuba suspended payment of its foreign debt with western countries and requested a rescheduling of such obligations through the Paris Club. As a result, Paris Club members essentially halted all fresh credits to Cuba, an impasse that continues to this day. In the United States, the Reagan and Bush administrations relentlessly continued the trade embargo on Cuba, providing a justification for the Cuban leadership to tighten their control under the guise of defense against imperialism and capitalism.

It would have been reasonable to expect that, in view of domestic economic improvement and mounting external economic pressures coming from the USSR, Cuba would have swum with the tide toward the market rising in the USSR and eastern Europe. But Castro and the old guard feared that such policies would threaten the revolutionary spirit, provoke social tensions, destabilize the political situation, and weaken their grip on power. In fact, a new idealist cycle, called Rectification of Errors and Negative Tendencies, was launched by Castro in mid-1986 and lasted until 1990. In theory, it was intended to recalibrate socialist policies to find an optimal middle road between the "idealistic errors" of 1966–70 and the "economicist" excesses of 1971–85 (the head of the planning agency who had led the successful development of the economy during the 1970s and 1980s was fired and put on trial for mechanically copying a model not suitable for Cuba). In practice, most of the Rectification policies resembled the anti-market ones of the previous idealist cycle, although not as extreme: the elimination of private farms was accelerated; peasant free markets and self-employment were abolished (the rationale being that they were unneeded and the state would carry out their functions); private housing construction and swaps were considerably restricted; incipient decentralization policies were halted and decision making returned to the top political elite; rationing was expanded again and parallel markets were eliminated; voluntary labor was reintroduced in the form of military-style construction brigades and massive labor mobilization in agriculture; material incentives were sharply reduced and moral incentives reinstated (the figure of Guevara and his quest to eliminate money and greed was resurrected to support moral incentives); and there was renewed emphasis on egalitarianism and free social services.

The new development strategy was centered on a food program with unrealistic targets: to reach food self-sufficiency in five years and generate a surplus of food production for export. A second strand of the strategy was to promote biotechnology, banking on this becoming a significant source of export revenue and on Cuba becoming a world power in this industry in a short time. The third strand of the strategy—and the only one that has been successful to date—was the promotion of international tourism through the development of tourism enclaves.

This idealist cycle lasted about 4½ years. Although Cuba suspended publication of its statistical yearbook after 1989, sufficient information is available to show that this cycle brought about a recession and virtually all indicators of performance deteriorated: The rate of economic growth was negative; monetary liquidity expanded significantly; fiscal deficits returned and expanded; the merchandise trade deficit reached historical highs; and open unemployment continued to rise (unlike during the first idealist cycle, when unemployment contracted). There is no information regarding effects on inequality, but it probably declined in view of the measures taken.

Economic Crisis, Reforms, and Policy Paralysis and Reversal, 1991–2004

At the start of the 1990s, Cuba suffered its most severe economic crisis since the revolution and perhaps since the Great Depression. Two factors, one external and one internal, were the principal causes of the crisis and triggered a new pragmatist cycle.

The external—and most significant—factor was the disappearance of socialism in the USSR and eastern Europe and the dissolution of the CMEA. This resulted in the immediate loss for Cuba of price subsidies and soft loans that amounted to an estimated $65 billion from the USSR alone during the 1960–90 period; the halt of hundreds of Soviet investment projects that were underway and the return home of thousands of Soviet technicians; and a virtual end to trade relations and economic support for Cuba from the socialist countries. Cuban foreign trade fell by 75% because about 70% of it was with the USSR, which stopped importing nickel, citrus, cigars, and other Cuban products and selling consumer, intermediate, and capital goods to the island. The USSR also significantly reduced oil shipments to Cuba and halted the mechanism whereby Cuba could resell some imported Soviet oil that it did not consume domestically. In a matter of a few years, Cuban-Soviet trade relations deteriorated to the point that they were limited to barter of sugar for oil conducted at world market prices.

The internal factor was the economic recession of 1986–90, manufactured under the idealist Rectification process. Contrary to trends in the rest of the world and even in the socialist countries, Rectification had set aside the very modest pro-market reforms that had been put in place during 1975–85, returning to moral incentives to motivate workers and pursuing an economic strategy based on attaining food self-sufficiency that ended in failure. The ensuing recession placed Cuba in a very vulnerable position to confront the collapse of the USSR and the socialist bloc. Had Cuba continued in the second half of the 1980s the market-oriented policies it had pursued during the 1971–85 pragmatist cycle, arguably the economic crisis of the 1990s would have been less severe and the recovery less traumatic.

Another external factor contributing to the economic crisis was the strengthening of the U.S. trade embargo of Cuba through the Torricelli (1992) and Helms-Burton (1996) acts. The Torricelli Act banned foreign subsidiaries of U.S. corporations from trading or investing in Cuba and foreign ships used in the Cuba trade from entering U.S. ports. During the Clinton presidency (1992–2001), the political channel of the Torricelli Act (the so-called Track II, designed to promote cultural exchanges and visits as instruments to promote change in Cuba) was emphasized. The Helms-Burton Act, enacted in 1996, bans imports of Cuban products from third countries. Its most controversial provision authorizes U.S. citizens to sue in U.S. courts persons that "traffic" in property confiscated by the Cuban government, including potential foreign investors in joint ventures with Cuban enterprises that control confiscated properties. It also restricts the issuing of U.S. visas to persons convicted of such "trafficking" or their families.[1] The EU, Canada, and Mexico protested the extraterritorial application of the Helms-Burton Act, enacted countermeasures to confront potential U.S. actions against businessmen from their countries who had made investments in the island taking advantage of a more permissive attitude toward foreign investment by Cuban authorities, and threatened to pursue actions against the United States before the World Trade Organization (Pérez-López and Travieso-Díaz 2000). The dispute has been postponed because first President Clinton and then President George W. Bush have invoked a provision in the Helms-Burton Act that allows the president to waive application of sanctions for a six-month period.

The economic crisis reached bottom in 1993. Compared to 1989, by 1993 real GDP (that is, GDP adjusted for inflation) was 35% lower and real GDP per capita was 42% lower. Reductions in physical output levels between 1989 and 1993 were as follows: sugar, 48%; nickel, 36%; citrus, 32%; and fish and shellfish, 63%. Monetary liquidity rose from 22% of GDP in 1989 to 73% of GDP in 1993. Over the same time span, the inflation rate rose from 0.5% to 26% and the fiscal deficit from 6% to 34% of GDP; the value of exports decreased by 80% and the value of imports by 75%, resulting in shortages of food, fuel, consumer products, raw materials, spare parts, and all other imported goods. The only positive economic developments during this time were an increase in oil production and in revenue generated by international tourism and a relative reduction in the merchandise trade deficit.

The crisis also had other detrimental effects. The rationing system again expanded to cover virtually all consumer goods and rations were cut so that they now covered only one-half of the monthly needs of the average consumer. The black market grew by leaps and bounds and prices skyrocketed. The loss in the value of the peso and the reduction (by half) of the purchasing power of the average real salary, coupled with generalized shortages, spurred illegal activities and theft from state enterprises. These events also had a negative effect on worker effort, increasing absenteeism and decreasing labor productivity. These negative tendencies offset many of the gains of earlier years and fed a feeling of frustration, disenchantment, and alienation in the population, eroding the political foundation of the revolution. In August 1994, thousands of residents of Havana rallied in the streets to protest against the government, the first popular action of such nature and magnitude since the revolution.

The Economic Reform Debate: Reformers versus Hard-Liners

At the beginning of the 1990s, a discussion about economic policies and strategies took place in Cuba, the first since the 1964–66 debate over the appropriate socialist model. As it was framed, the debate of the 1990s was not about shifting from socialism to a market economy, but rather about the degree to which market instruments should be used and how they should be used within a socialist system in order to promote economic growth and avoid negative consequences. There were basically two positions: The most avid reformers supported deep structural changes and market-oriented reforms that in their mind would guarantee sustainable economic growth in the long term. In contrast, the hard-liners and more cautious reformers supported only minor market-oriented changes to arrest the economic decline, slow down the rate of inflation, strengthen the value of the peso, and promote economic growth, in order to minimize the threat of political instability and regime destabilization.

The first position was supported by academics (economists as well as other social scientists) and technicians who saw market-oriented reforms as the lesser of two evils. Some of them argued that repressing markets was futile, as markets would surge elsewhere, as had been demonstrated by the black market. Moreover, if the government was not able to satisfy the basic needs of the population, it should permit regulated markets or private enterprise do so. Mid-level technicians clamored for the privatization of personal services the government was unable to provide, as well as for the reestablishment of farmers' free markets, self-employment, and other mechanisms that had been abandoned or severely reduced during the Rectification process.

The avid reformers were however concerned about the adverse consequences that market reforms had had in the USSR and eastern European countries. They acknowledged that the private sector was capable of making positive contributions (for example, eliminating the state monopoly on certain products, promoting competition and raising efficiency, creating new sources of productive employment) but they feared a snowball effect as an expanded private sector would increase demand for inputs, accumulate wealth, and present a challenge to the state. The potential disappearance or substantial weakening of the social safety net was also a concern: (1) high

unemployment would create serious economic and social problems; (2) significant inequality in income and in access to goods and services would
weaken population unity; (3) price increases would adversely affect the consumption level of low-income groups; and (4) social services would deteriorate overall.

Fidel Castro initially opposed any market-oriented reforms and in several
speeches during 1990–92 rejected the facilitation of commercial relations
between, on one hand, state farms and state-owned enterprises and, on the
other, family-owned enterprises or groups of workers; farmers' free markets;
the privatization of small businesses; and even the possibility of authorizing
self-employed street vendors. He warned that the revolution would continue
to expand state ownership of the means of production, bringing privately
owned farms under state control, and all economic problems would be addressed through government action. He attacked supporters of reforms
within the island, accusing them of being disaffected, defeatists, pseudo-revo-
lutionaries, and traitors.

Economic Reform during the Special Period in Time of Peace, 1991–96

To confront the economic crisis, the government put in place an emergency
plan (euphemistically called the Special Period in Time of Peace) that assigned
scarce resources to the most vital needs of the country. The Special Period
economic strategy had many of the features of an orthodox structural adjustment program, although it also attempted to protect social services. In an
attempt to slow down the economic decline and promote growth, several
market-oriented measures were implemented to stimulate the external sector:
promotion of the tourism industry, efforts to attract foreign investment, and
attempts to develop new markets for exports (with the dissolution of the
CMEA, the world market was Cuba's only alternative forum for trade). This
strategy tried to maintain market-oriented changes within foreign enclaves in
order to avoid contaminating the domestic economy and the socialist system.
Although tourism did expand and some new export markets were developed,
the overall volume of exports did not grow and foreign investment trickled in
slowly; therefore, the strategy was not able to stop the economic decline. The
worsening of the crisis in 1993 made it evident that drastic domestic reform
measures could not be put off any longer, no matter how distasteful they were
to the leadership. Castro and the hard-liners would agree only to the most
essential measures, implement them piecemeal, and maintain strict control
over their application to avoid their "getting out of hand."

The most significant reform measures were enacted between August 1993
and September 1994. They included:

• the legalization of the holding and circulation of hard currencies (principally U.S. dollars), and the promotion of remittances to Cuban citizens from relatives and friends residing abroad, including greater flexibility for Cubans abroad to travel to the island, the establishment of stores selling merchandise priced in dollars to which all residents would have access, and a network of exchange houses where the public could exchange hard currency for pesos and vice versa (see below);
• authorization of self-employment in selected occupations, including taxi driving, and home food preparation and sale in home restaurants (*paladares*);
• transformation of state farms into a new type of cooperative (Unidades Básicas de Producción Cooperativa, UBPC) and assignment of small plots of land within cooperatives to members for family use in growing food for self-consumption;
• reestablishment of agricultural free markets authorized to sell a wide range of agricultural commodities and establishment of artisan markets;
• measures to reduce the fiscal deficit and soak up excess monetary liquidity, such as new taxes, charging for certain public services that used to be free, and reducing the ration allotments that formerly provided the bulk of household food;
• creation of a "convertible peso" and establishment of currency exchange houses (*casas de cambio*, CADECA);
• enactment of a new foreign investment law in 1995 that provided more flexibility and incentives to attract foreign investors than the 1982 law had done, and of legislation establishing export processing zones; and
• authorization for foreign citizens to purchase commercial and residential real estate—including offices, dwellings, and tourism facilities—and for Cuban citizens to rent rooms in their houses or apartments to foreign tourists.

Returning to table 1, the pragmatist cycle that began in 1991 encompassed by far the most significant move toward the market during the revolutionary period, particularly through the following measures:

• modest diminution of collectivization achieved by the distribution of small parcels of land to families;
• transformation of state farms into UBPCs;
• reestablishment of agricultural free markets;
• wider opening of the economy to foreign investment;
• authorization of self-employment;
• modest decentralization of decision making, initially only with re-

spect to external-sector activities and eventually also with respect to the domestic economy, including the creation of quasi-private firms (*sociedades anónimas,* or S.A.) and joint ventures with foreign investors;
• reestablishment of the national budget as the key financial control tool and implementation of policies to reduce public expenditures and increase revenues (including new taxes) in order to reduce the fiscal deficit;
• more extensive use of markets (including agricultural free markets, artisans' markets, and dollar stores) where prices were determined by demand and supply, in order to provide goods to the population and reduce reliance on the rationing system;
• virtual elimination of voluntary work and significant reduction of labor mobilization;
• decreased reliance on moral incentives and greater emphasis on material incentives (the role of the latter reached its peak for the entire revolutionary period during this time);
• drastic reduction of the emphasis on egalitarianism and acceptance of income disparities; and
• increases in the prices of certain public services, including for some that used to be free of charge, although education and public health continued to be free.

This pragmatist cycle lasted about six years, although most of the market-oriented policies were introduced during the three-year period from 1993 to 1996. The implementation of these policies resulted in positive economic growth beginning in 1994. Compared to 1993, when the economic crisis was at its worst, most macroeconomic indicators showed marked improvement by 1996: The growth rate in 1996 was 7.8%, the best performance since 1985; monetary liquidity was 42% of GDP, compared to 73% in 1989; inflation had fallen sharply from 26% in 1989 and there was actually some deflation in 1996; the fiscal deficit was 2.5% compared to 34% in 1989; exports grew by 72% and imports by 80%; and the value of the peso in terms of U.S. dollars—based on the exchange rate in the CADECA currency exchange houses—appreciated to 19 for 1 U.S. dollar in 1996 from 95 for 1 U.S. dollar in 1989. The only macroeconomic indicator that deteriorated was the open unemployment rate, which rose from 6.2% to 7.6%, and there probably also was an increase in inequality (see chapter 2).

Slowdown, Halting, and Reversal of Reforms, 1997–2004

Despite the positive economic results, Castro and the hard-liners harbored suspicions about the reforms, fearing that the diminution of collectivization, loss of economic power by the state, and growing economic independence of farmers, self-employed workers, and other sectors of the population would weaken the state and erode the power of the leadership. Moreover, the growing unemployment rate and increase in inequality ran counter to the ideological proclivities of Castro and the hard-liners.

Thus, many of the pragmatic policies implemented in 1993–96, which could have formed the basis for further reforms, were subjected to strict regulation, backtracking, and reversals, thereby reducing their effectiveness. For example, the foreign investment law establishes that any foreign investment exceeding $10 million has to be approved by the executive committee of the Council of Ministers; most foreign investors are allowed to control no more than 49% percent of joint ventures; joint ventures are not permitted to directly hire their employees nor pay them in dollars; an agency of the Cuban government hires and fires employees, collects the workers' salaries in dollars from the joint venture, and pays Cuban workers in pesos (at the official exchange rate of 1 peso equivalent to 1 U.S. dollar). These rules have been strictly enforced and the approval process has taken so long that potential foreign investors have protested; only one wholly foreign-owned investment has been allowed and foreign investment slowed down considerably. The new agricultural cooperatives, unlike their counterparts in China or Vietnam, have not been allowed to decide which crops to grow, to whom to sell their output, or at what price; the state determines the crops to be planted and buys the bulk of the output at fixed prices, generally substantially below market prices. This behavior creates disincentives to production and contributes to UBPC losses.

Finally, high taxes and fees have been assessed on self-employed workers, and their workplaces have been singled out for frequent inspections by government officials, who are quick to level fines for supposed violations. The small family restaurants (or *paladares*) were first allowed, then closed down, and finally allowed to reopen but subject to strict restrictions: A maximum of twelve customers can be served at one time, owners cannot hire workers other than family members, and they must pay high taxes. Private taxis experienced the same uncertainty as the *paladares*, and currently they are not allowed to carry foreign tourists.

In March 1996, Vice President Raúl Castro strongly criticized the market-oriented reform process. Several of the economists who had expressed favorable views about reforms were censured and removed from their positions, among them three economists known outside the island who had written an important book about the need to expedite and deepen economic reforms (Carranza, Gutiérrez, and Monreal 1995). This purge put an end to the public debate on reforms. Although there have been reforms since 1996—for example, enactment of a new banking law—for all practical purposes the reform process was halted that year. Several of the measures that were under discussion in 1995–96—enterprise reform, elimination of redundant workers from the state payroll, real convertibility of the peso, authorization to establish small businesses and hire workers outside the family, general price reform, social security contributions by all workers—had disappeared into policy limbo and had not been implemented by 2004.

The negative effects on economic performance of halting and reversing the reform process can be illustrated by examining economic outcomes for the 1996–2003 period: The rate of growth of GDP slowed down; monetary liquidity began to grow again, reaching record levels; the price stability (actually deflation) that had been reached vanished and inflation began to rise again; the fiscal deficit expanded; and the merchandise trade deficit ballooned, reaching historical record highs. The only positive indicator in this otherwise bleak panorama was a reduction in open unemployment but, as we discuss elsewhere in this volume, the unemployment figures provided by Cuban officials are of questionable validity. Our analysis suggests that inequality has increased by leaps and bounds since 1996 (see chapter 3).

In our view, the leadership's decision to halt the reform process resulted from its (erroneous) judgment that the economic crisis had been overcome and therefore the threat of a popular uprising because of declining standards of living had disappeared. Continuing on the path of economic reforms, the leadership reasoned, would loosen its reins on economic and political control. As in 1986, the political logic of Castro and the hard-liners prevailed over the economic logic of the reformers, leading to the halt of reforms and the shift away from the market. To deal with potential popular dissatisfaction and the emergence of peaceful dissidents, in February 1999 the National Assembly passed Law No. 88, the Law for the Protection of Cuba's National Independence and Economy (Ley de la Protección de la Independencia Nacional y la Economía de Cuba). Referred to in Cuba as the "gag law" (*ley mordaza*), it established jail sentences of between 8 and 20 years and seizure of assets for citizens convicted of political crimes such as collaborating with foreign journalists, accepting payment for such collaboration, and having or distributing "subversive materials" (that is, publications not authorized by the government), disrupting the peace by participating in demonstrations, and otherwise seeking to destabilize the country.

The Varela Project, directed by human-rights activist Oswaldo Payá, winner of the 2003 Shakarov Prize for Freedom of Thought awarded by the European Parliament, collected more than 11,000 signatures of Cuban citizens in 2002 requesting a referendum (in accordance with the Cuban Constitution) to allow freedom of expression, hold free elections, grant amnesty to political prisoners, and permit the creation of small businesses. Former U.S. President Carter, during a visit to Cuba in 2002, used the opportunity of a televised speech to the Cuban people to describe (in Spanish) the tenets of the Varela Project. Along the same lines, a pastoral letter issued by Roman Catholic Cardinal Ortega (2003) called on the government to allow a political and economic opening, making some of the same proposals embodied in the Varela Project petition. The government mounted a major campaign against the Varela Project referendum and, in this context, the National Assembly not only rejected the referendum request in July 2002, but it also amended the constitution to explicitly state that Cuba's socialist system is irrevocable. In March 2003, 75 dissidents (including independent journalists, economists, librarians, human-rights activists, trade unionists, and supporters of the Varela Project) were arrested, charged with violating Law No. 88, and sentenced through summary trials to a combined 1,400 years in prison. This crackdown on peaceful dissidents resulted in a strong and swift reaction from the international community, including from individuals who to that point had supported the revolutionary government.[2] At about the same time, Minister of Economics and Planning José Luis Rodríguez (who implemented the 1993–96 reforms) was removed from the powerful Council of State and replaced by Ramiro Valdés, a hard-liner and former minister of the interior. In June 2003, Minister of Finance and Prices Manuel Millares, also a supporter of reforms, was dismissed from his post. In October 2004, Marcos Portal, minister of basic industry, another reformer and proponent of modern managerial techniques, was removed and blamed for the collapse of the electricity grid.

In mid-2004 José Ramón Machado Ventura, a member of the political bureau of the Communist Party, warned at a meeting of top party officials that Cuba was copying capitalistic management methods and style. He criticized "those who have copied capitalist methods so well that they have become capitalists themselves" and concluded that "liberalism, lack of control and tolerance" are affecting the entire country (cited by Frank 2004d). A series of measures enacted in 2003–4 imposed recentralization of decision making.

In July 2003, the government decreed that all operations of state enterprises must be conducted in convertible pesos, all hard currency that such enterprises have or receive from exports must be sold to Cuba's Central Bank (Banco Central de Cuba, BCC), and purchases of hard currency needed for imports must be approved by the BCC. State enterprises must pay to the BCC from 1% to 2% of the value of hard currency they buy (Resolución 65 of the BCC, July 16, 2003). These regulations reduced the flexibility of state enterprises, caused delays in their operations, and resulted in lost opportunities;

many negotiated deals were cancelled and creditors could not collect payments. Under the new regulations, an enterprise may negotiate the purchase of a product from a foreign firm, but the BCC may refuse to approve it. As a practical matter, the BCC bureaucracy is not prepared to take on the new functions and the criteria for making decisions to approve or reject individual transactions have not been released ("Marcha" 2003). Minister of Economics and Planning José Luis Rodríguez declared to the National Assembly in December 2003, "The decentralization of hard currency has gone further than planned and has begun to result in unnecessary expenses." But a Cuban scholar has warned that the previous mechanism led to a significant decentralization in the management of state enterprises and, if the new regulations are not successful in achieving an adequate proportion of convertible pesos and hard currency, "a return to a centralized allocation of resources would occur, resulting in rigidity and inefficiency" (González Gutiérrez 2003: 18–19).

Meanwhile Minister of Foreign Trade Raúl de la Nuez stated that commerce is being recentralized from state enterprises in order to control imports (cited by Frank 2004a, 2004b). The Foreign Trade Ministry (MINCEX) has retaken control of exports and imports that were in the hands of state enterprises, and is organizing committees to regulate and approve foreign trade transactions, as well as to buy goods for duty-free stores after branches of foreign firms performing this function were closed. In March 2004, MINCEX reduced from 43 to 10 the number of enterprises authorized to import videos and cancelled the permit of 61 enterprises to import computers and their components (Cancio 2004a).

Also in March 2004, the Ministry of Finance was empowered to control the purchase of automobiles in hard currency; only government officials, technicians, university professors, artists, or athletes can apply to purchase a vehicle, and they must prove that they have earned the hard currency to effect the purchase from work assigned by the state in the last two years (Resolución 54 of the Ministerio de Finanzas y Precios, March 15, 2004). Managers of state enterprises were simultaneously forced to turn in "luxury cars" (such as Toyotas and Mitsubishis) to the state and inspectors began to confiscate forbidden vehicles (Frank 2004a). In April 2004, the government prohibited state enterprises from conducting 87 types of services that they used to provide as side businesses to earn hard currency, in order to control those operations directly and obtain the corresponding revenue, which is needed to finance imports (Circular 2000 of the Ministerio de Economía y Planificación, April 1, 2004). In the fall, the government placed four decentralized state tourist companies directly under the central Ministry of Industry.

Other measures enacted in 2004 reversed reforms introduced in 1993–96. In March, the government restricted self-employment to state officials and administrators as well as members of the military; in addition, in October, it cancelled permits and halted the issue of new licenses for 40 occupations that were previously authorized for self-employment (Resolución 11 of the Ministerio del Trabajo y Seguridad Social, March 13, 2004). Purportedly in response to a set of measures announced by the U.S. administration in mid-2004 that tighten the rules on sending off remittances and on travel to the island, in November the Cuban government banned the use of the U.S. dollar and stipulated that only convertible pesos would be accepted by all state entities such as hard currency shops, hotels, restaurants, bars, cafeterias, taxis, and auto rental agencies. Nationals, foreign tourists, and senders of remittances who need to convert dollars to convertible pesos are charged a 10% fee at exchange houses, banks, hotels, and hard currency shops. Existing banking accounts in dollars (owned by individuals, diplomats, national enterprises, and joint ventures) cannot receive new deposits or transfers (opening of new accounts is allowed); withdrawals from such accounts are permitted without charge, as is the receipt of interest from certificates of deposit (CDs). Four foreign currencies, Canadian dollars, euros, British pounds, and Swiss francs, can be converted without the 10% charge, and bank accounts in those currencies can receive deposits and transfers (Resolución 80 of the BCC, October 23, 2004).

Conclusion

This chapter has shown that the economic policies pursued by socialist Cuba have followed a pattern of successive idealist and pragmatist cycles, sometimes moving toward and sometimes away from the market. We have identified six cycles averaging about seven years each; if the long pragmatist cycle 1971–85 is excluded, the average length of the cycles was about 5½ years. The frequent swings in economic philosophy have created confusion and instability, with adverse consequences for economic performance. The recurrent policy shifts have meant that insufficient time transpired for the policies to take hold and bear results. It is worth noting that the best economic results were obtained during the longest cycle, the pragmatist one from 1971 to 1985.

The two best-defined idealist cycles—the application of the Guevara-Castro model during 1966–70 and the Rectification process during 1986–90—resulted in deterioration of economic and social conditions, with adverse implications for political stability. The precarious situation that arose forced Castro and the hard-liners to shift gears and implement market-oriented policies. The two pragmatist cycles that ensued after those idealist cycles brought about economic recovery and overall improvements in the standard of living, but widened social disparities and, during the first pragmatist cycle (1971–85), also open unemployment. The excessive emphasis on egalitarianism during the idealist cycles wreaked havoc on incentives and adversely affected economic performance. The reductions in unemployment have been accomplished by bloating the payrolls of state enterprises, increasing underemployment, and lowering worker productivity. Finally, while advocating egalitarianism, Castro and the ruling elite have isolated themselves from the painful effects of the key instruments of egalitarianism, such as the rationing system (see chapter 3).

Despite the generally favorable economic results achieved during pragmatist cycles, time and time again the leadership has turned away from market-oriented policies and embraced idealist policies, in recent years halting and reversing the pro-market reform process to the detriment of the economic and social situation. Castro, with prompting from external factors, has played a key role in the start and end of the cycles. We believe the core reason why the leadership limits, slows down, and eventually reverses pro-market, pragmatist cycles and launches idealist cycles—certain to bring about adverse economic performance—is the fear of losing political control as a result of a rise in the private sector, decentralization of economic policymaking, and surge in economic behavior independent of the state and associated with the market. Political logic, therefore, trumps economic logic even though this results in deterioration of economic conditions and standard of living. To a large extent, the leadership is insulated from the economic hardships that result from their actions by a system of perquisites associated with their position. They are likewise insulated from public accountability for their actions and have no fear of being removed from their posts for malfeasance of duty since there is no electoral process to do so. The very few, very small political spaces that existed at the beginning of 2003 were shut down tight by the government, silencing peaceful internal dissidence, blocking any possibility of peaceful change, and demonstrating lack of concern about how such decisions affect the economic and social well-being of the Cuban population.

2

The Economic Crisis, Partial Recovery, and Stagnation

This chapter assesses Cuban economic and social performance during the 1990–2004 period, comparing it with 1989 (the year before the start of the economic crisis) and 1993 (the trough of the crisis). First, we examine the performance of selected macroeconomic, physical production, labor market, and social indicators. Second, we compare economic and social goals for 1998–2003 with actual performance and analyze goals for 2004. Third, we summarize the views of several Cuban economists on the current problems ailing the economy. And fourth, we analyze whether the economic slowdown since 2001 has been caused by external factors, as posited by the Cuban government, or by structural factors that have not been addressed because of the paralysis of the reform process.

We rely for our analysis mainly on official statistics from government agencies such as the Oficina Nacional de Estadísticas (ONE), the Banco Central de Cuba (BCC), and various ministries. Other information comes from Cuban academic economists, whose output has expanded significantly and improved in quality in recent years, the Economic Commission for Latin America and the Caribbean (ECLAC), and other United Nations (UN) agencies. In addition, we have relied on information from the press, including articles published in the official Cuban press and by independent journalists and economists who reside in the island.

Economic and Social Performance

To begin, we focus on indicators of domestic macroeconomic performance, external-sector performance, physical output, and labor and social conditions.

Domestic Macroeconomic Indicators

In this section we assess performance of several key domestic macroeconomic indicators: economic growth (GDP growth), investment, and financial stability (inflation, monetary liquidity, and fiscal balance). Data on these indicators are presented in table 2.

Economic Growth

GDP fell by 35% between 1989 and 1993. Beginning in 1994, the GDP growth rate turned positive and peaked at 7.8% in 1996. Subsequently, GDP growth steadily slowed down, to 6.2% in 1999, 5.6% in 2000, 3.0% in 2001, and 1.5% in 2002; there was a small improvement to 2.6% in 2003. Cuba's annual growth rate for 1990–2000 averaged –1.2%, the worst performance in the region (ECLAC, *Balance preliminar,* 2000). In 2001, Cuba's GDP at constant 1981 prices was still 13% below the level of 1989 and, in per-capita terms, was 18% below 1989. Cuba's minister of economics and planning José Luís Rodríguez has stated that Latin America lost half a decade of growth from 1997 to 2002 (Rodríguez 2002), but Cuba has lost 15 years since 1989. At the average growth rate for the 1994–2003 period, it would take Cuba at least until 2010 to return to the level of GDP per capita reached in 1989.

Change in GDP Series and Cuban Criticism of GDP Methodology

Cuba's GDP series at constant prices for 1985–2000 was based on the structure of prices in 1981. The 1981 price base was maintained for 20 years, prompting criticism from foreign scholars and ignoring United Nations recommendations regarding periodic updating of base periods in national account statistics. Beginning with GDP statistics for 2001, the base year was shifted from 1981 to 1997 and the new series was recalculated back only to 1996 (BCC 2002). A Cuban economist has noted three significant problems associated with that shift: (1) comparisons between the 1981 and 1997 series are impossible prior to 1996; (2) the series at current prices differs from the 1981 series although they should not because current-price statistics presumably did not change; and (3) gross capital formation increased significantly in the new series, by as much as 146% in one year, without explanation (Espinosa Chepe 2003a).

Absolute and per-capita GDP for the old series (1981 price base) for 1989–2001 and for the new series (1997 price base) for 1996–2002 are given in table 3. Annual values for GDP are higher for 1996–2001 in the new series than in the old series by an average of 60%.[1] Such an astounding jump in the value of GDP casts doubt on the reliability of that data.

Table 2. Cuban Macroeconomic Indicators, 1989–2003 (in percentages)

Indicator	1989	1993	1994	1995	1996	1997	1998	1999	2000	2001	2002[a]	2003[a]
GDP growth rate[b]	1.2	−14.9	0.7	2.5	7.8	2.5	1.2	6.2	5.6	3.0	1.5	2.6
GDP per capita (pesos)[b]	1,585	1,172	1.175	1,201	1,290	1,317	1,327	1,405	1,478	1,518	1,538	n/a
Gross capital formation/GDP[b]	26.7	5.4	5.5	7.2	8.2	9.5	13.0	13.1	12.6	12.8	11.5	n/a
Inflation rate[c]	0.5[d]	19.7	25.7	−11.5	−4.9	1.9	2.9	−2.9	−2.3	−1.4	5.0	n/a
Monetary liquidity/GDP[e]	21.6	73.2	51.8	42.6	42.0	41.1	40.6	38.8	37.9	41.7	44.3	42.7
Fiscal balance/GDP[e]	−7.2	−33.5	−7.4	−3.5	−2.5	−2.0	−2.3	−2.4	−2.5	−2.7	−3.2	−3.4

Sources: CEE 1991; ONE 1998–2003; BCC 2000–2002; ECLAC, *Cuba* 2004, *Política social* 2003.

a. Most 2001–2003 data are not comparable with previous data because of a change in price base.

b. At constant 1981 prices through 2000; in 2001 shifted to 1997 prices (see text); the 2001–2002 rates are authors' estimate based on ECLAC, *Balance preliminar* 2001, 2002.

c. Annual variation of the CPI.

d. Year 1988.

e. At current prices.

Table 3. Comparison of Cuban Absolute and Per Capita GDP at Constant Prices of 1981 and 1997, 1989–2002

| | GDP (Million Pesos) | | | | GDP Growth Rates (%) | | | | |
| | Absolute | | Per Capita | | Absolute | | Per Capita | | Absolute GDP |
Year	1981	1997	1981	1997	1981	1997	1981	1997	Difference (%)[a]
1989	19,586	n/a	1,852	n/a	1.2	n/a	0.1	n/a	n/a
1990	19,008	n/a	1,777	n/a	−2.9	n/a	−4.0	n/a	n/a
1991	16,976	n/a	1,573	n/a	−10.7	n/a	−11.6	n/a	n/a
1992	15,010	n/a	1,381	n/a	−11.5	n/a	−12.3	n/a	n/a
1993	12,776	n/a	1,172	n/a	−14.9	n/a	−15.4	n/a	n/a
1994	12,868	n/a	1,175	n/a	0.7	n/a	0.2	n/a	n/a
1995	13,184	n/a	1,201	n/a	2.5	n/a	2.2	n/a	n/a
1996	14,218	22,819	1,290	2,071	7.8	n/a	7.4	n/a	60.5
1997	14,572	23,439	1,317	2,118	2.5	2.7	2.1	2.3	60.8
1998	14,754	23,476	1,327	2,112	1.2	0.2	0.8	−0.3	59.2
1999	15,674	24,956	1,405	2,236	6.2	6.3	5.8	5.9	59.1
2000	16,556	26,482	1,478	2,365	5.6	6.1	5.2	5.8	60.0
2001	17,053	27,274	1,518	2,428	3.0	3.0	2.6	2.7	59.9
2002	n/a	27,573	n/a	2,462	n/a	1.1	n/a	1.4	n/a

Sources: GDP at 1981 prices from ONE 1998, 2001; for 2001, authors' estimate based on ECLAC, *Balance preliminar* 2001, *Cuba* 2002. GDP at 1997 prices from ONE 2002 and 2003.

a. 1997 prices/1981 prices.

At the end of 2001, two top Cuban economists (the minister of economics and planning and the president of the Commission of Economic Affairs of the National Assembly) argued that 2002 had been a year of low economic growth but high development and, citing Fidel Castro, openly criticized the GDP methodology developed by the United Nations, which has been used internationally for more than six decades and was adopted by Cuba in the early 1990s:

> On several occasions comrade Fidel has referred to the deficiencies of GDP to measure economic development . . . an indicator designed for a market economy, incapable of reflecting the social accomplishments, wealth distribution, and social welfare of a given country. . . . [Neo-liberal economies] utilize GDP ignoring those variables and try to impose it as a standard criterion for development [and yet] GDP may grow despite social and economic deterioration and increasing poverty. . . . [Fidel's criticisms are evident in Cuba] because such international methodology, in addition to GDP's intrinsic deficiencies, underestimates our performance in comparison with other countries, given the higher proportion of free and subsidized consumption in Cuba, hence,

placing us in a notoriously unequal position. . . . In order to solve some of those deficiencies we have worked to achieve both a more just international comparison and a proposal to measure services within GDP to provide a more realistic vision of our society (Rodríguez 2002, our translation).

Minister Rodríguez (2002) added that Cuba's GDP should be estimated based on the purchasing power parity (PPP) of the peso, compared with other currencies, to buy a given basket of goods rather than on conventional exchange rates. (There is no information on how the PPP exchange rates for Cuba have been estimated.) According to him, Cuba's GDP in 2002 was 57.7 billion pesos based on PPP exchange rates compared to 27.6 billion pesos using conventional exchange rates (5,200 and 2,445 pesos per capita, respectively). Moreover, he argued, Cuba's GDP PPP is underestimated because it does not take into account the value of free social services and consumption subsidies to the population, a correction that he reported would be incorporated in 2003.

Actually, Cuba's GDP PPP in international dollars has been calculated since the late 1980s by the United Nations Development Programme (UNDP) in the Human Development Index (HDI), which includes imputations for the value of certain services provided free by the government, something that Cuban officials state they plan to add to the GDP PPP estimates. In its latest report the UNDP estimated Cuba's GDP at $4,519 per capita (UNDP 2002). In chapter 4 of this volume, however, we demonstrate that such estimations are flawed. Furthermore, a report prepared by a Cuban institution with support from the UNDP criticized the HDI methodology and proposed to replace it with a new Human Development and Equity Index, in which Cuba would rank second among 23 countries of Latin America and the Caribbean (CIEM 2000); this may well be the methodology Rodríguez refers to.

At the December 2003 session of the National Assembly, Castro criticized again the conventional GDP methodology ("Sesión" 2003), while Minister Rodríguez gave two rates of GDP growth for that year: 2.6% based on the conventional method and 3.8% based on the new method that adds the value of free social services, price subsidies, and the "real purchasing power of the Cuban population" (Rodríguez 2003). If previously we had serious concerns about the reliability of Cuban GDP statistics, the methodological changes already introduced or under development make official figures since 2001 virtually worthless.

Investment

Gross capital formation as a percentage of GDP fell from 26.7% in 1989 to 5.4% in 1993, but rose to 13% in 1998 and 1999; it later declined to 12.8% in 2001 and to 11.5% in 2002.[2] Domestic investment averaged 9.8% of GDP for 1997–2000, declining to 9.2% in 2001 and to 7.8% in 2002 (ONE 2003), a trend that two economists have described as a process of decapitalization of the economy while some recovery was occurring (Brundenius and Monreal 2001: 130). A Cuban economist has concluded that a strong economic recovery would require an investment rate of 25% of GDP, similar to that reached for 1975–89 (Marquetti 2000). Another Cuban economist has noted that future increases in investment would have to be generated by increases in GDP, as it is not feasible to make further cuts to population consumption to shift resources from consumption to investment (Triana 2001).

Financial Stability

Inflation, based on changes in the official consumer price index (CPI), peaked at 25.7% in 1994 and turned negative (that is, became deflation) for 1999 through 2001. There is very little information on the methodology for computing the CPI, including the basket of commodities and services that might be included and the relative importance of each, whether the index is intended to measure price change at the national level or only in urban areas, and whether price changes refer to all outlets in which Cuban consumers can make purchases. The official CPI statistics indicating deflation during this period are questionable for two reasons: (1) in 2000–1 prices in agricultural free markets and state retail outlets increased significantly; and (2) monetary liquidity (monetary overhang) fell from 11.0 to 9.2 billion pesos between 1993 and 1995 (to 42.6% of GDP in 1995), but rose again subsequently, reaching 9.9 billion pesos in 1999 (38.8% of GDP), 10.5 billion pesos in 2000 (37.9% of GDP), 12.3 billion pesos in 2001 (41.7% of GDP), and 13.6 million pesos in 2002 (44.3% of GDP); the last figure is more than three times its absolute value in 1989 (CEE 1991; ONE 1998–2003). How there could have been deflation from 1999 to 2001 while monetary liquidity was rising is an interesting question.

For 2002, Cuban official statistics reported a 5% increase in inflation and a 10% increase in monetary liquidity, to 44.3% of GDP (ONE 2003), whereas ECLAC (*Balance preliminar,* 2003) estimated inflation at 7% and monetary liquidity at 44.5% of GDP. For 2003, ECLAC (*Cuba,* 2004) estimated a deflation rate of 1% and a 4% reduction in the monetary liquidity, to 42.7% of GDP, while a Cuban scholar gave the monetary liquidity as 45% of GDP (Triana 2004).

The fiscal deficit as a percentage of GDP fell from 33.5% in 1993 to 2.0% in 1997 as a result of an austerity program consisting of aggressive cuts in spending coupled with increases in revenues from higher prices and fees for government-provided goods and services. Yet it rose to 2.5% in 2000, 2.7% in 2001, 3.2% in 2002, and 3.4% in 2003. For the Latin American region as a whole, the fiscal deficit averaged 2.4% of GDP in 2003 (ECLAC, *Balance preliminar,* 2003).

External-Sector Indicators

In this section we analyze changes during the 1989–2003 period in eight external economic indicators: merchandise trade (exports, imports, and balance of trade), terms of trade, composition of exports and imports, leading trading partners, external debt, foreign investment, exchange rate, and revenue from international tourism. Data on most of these indicators are presented in table 4.

Merchandise Trade

Following a fall of 79% between 1989 and 1993, the value of merchandise (goods) exports increased modestly for 1994 through 1996, but declined and remained stagnant thereafter, falling sharply in 2002 to 1.4 billion pesos (albeit recovering somewhat to 1.6 billion pesos in 2003). By 2003, the value of exports was still 70% below their 1989 level. Meanwhile, merchandise imports shrank by 75% between 1989 and 1993, then rose steadily thereafter; in 2003, the value of merchandise imports was 4.6 billion pesos, still 43% below the 1989 level.

Because merchandise imports rose much faster than exports, the merchandise trade deficit skyrocketed, increasing fourfold between 1994 and 2001, reaching a historical record of –3.2 billion pesos in 2001; the merchandise trade deficit fell moderately to 3.0 billion pesos in 2003, 11% higher than its level in 1989. According to a Cuban economist, "these results confirm the traditional weakness of Cuba's external sector, which after more than ten years of economic transformations has been unable to substantially change its patterns of integration into the world market" (Triana 2002: 13). Furthermore, Cuba no longer benefits from the long-term loans to cover its bilateral trade deficit that the Soviet Union automatically issued until the end of the 1980s. These loans carried very low interest rates and were never repaid. At present, in order to finance its imports, Cuba has to resort to short-term loans from foreign banks and other financial institutions that charge relatively high interest rates: 5% to 8% above prevailing international interest rates (Triana 2004).

Cuba's balance of payments statistics, available only through 2001,[3] suggest that the very large merchandise trade deficits have been partly offset by substantial surpluses in services trade, due mainly to rapidly growing exports of tourism-related services (described later). Nevertheless, the goods and services trade account deficit reached an all-time high in 2000 of 894 million pesos.[4] Amortization of foreign debts (interest and principal repayments) and profits earned by foreign investors constituted significant payments out-

Table 4. Cuban External-Sector Indicators, 1989–2003

Indicator	1989	1993	1994	1995	1996	1997	1998	1999	2000	2001	2002	2003	2003/1989 (%)
Exports (billion pesos)	5.4	1.1	1.3	1.5	1.9	1.8	1.5	1.5	1.7	1.6	1.4	1.6	−70
Imports (billion pesos)	8.1	2.0	2.1	2.8	3.6	4.1	4.2	4.3	4.8	4.8	4.1	4.6	−43
Trade balance (billion pesos)	−2.7	−0.9	−0.8	−1.3	−1.7	−2.3	−2.7	−2.8	−3.1	−3.2	−2.7	−3.0	+11
Terms of trade (1989 = 100)	100.0	54.4	65.9	71.2	65.1	67.0	64.2	53.2	47.4	45.9	41.7	44.3	−56
External debt (billion $)	6.2	8.8	9.1	10.5	10.5	10.1	11.2	11.1	11.0	10.9	11.0	11.0	+77
Foreign investment (billion $)	n/a	n/a	n/a	2.1	n/a	n/a	2.2	n/a	2.2[b]	2.5[b]	2.5[b]	n/a	+19[c]
Exchange rate (pesos/1$)[a]	7	78	95	32	19	23	21	20	21	26	26	26	+271
Gross revenue from tourism (billion $)	0.2	0.7	0.8	1.1	1.4	1.5	1.8	1.9	1.9	1.9	1.7	2.0	+185

Sources: Exports, imports, and trade balance from CCE 1991; ONE 1998–2003. Terms of trade from ECLAC, *Cuba* 2002, 2003; ECLAC, *Statistical Yearbook* 2002 (the series for 1995–2001 was changed). External debt from BCC 1999–2002; ECLAC, *Estudio económico* 2003. Foreign investment from Rodríguez 2000, 2001; Triana 2003. Exchange rates from Mesa-Lago 2000; ECLAC, *Balance preliminar* 2001; ECLAC, *Cuba* 2002, 2003; ECLAC, *Statistical Yearbook* 2002. Gross revenue from tourism from Mesa-Lago 2003c.

a. Unofficial rate in CADECA, annual average.

b. Disbursed investment rather than committed investment; the latter was estimated at $4.3 billion in 2000 and $5 billion in 2001.

c. 2002/1995.

flows. On the other side of the ledger, Cuba benefited from substantial "net transfers," mostly remittances from Cubans abroad, which according to ECLAC estimates, grew from virtually nil in 1990 to $915 million in 2003 (ECLAC, *Cuba*, 2002, and *Balance preliminar*, 2003), although these estimates are questionable (see chapter 3). The current account deficit reached 776 million pesos in 2000 and 573 million pesos in 2001 (ONE 2003; ECLAC, *Cuba*, 2002; for different estimates see BCC 2001, 2002).

Terms of Trade

Cuba's merchandise terms of trade deteriorated by 56% during the 1989–2003 period (see table 4) as a result of steady decreases in the price of sugar, a fall in the price of nickel in 2001, and increases in the price of oil since 1999 (with the exception of 2001). The terms of trade deteriorated by 9.1 percent in 2002 because although nickel prices recovered, oil prices rose more than proportionally (ECLAC, *Statistical Yearbook*, 2002, *Cuba*, 2002). There was an improvement in the terms of trade in 2003 mainly because of a recovery in the price of nickel.

The terms of trade were favorably affected by a very beneficial trade agreement signed in October 2000 with Venezuela's state oil corporation, Petróleos de Venezuela S.A. (PDVSA), guaranteed by President Chávez. Through this agreement, effective for five years with the possibility of a five-year renewal, PDVSA committed to deliver to Cuba 53,000 barrels of oil per day, or about 2.7 million tons of oil per annum—about 30% of domestic needs—under the following terms: 80% of imports are contracted at prevailing world market prices payable in 90 days, while the remaining 20% are contracted at the average annual price of oil, payable in 5 to 20 years, and up to one-fifth of the latter volume can be paid through medical and sports-related services. Over the five-year life of the agreement, it is estimated that Cuba would receive transfers of about $2.6 billion. Moreover, Cuba has reportedly resold a portion of the Venezuelan oil at market prices, earning a sizeable profit. Cuba's special relationship with Venezuela has partially shielded the island from the record-setting world market oil prices.

At the end of 2001, Cuba was in arrears in paying for the Venezuelan crude purchases and had run up a debt of $95 million. PDVSA suspended shipments in April 2002 for lack of payment, an action that led President Chávez to dismiss the president of the corporation. After a period of irregular shipments associated with the brief overthrow of President Chávez, regular shipments resumed in September 2002 after Cuba agreed to restructure its oil debt, which by then had grown to $142 million. A general strike in Venezuela during December 2002 and January 2003 led to further shipping irregularities and widespread blackouts in the city of Havana. In March 2003, the general auditor of Venezuela estimated the Cuban debt for oil shipments through the end of February 2003 at $266 million (Montiel 2001; Rodríguez Castellón 2001; "Quiet Deal" 2002; "Cuba adeuda" 2003; Mogollón 2003). Based on interviews with PDVSA officials and company documents, two journalists reported in February 2004 that (1) Cuba owed Venezuela $752 million for oil deliveries for the 2001–3 period; (2) the Cuban debt represents 80% of the total debt owed PDVSA by its foreign clients; but (3) the Venezuelan government claims that Cuba is honoring the terms of the agreement (Barrionuevo and de Córdoba 2004). Furthermore, in 2004 PDVSA reportedly increased deliveries to Cuba from 53,000 to 82,000 barrels per day (from 2.7 to 4.1 million tons per annum) and the Cuban oil debt to Venezuela projected for that year was $992 million (ICCAS 2004). Cuba's Ministry of Foreign Trade has stated that it has met all terms of the agreement with Venezuela, that Cuba is not in arrears, and that irregularities in oil shipments from Venezuela in 2002 forced Cuba to purchase high-priced oil in the spot markets at a cost of $100 million ("Declaración del MINREX" 2003).

Composition of Trade

Sugar's share of merchandise exports steadily decreased from 73% in 1989 to 32% in 2002 (ONE 2003) due to the fall in the volume and value of sugar exports "because there was an acute production crisis in the sector and not because other export activities grew (with the exception of tobacco)" (Monreal 2001: 21). Thus, the export share of nickel (and to a lesser extent of tobacco) rose not only because of increases in export volumes, but also because of the sharp decline in sugar's share. The export shares of fish, citrus, and rum also fell. Turning to imports, the share of food within total imports rose from 13% in 1989 to 19% in 2002, while the share of manufactures rose from 14% to 23% over the same period. Meanwhile, the share of capital goods (machinery and transportation equipment) imports fell from 31% to 24% (CEE 1991; ONE 1999–2003). These import trends clearly illustrate (1) Cuba's decline in food self-sufficiency, as more food is being imported, and (2) the decrease in industrialization, as fewer capital goods from abroad are purchased.

Trading Partners

In 1989, 79% of Cuba's total merchandise trade was with the USSR and other members of the CMEA. After the collapse of the socialist camp, the island was forced to significantly diversify its trading partners. In 2002, Cuba's main trading partners (based on the value of two-way trade) were Venezuela (14%), Spain (13%), China (11%), Canada (8%), Russian Federation (6%, compared to 65% with the USSR in 1989), Netherlands (6%), France and Italy (5% each), and Mexico (4%; ONE 2003). Cuba is the only country in Latin America and the Caribbean that is not a full member of any of the regional trading blocs. (Cuba has observer status in CARICOM—the Caribbean Community and Common Market—but its trade with this region is minuscule.)

In December 2000, Cuba was formally accepted by Asian, Caribbean, and Pacific (ACP) countries of the European Union (EU) as a member. This was a requirement for Cuba to accede to the Cotonou Accord and therefore be eligible for aid from the $15.5 billion fund created by the EU to support development programs in ACP countries. Over the 1992–2001 period, the EU provided 145 million euros in assistance to Cuba, of which about 60% (90 million euros) was in humanitarian assistance. In 2000, the EU Commission decided to phase out humanitarian assistance to Cuba because the island was no longer in "a state of generalized emergency" (Carbone 2003: 7). These cuts made it more important for Cuba to tap into the larger pool of resources for development available to Cotonou Accord members. However, Cuba disengaged from negotiations to accede to the pact in response to some EU countries' support of UN Commission on Human Rights resolutions that in 2000–1 censured Cuba for repressing dissidents and religious groups.

In December 2002, Cuba formally applied for accession to the Cotonou Accord. Negotiations started in early 2003 and EU Commissioner for Development and Humanitarian Aid Poul Nielson visited the island in March of that year to advance the negotiations and preside over the opening of an EU diplomatic delegation office in Havana. A mere five days after Nielson's departure, the Cuban government detained 75 peaceful dissidents and sentenced them to jail sentences of 6 to 28 years. In addition, three citizens who tried to hijack a boat to flee the island were executed by firing squad. In response to these human-rights violations, the EU demanded freedom for prisoners of conscience, closed its office in Havana, suspended negotiations on Cuba's accession to the Cotonou Accord, and imposed political sanctions on the Cuban government. Castro indirectly accused the EU of being a "little band of gangsters or *mafiosos* shamefully serving the Nazi-fascist government of the United States." Fidel and Raúl Castro led demonstrations in front of the Spanish and Italian embassies in Havana and insulted the chiefs of government of both nations.[5] (Spain's Prime Minister Aznar was called "donkey"—a play on words: *asno* and Aznar—and "little fuehrer," while Italy's Prime Minister Berlusconi was christened "Benito Burlesconi.") Anticipating rejection from the EU, in May 2003 Cuba withdrew its application to accede to the Cotonou Accord. The foreign ministers of the 15 EU member states unanimously condemned the outrageous behavior of the Cuban government and reiterated their demand for the release of the 75 political prisoners and an end to repression of dissidents (Vicent 2003).

In 2000, the United States enacted the Trade Sanctions Reform and Export Enhancement Act (TSRA), which modified the U.S. trade embargo to allow direct exports to Cuba of food provided they were paid for in cash. Initially, the Cuban government rejected the U.S. initiative because it wanted to buy on credit, but later accepted offers from U.S. agriculture exporters in the aftermath of Hurricane Michelle. According to the Cuban food procurement agency Alimport, Cuba purchased U.S. food and agricultural products valued at $4 million in 2001, $176 million in 2002, and $344 million in 2003 (Luxner 2004). The U.S.-Cuba Trade and Economic Council has estimated that Cuba purchased $391.9 million U.S. agricultural commodities in 2004, making Cuba the 25th largest agricultural export market for the United States last year ("Cuba Is the 25th" 2005).[6] Although Cuba does not separate out trade with the United States in its official trade statistics, the reported $176 million in agricultural imports in 2002 would make the United States the island's eighth largest source of imports (behind Venezuela, Spain, China, Italy, Canada, France, and Mexico; ONE 2003).

According to Cuban Minister of Foreign Trade Raúl de la Nuez, in 2003 the United States became the island's seventh largest trade partner and the main supplier of food (*Granma International*, January 7, 2004). Vice Minister of Foreign Relations Ángel Dalmau declared that "at this time, every purchase of food from the United States has the political purpose of defeating the U.S. embargo." This assessment prompted an official statement clarifying that Dalmau was not authorized to make such a pronouncement and that the purchases were made in response to the needs created by Hurricane Michelle ("Nota oficial" 2003). Yet all U.S. enterprises that export to Cuba must sign a memorandum of understanding with Alimport making a commitment to lobby the U.S. Congress in favor of lifting the embargo (Cancio Isla 2003).

The Cuban government's crackdown against dissidents in March 2003 did not slow down agricultural sales to the island. (Three U.S. states cancelled trade missions to Cuba, but the rest continued to promote exports to the island and Cuba signed several agreements with U.S. states and ports.) Cuban cumulative food purchases from U.S. farmers from 2001 through 2004 exceeded $1 billion. Such a volume suggests that the agricultural interests and their allies in Congress that favor liberalizing the embargo and increasing sales to Cuba have gained the upper hand over those favoring the continuation of the embargo. It is interesting that in spite of hard rhetoric against President Bush and American imperialism, Castro has continued to purchase food products from the United States and has not taken steps to close the U.S. Interests Section in Havana.[7]

External Debt

Cuba's hard currency external debt jumped from $6.2 to $11.2 billion between 1989 and 1998, due primarily to accumulation of unpaid interest. It declined slightly to $10.9 billion in 2000 because of the depreciation vis-à-vis the dollar of the yen and the mark (the two currencies that make up most of Cuba's debt), and rose again to $11 billion in 2002 and 2003 (table 4). Cuba's debt represented 226% of the value of exports of goods and services in 2003, well above the average of 172% for the Latin American and Caribbean region (ECLAC, *Balance preliminar,* 2003, *Cuba,* 2004). About 75% of the debt has matured and Cuba is in default (BCC 2001, 2002). In 1986 Cuba stopped payments on its debt to foreign governments and sought rescheduling through negotiations with the Paris Club. These negotiations were unsuccessful, and since then Cuba has not had access to fresh government loans. Cuba made another effort to renegotiate the official debt in 1999, but again the rescheduling efforts failed and the negotiations with the Paris Club terminated in 2001 without an agreement. The debt with Russia—which assumed the debt of the former Soviet Union—and the former socialist countries of eastern Europe, estimated at $26.7 billion in 1989 (Mesa-Lago 2000), is also outstanding and there is no agreement on even a framework for repayment. Cuba argues that such debt is not "convertible in hard currency . . . and those countries unilaterally did not fulfill the terms and conditions of the debt" (BCC 2002: 40) and therefore Cuba is not obligated to repay it. At the beginning of 2004, Cuba's total external debt has been estimated by a U.S.-based research institution at $35.8 billion, $13.7 billion in hard currency obligations and an additional $22.1 billion to former socialist countries ("Cuba's Hard Currency" 2004).

In 2001, about 29% of Cuba's hard currency debt had short-term maturity, mostly one year or less, and carried high interest rates, which imposed a heavy burden on the island's finances (BCC 2000, 2002). Most of this debt consisted of supplier credits to finance exports of goods or services to Cuba. During 1996–2001, some foreign banks granted short-term (one-year) loans to finance the sugar harvests. The low sugar production levels in those years were insufficient to cover repayment of the loan principal plus the very high finance charges. As sugar output has steadily declined, it has become increasingly difficult to secure loans to finance sugar production and modernization of the sugar industry (Triana 2000).

Between 1998 and 2000, Cuba signed debt rescheduling agreements with creditors in Japan, France, the United Kingdom, Belgium, and Mexico. Cuba's performance in fulfilling these agreements was abysmal. In fact, in February 2002, Cuba's Ministry of Foreign Trade asked for the creation of a consortium of foreign creditors to restructure about $150 million in loans, a debt that had been partly restructured earlier ("Balance" 2002), but creditors were not receptive. Cuba's failures to repay foreign debts include the following:

- In 2000, Cuba rescheduled loans that had been secured to purchase French agricultural products and capital goods and agreed to a new repayment schedule; in 2001, France's export financing agency, COFACE, suspended a $175 million credit line after Cuba fell behind in repayments.
- This was followed by defaults on debts with Spain, South Africa, and Chile. Cuba is at the top of Spain's list of debtor countries in default; Cuba's debt to Spain—$810 million in 2003–represented 32.5% of Spain's overall debt in default (*Europa Press* [Madrid], May 15, 2003).
- In April 2002, Cuba suspended payments on $380 million owed to Bancomext, Mexico's export financing bank. The debt had been renegotiated a few months earlier such that repayment would occur over a 10–year period guaranteed by income from the telecommunications enterprise ETECSA, a joint venture between Cuba and Italy's Telecom Italia. In April 2004, Bancomext closed its offices in Havana and stopped doing business on the island.
- In October 2002, Cuba defaulted on a $750 million debt agreement with Japan's private sector and requested a new restructuring of it (Frank 2002a).
- In May 2003, Cuba suspended payment of $100 million to a consortium of Panamanian banks.
- Cuba owes $1.9 billion to Argentina and at the end of 2003 recognized only $1.2 billion in principal, but not the accrued interest. At the start of 2004, the Argentinean government forgave 75% of the Cuban debt, the remaining $475 million to be paid by Cuba in five years through exports of medicines and medical assistance to low-income Argentineans (Alemann 2004).

This pattern of lack of repayments and defaults has greatly reduced Cuba's ability to obtain fresh credits. At the end of 2002, Moody's, an international financial rating service, lowered Cuba's credit rating to "speculative grade, very poor" (ICCAS 2003). While defaulting on obligations to traditional suppliers, Cuba has made cash purchases of U.S. agricultural products estimated at more than $1 billion during 2001–04, hoping to draw the United States into financing food exports, credits that would be likely to experience the same fate as those of other lenders.

Foreign Investment

The value of the stock of foreign direct investment (FDI) increased modestly, from a reported $2.1 billion in 1995 to $2.5 billion in 2002 (table 4). Much higher estimates have also been reported however: $4.3 billion in 2000, $5 billion in 2001, and $5.9 billion in 2002 (Triana 2001; *Granma International*, February 3, 2003). This very large difference probably arises because the second set of estimates refers to committed investments while the first refers to actually disbursed investments (ECLAC, *Cuba*, 2001).

In 2002, the EU, through its embassies in Havana, transmitted a document to the Cuban government complaining about the lack of transparency of the legal framework for foreign investment; costly banking services, customs procedures, and public utility charges; unilateral changes to joint venture agreements favoring the Cuban partner; the requirement to pay Cuban workers' salaries to the state in dollars, while the salaries that workers receive are in pesos converted at the official exchange rate; and the short duration of work permits and visas for foreign workers, which requires very frequent renewals. In part because of these problems, foreign direct investment has slowed in recent years. Between 1988 and 2000, 540 joint ventures between Cuban and foreign enterprises were established on the island (Pérez Villanueva 2002b). At the end of 2002, 407 joint ventures were active, and there were 342 at the end of 2003 ("Menos empresas" 2004). Meanwhile, the flow of incoming FDI, according to official statistics, fell from 449 million pesos in 2000 to 39 million in 2001 (ONE 2002). Cuba did not publish FDI flows in the statistical yearbook for 2002, but an analyst has reported that they amounted to $100 million (Triana 2003).

Exchange Rate

Although the official exchange rate is one peso to one U.S. dollar, the Cuban currency is not convertible in international markets. Since the 1960s, there has been a black market for U.S. dollars in Cuba, with the exchange rate jumping from 7 pesos per dollar in 1989 to 95 pesos in 1994. Subsequently, the value of the peso strengthened, and the CADECAs created in 1995 exchanged 19 pesos for one dollar in 1996, 21 pesos in 2000, and 26 pesos in 2001–3 (table 4; ECLAC, *Estudio económico*, 2003). Reports from Cuba in October 2004 indicate that the exchange rate increased to 27 pesos ("Ofrecen" 2004). A Cuban economist has stated that the exchange rate would have been 40 pesos or more per dollar if not for government manipulation of the exchange rate (cited in Frank 2002b). Some Cuban scholars argue that the policy of artificially maintaining parity between the peso and the dollar results in severe overvaluation of the domestic currency, which in turn gives rise to disincentives for exports and productivity; therefore, they advocate an exchange rate that more closely reflects market conditions (Carranza 2001; Triana 2000).

International Tourism

The number of foreign tourists visiting Cuba rose from 270,000 in 1989 to 1,773,986 in 2000, but stagnated at 1,774,541 in 2001 and declined to 1,686,162 in 2002 because of the September 11 attacks and the subsequent decrease in international tourism (Rodríguez 2002). Over this period, gross revenue from international tourism jumped tenfold, from less than $0.2 billion in 1989 to $1.9 billion in 1999–2001, but declined to $1.7 billion in 2002; in 2003, Cuba for the first time reached the $2 billion tourist gross revenue mark, based on 1.9 million tourists (table 4). Cuba has not published information on the value of imported hard currency inputs, which would be necessary for independent calculations of net revenue from tourism. One of the authors has estimated that net revenue from tourism increased from 99 million pesos in 1992 to 1,196 million pesos in 2002 (Mesa-Lago 2003c), but there are other estimates as well (Brundenius 2002). Pérez Villanueva (2000) has argued that the nation must produce domestically a larger share of the inputs demanded by the tourism industry or the development plans of the tourism sector would induce imports valued at $3 billion per annum, roughly the magnitude of the overall merchandise trade deficit in 2001.

The international tourism industry faces other challenges, including vulnerability to changes in external factors. At the end of 2001, for example, 20 hotels out of a total of 225 and one-third of the 38,000 rooms suitable for international tourism were closed because of the fall in tourism after September 11. The occupancy rate of hotel rooms for international tourists declined from 78% in 1997 to 69% in 2001 and to 50% in 2002 (ECLAC, *Balance preliminar,* 2002, *Cuba,* 2002; BCC 2000, 2002; ONE 2001; Lage 2003b). Average expenditures, average length of overnight stay at hotels, and average receipts per visitor have all declined since the mid-1990s (Espino 2001).

Physical Output

Table 5 reports output statistics for 13 of Cuba's principal commodities for domestic production as well as for export for the period 1989–2003. For nine of the commodities, production was lower in 2003 than in 1989 (the exceptions were nickel, oil, electricity, and cigars).

Sugar

Over the 1994–2003 period sugar production averaged 3.7 million metric tons per annum, less than half the average production level of the 1980s.

Table 5. Cuban Physical Output Indicators, 1989–2003 (1,000 metric tons, unless otherwise specified)

Indicators	1989	1993	1994	1995	1996	1997	1998	1999	2000	2001	2002	2003	2003/1989 (%)
Sugar	8,121	4,246	4,016	3,258	4,528	4,318	3,291	3,875	4,057	3,748	3,522	2,200	−73
Nickel	47	30	27	43	54	62	68	66	71	77	76	72	+53
Oil	718	1,107	1,299	1,471	1,476	1,438	1,658	2,104	2,621	2,773	3,533	3,691	+414
Electricity[a]	16	11	12	12	13	14	14	14	15	15	16	16	0
Cement	3,759	1,049	1,085	1,456	1,438	1,701	1,713	1,785	1,633	1,324	1,327	1,331	−65
Textiles[b]	220	51	56	45	48	54	54	51	47	47	30	n/a	−86
Fertilizers	898	94	136	217	241	184	156	138	118	93	95	n/a	−89
Cigars[c]	308	208	186	192	194	214	264	284	246	339	327	310	0
Fish catch	192	94	88	102	106	108	93	98	79	90	67	n/a	−65
Citrus[d]	1,016	644	540	585	690	835	744	795	998	957	478	817	−20
Rice[e]	532	177	387	396	573	419	280	369	306	325	307	272	−49
Milk (cow)[e]	1,131	585	636	638	640	651	655	618	614	621	590	607	−46
Eggs[e]	2,673	1,512	1,647	1,542	1,412	1,632	1,416	1,753	1,722	1,525	1,778	1,785	−33

Sources: CCE 1991; ONE 1998–2003; ECLAC, Cuba 2001, 2004.

a. Billion kilowatt hours.

b. Million square meters.

c. Million units.

d. The series was adjusted downward for 1996–2001 by ONE (2002), without explanation.

e. The series was adjusted downward for 1999–2003 by ECLAC, Cuba 2001, 2004.

Meanwhile per-capita sugar production fell from 0.76 tons in 1989 to 0.19 tons in 2003. Sugar production in 2002–3 was 2.2 million tons, 73% below the production volume in 1989.

Several factors contributed to this dismal performance: between 1988–89 and 2001–2, sugarcane area harvested decreased by 33% and sugarcane lands under irrigation by about 40%.[8] Partly because of a shortage of imported herbicides, weeds expanded to cover as much as 15% of the cultivated area. Shortages of imported and domestic chemical fertilizers affected sugarcane yields, which fell by 46%. Because of fuel shortages, most of the sugarcane is being transported by animal traction. The scarcity of fuel, combined with a lack of spare parts, has reduced the number of mechanical sugarcane combines and sugarcane cleaning centers in operation. Finally, the industrial yield has steadily fallen from 12.5% in 1961–65 to 10.9% in 1996–2000, 10.7% in 2001, and 10.1% in 2002 (CEE 1991; ONE 1999–2003). At the end of the 2001–2 sugar harvest, the government announced that it would shut down 45% of the sugar mills because of their low efficiency combined with low world sugar prices. This action affected more than 120,000 workers, about one-third of the total, who are continuing to draw their salaries while being retrained or relocated to other jobs, mainly in the agricultural sector. The 2002–3 sugar harvest, at 2.2 million tons, was the lowest since 1933, when about 2 million tons were produced (Grupo Cubano 1963: 656).

Nickel

There are three nickel processing plants in operation: René Ramos Latour (formerly Nicaro, built by the United States in the 1940s), Pedro Sotto Alba (formerly Moa, the most technologically advanced plant, built by the United States in 1957), and Ernesto "Che" Guevara (built with Soviet assistance in the 1980s). A fourth plant, Las Camariocas, has not been completed. In 1989, the combined installed capacity of the three plants was 76,500 tons of nickel per annum, but production was only 47,000 tons, in part because the Che Guevara plant was still very new, consumed a lot of energy, and needed modernization; the Ramos Latour plant was also plagued by overconsumption of energy and lack of modernization (Mesa-Lago 2002a).

Nickel production decreased by 43% between 1989 and 1994, but an investment of $350 million from Canadian corporation Sherritt International in the Pedro Sotto plant (through the joint venture Moa Nickel S.A. between Sherritt and the Cuban enterprise General Nickel Company) stimulated production. Overall nickel output set a new record in 1996 and rose thereafter. Production peaked in 2001 at 76,529 tons, very close to the rated capacity of the plants and 63% above the 1989 production level. World nickel prices declined by 31% in 2001, however, and the value of nickel exports fell by $210 million compared with 2000. Production in 2002 fell to 75,600 tons as a result of poor performance by the Ramos Latour plant (plagued by very old technology and depletion of deposits; Triana 2004) and the Che Guevara plant; the latter plant consumes 18 tons of oil per ton of nickel, a very high energy consumption level and a very costly proposition at a time of high international oil prices (Marquetti 2002; Martínez 2002). Output in 2003 fell again, to 71,590 tons, still 53% above the 1989 level, but the world price of nickel was 42% higher in 2003 than in 2002. A Cuban economist has noted that the nickel industry needs to modernize (the Ramos Latour and Che Guevara plants, in particular), reduce overall costs, recover more nickel from the ore, and increase its world competitiveness in terms of both quality and costs (Pérez Villanueva 2003).

Oil

Oil extraction reached almost one million tons in 1986 then declined by 44% between 1986 and 1991. Spurred by $450 million in foreign investment by Sherritt Ínternational (Triana 2000) and involvement in oil exploration and extraction by foreign oil companies, oil production has increased steadily, reaching 2.77 million metric tons in 2001, 3.53 million tons in 2002, and 3.69 million tons in 2003, more than five times the level of production in 1989. Despite these impressive gains, Cuba still depends heavily on oil imports, which accounted for 20% of the total import bill in 2002.

In 1999, about 42% of Cuba's total energy needs were met through domestic production of bagasse (25%) and crude oil (17%), with minimal contributions from domestic natural gas production and hydroelectric power, so that imports accounted for 58% of national energy needs (Rodríguez Castellón 2001). As a result of the increase in domestic oil production, Cuba's dependence on imported oil has fallen substantially, but oil imports still accounted for 58% of apparent oil consumption in 2003 (ECLAC, *Cuba*, 2004).

Expectations ran high on the island in the summer of 2004 about the possibility of a significant, high-quality oil strike in an offshore area about 30 kilometers northeast of Havana, within Cuba's economic zone in the Gulf of Mexico. Spanish oil company Repsol YPF, which the Cuban government had awarded exploration rights to the area, leased the Norwegian exploration platform Erik Raude, reportedly at a cost of $195,000 per day, to carry out deep-water exploration ("Plataforma petrolera" 2004; Alfonso 2004a; "Gran expectación" 2004). Dashing Cuba's hopes, in early August Repsol YPF announced that the drilling activities had confirmed the existence of high-quality oil, but the deposit was considered noncommercial, meaning that insufficient quantities were present to justify exploration and production expenditures

("La primera exploración" 2004). Although Repsol YPF officials have indicated that they intend to continue exploration activities on the island, the disappointing results have tempered the hopes for a significant oil find ("Repsol reanudará" 2004).

Manufacturing

Overall non-sugar manufacturing output in 2002 was 56% below the 1989 level (ONE 2003). Five manufactured products shown in table 5 played a key role in Cuba's industrialization process before the economic crisis: fertilizers, textiles, cement, electricity, and cigars. These products were consumed domestically and also exported. Output of all five manufactured products fell sharply between 1989 and 1993. Although output subsequently recovered for three of the products, production in 2003 was below the 1989 level by the following percentages: 89% for fertilizers, 86% for textiles, and 65% for cement. For electricity, production in 2002 finally regained its 1989 level and remained at that level in 2003;[9] cigar output in 2002 was 6% higher than in 1989 but dropped to near the 1989 level in 2003.

Several factors have contributed to the poor performance of the manufacturing sector: shortages of fuel, lack of spare parts (most Cuban factories were equipped with machinery from the USSR and other eastern European countries and obtaining spare parts is difficult), difficulties in acquiring necessary raw materials abroad, and lack of foreign markets for Cuban manufactured products (except for cigars).

The frailty of the Cuban industrial sector resulting from postponement of critical maintenance and failure to invest in modernization and expansion can be illustrated by the severe problems faced by the electricity industry in 2004. The temporary shutdown of one of the country's major power generation plants, the Antonio Guiteras plant in Matanzas, reportedly for routine maintenance, resulted in unforeseen problems, and the unit was slow to return to operation. As a result, the poorly maintained and overtaxed electric generation system was unable to cope with demand, and electricity blackouts—lasting as long as six to eight hours per day in some areas—multiplied. In August, the government enacted conservation measures that included the shutting down of nonessential activities of state enterprises, the granting of administrative leave (vacation) to nonessential workers, the elimination of air conditioning in state offices during peak demand hours, the turning off of lights, and the scheduling of irrigation activities during evening and dawn hours ("Adoptan más medidas" 2004). In late September, the Gran Caribe tourism enterprise was forced to shut down 4,000 hotel rooms in Havana, Varadero, Cayo Largo del Sur, Las Tunas, Trinidad, and Santiago for lack of electricity (Rodríguez 2004). The Cuban government ordered 188 factories, including the largest steel-making plant in the country, sugar mills, paper producers, and citrus-processing plants, to shut down for the entire month of October in order to reduce electricity demand (García-Zarza 2004). Moreover, starting on October 25, 2004, and running through February 28, 2005, the government shortened the workday by 30 minutes ("Información del Ministerio" 2004). The impact of the electricity industry crisis on economic performance in 2004 (and beyond) is not known at this time, but it could be considerable. The costly crisis led to the dismissal of Minister of Basic Industry Marcos Portal, who had held the post since the early 1980s and was considered one of the country's top leaders ("Destituyen" 2004). In a note published in the official newspaper *Granma* on October 14, 2004, the Council of State publicly chastised Portal for character flaws and errors in judgment, specifically his failure "to alert the top leadership of the Communist Party and of the government of the risks associated with a crisis that could have been prevented . . . and has forced the nation to undertake urgent and costly measures" ("Nota oficial" 2004).

Fishing

The fishing industry, one of the major economic successes of the revolution, began to confront serious problems even before the economic crisis of the 1990s. Fish catch peaked at 244,000 tons in 1986 and by 1989 had declined to 192,000 tons. The crisis further reduced the fish catch to 88,000 tons in 1994. A gradual recovery ensued, with output increasing to 108,000 tons in 1997, but the trend subsequently reversed, decreasing to 90,000 tons in 2001 and 67,000 tons in 2002. Output in 2002 was 65% below the 1989 level and 73% below the 1986 peak. (ONE 2002 adjusted the fish catch series downward for 1997–2001 without explanation.) The industry is plagued by serious problems, among them very high indebtedness, lack of liquidity in both pesos and dollars, poor image in credit markets, and allegations of corruption. (The minister in charge of the industry was removed in March 2001.)

Agriculture

The recovery of the non-sugar agricultural sector (producing for both domestic consumption and export) has been sluggish and unsteady since the 1993 trough. In 2003, output was below the 1989 level for milk (by 46%) and eggs (by 33%), two agricultural staples listed in table 5. Citrus production, which fell sharply in 2002 (by 51% compared with 2001) as a result of three hurricanes, bounced back in 2003 but was still 20% below 1989 levels. Coffee production was 48% below the 1989 level (García Alvarez 2004). A similar pattern is evident with respect to tobacco leaf: Production peaked at 53,696 tons in 1981, declined to 16,890 tons in 1994, then increased to 34,494 tons in 2002, still 36% below the 1981 level. Meanwhile, the output of vegetables, tubers, corn, and beans recovered more robustly, although their production in per-capita terms was either stagnant or lower than in 1989 (CEE 1991; ONE 1999–2003; BCC 2002; ECLAC 2000a). Rice production recovered fully by 1996 but subsequently declined; in 2003 production was 49% below the 1989 level.[10]

The cattle herd peaked at 6.8 million head in 1967 but was less than 4 million head in 2002; the ratio of head of cattle per capita fell from 0.83 to 0.35 over this period. The reduction in the cattle herd lowered beef and milk production; consequently, beef output in 2002 was 54% below its 1989 level and milk 48% below (Mesa-Lago 2000; ONE 1999–2003). Another factor responsible for the lower milk and dairy production was a shortage of animal feed (for both cattle and poultry), imports of which declined by 52% over the 1989–2000 period, thus poultry production in 2002 was 62% below its 1989 level (Espinosa 2002c; García Alvarez 2004). Moreover, Hurricane Michelle, which battered the island in November 2001, caused agricultural losses estimated at $317 million pesos, primarily to sugarcane, banana, and citrus production; Hurricanes Isidore and Lili, which hit the island in 2002, damaged tobacco plantations and tobacco storage facilities.

The 1993–94 agrarian reform has not solved key agricultural problems such as inefficiency and lack of incentives. The new agricultural cooperatives (UBPCs), created from the breakup of state farms inherited many of the same problems and engendered new ones: They tend to be too large and to depend too heavily on the state, which "sold" them the structures and equipment they use, directs their production plans, provides them with necessary inputs, and purchases nearly all of their output at below-market prices. In addition, UBPC sales to agricultural free markets are subject to price ceilings (*topados*) that, although they provide consumers with a lower-priced alternative to sales by private farmers, reduce UBPC profits and incentives. In 1997, the UBPCs controlled 58% of total cultivated land, but as a result of state-imposed restrictions, their share of sales in the agricultural free markets was only 4%. In contrast, private farmers, who controlled only 17% of cultivable land, were able to sell their output at much higher prices, accounting for 73% of the sales in the agricultural free markets. In 2003, private farmers combined with the more traditional cooperatives[11] controlled 35% of the total cultivated land, while UBPCs controlled 46% of such land. Yet the traditional cooperatives produced 96% of total tobacco output, 75% of corn, 72% of beans, 70% of pork, 64% of cocoa (versus 36% for the UBPCs), 56% of vegetables (10% for the UBPCs), and 48% of tubers (20% for the UBPCs; ONE 2003; Pagés 2004c; "La UBPC" 2004).

In 2003, 40% of the UBPCs recorded financial losses and required state subsidies. Seventy-four percent of the land controlled by UBPCs is devoted to sugarcane and 62% of sugarcane UBPCs suffered losses in 2003, which largely explains the financial woes of the sugar sector (ECLAC, *Cuba*, 2000; Nova 2001; Varela Pérez 2003). A law enacted in 2002 to stimulate agricultural production provided traditional cooperatives with slightly more autonomy in planning production as well as higher profit sharing, but the change did not extend to UBPCs, which control the bulk of agricultural land (Mayoral 2002).

Between 2002 and 2004 the government took some measures that harmed private farmers. In 2002 the state, which owed them 300,000 pesos for sales of products to the state procurement system (*acopio*), delayed payments for seven months and froze farmers' accounts, allegedly to review their books for tax purposes (Cosano Alen 2004). In September 2003 a government regulation ordered a price reduction for products sold at agricultural free markets, which led to some markets closing and others not being able to carry produce because farmers could not sell at the lower prices and realize a profit. In several municipalities, PCC authorities demanded that farmers return to the markets, even if they offered only a single product for sale, or risk revocation of their licenses on the grounds that their failure to participate was tantamount to a strike action. As a result, UBPCs dominated the supply in the agricultural markets but the quantity, quality, and assortment of products available decreased significantly. Because of protests from consumers, the government revoked the price regulation and private farmers returned to the markets in April 2004 ("Disposición" 2004; Fornasis 2004).

Labor and Social Indicators

This section summarizes changes between 1989 and 2003 in three indicators: unemployment, real wages, and social security. Table 6 presents supporting statistical series. Other social indicators will be analyzed in detail in chapter 3.

Unemployment

Open unemployment fell from 7.9% in 1989–95 to 4.5% in 2001 (a decline of 43%) and to 3.3% in 2002. For 2003, Cuba has reported an unemployment rate of 2.3%. How was this feat accomplished when in 1995 between 500,000 and 800,000 state workers were identified as redundant and slated for dismissal, the small self-employed private sector is stagnant under increasingly tight regulations and taxes, and more than 120,000 sugar workers lost their jobs in 2002? A possible explanation is disguised unemployment. According to ECLAC, the "equivalent unemployment rate" (open unemployment plus displaced workers receiving compensation) amounted to 35%

of the labor force in 1993 and 25% in 1998 (ECLAC 1998, 2000a; ECLAC has not published more recent estimates). Furthermore, inspections conducted in 2002 by the Cuban Workers Central (Central de Trabajadores de Cuba, CTC) in workplaces with combined employment of more than one million workers found violations of labor contracts in 35% of them, mostly hiring of additional personnel to cover workers absent because of military mobilizations, participation in international assistance missions, or authorized paid leave (Maseda 2002b). Finally, according to an independent economist, the unemployment figures are distorted because individuals seeking jobs do not typically register with the municipal authorities because the only jobs to which the authorities refer them are undesirable jobs in agriculture and community services. Instead, the jobless gravitate toward illegal economic activities and "disappear" from the official job market (Ramos Lauzurique 2003).

The very low official unemployment rate probably also involves some manipulation of the number of persons who are productively employed. Since 2001, the government has created five new special employment or "study as employment" programs that in 2002 enrolled 752,729 persons, or 16% of the economically active population: (1) 326,000 persons growing vegetables full- or part-time in their backyards or in urban gardens, mostly for family consumption; (2) 238,000 persons with disabilities in regular or sheltered jobs, working at home, or working in vegetable gardens; (3) 116,000 youths from 17 to 30 years of age enrolled in evening classes four times per week and receiving compensation from the government; (4) 44,000 sugar workers who are enrolled in educational institutions ("study as employment") and receive a stipend, and 20,000 additional sugar workers who are enrolled in higher education courses; and (5) 8,500 persons enrolled in ten-month social work courses who are guaranteed a job or admission to one of eight academic careers in humanities fields upon completion of the course. To this number should be added 10,514 workers temporarily dislocated (*interruptos*) from their jobs because of the closure of their workplaces and continuing to receive 60% of their salary as well as 1,654 permanently dislocated workers (*disponibles*). All of these workers are probably considered as employed for purposes of official employment and unemployment statistics (Mesa-Lago 2005). Treating at least some of these workers as unemployed would bring the national unemployment rate to a level more in line with the results of a survey on poverty conducted in Havana in 2002: 14% of those interviewed considered themselves "poor" in employment and 13% "almost poor" (Ferriol 2003).[12]

In the 1996–2004 period, the government took several actions to restrict self-employment and other private-sector activities. These actions included (1) raising the cost of licenses to engage in self-employment by 300% and raising fees by 650%; (2) imposing a monthly tax of $850 on operators of

Table 6. Cuban Labor and Social Security Indicators, 1989–2003

Indicator	1989	1993	1994	1995	1996	1997	1998	1999	2000	2001	2002	2003	2003/1989 (%)
Open unemployment[a]	7.9	6.2	6.7	7.9	7.6	7.0	6.6	6.0	5.5	4.5	3.3	2.3	–71
Real salary (index)[b]	100	78	60	58	57	58	57	63	66	66	68	n/a	–32[c]
Social security expenses[d]	10.1	15.8	13.2	12.3	12.1	12.2	13.4	13.4	12.8	13.1	14.5	15.4	+52

Sources: Open unemployment from ECLAC, *Balance preliminar* 2000, *Cuba* 2004; ONE 2001–2003. Real salary from ECLAC 2000a, and authors' calculations based on the nominal wage and the inflation rate. Social security includes health, pensions and social assistance, from Mesa-Lago 2003c, updated with ONE 2003 and ECLAC, *Cuba* 2004.

a. As a percentage of the labor force.

b. 1989=100.

c. 2002/1989.

d. As a percentage of GDP.

paladares and suspending licenses for new such outlets; (3) establishing a monthly tax of $250 for renting one room to tourists and fines ranging from $1,000 to $1,800 for violations of this regulation; (4) banning private taxi drivers from offering their services to tourists and, in 2003, imposing on violators fines of up to 1,500 pesos and seizure of their vehicles; (5) conducting raids at the end of 2003, by teams composed of Ministry of the Interior officials, police, and members of the Committees for the Defense of the Revolution (Comités de Defensa de la Revolución, CDRs), to detect thousand of illegal activities supposedly committed by self-employed workers, transportation service providers, sellers in agricultural markets, leasers of dwellings, and others; and (6) suspending licenses, starting in October 2004, for 40 occupations previously authorized for self-employment (such as clowns, newspaper street vendors, *paladares*) and toughening regulations on self-employment overall (Bauzá 2001; Henken 2002; "Investigan" 2004; Resolución 11 of the Ministerio del Trabajo y Seguridad Social, March 13, 2004). These measures led to a sharp decline in the number of workers officially registered as self-employed, from 208,500 at the end of 1995 to 152,900 in 2002 and 149,990 in 2003, as well as a reduction in operators of *paladares* from 600 in 1995 to 150 in 2003 (ECLAC 1998; Boadle 2003; ONE 2003).

A law drafted in 1995 that would allow Cuban citizens to own and operate small businesses remains in limbo and has not been discussed in nine years. Both the Proyecto Varela (in 2002) and Roman Catholic Cardinal Ortega (2003) have called for more flexibility on the part of the state vis-à-vis the private sector, including lower taxes and legislative changes that would encourage entrepreneurship and personal and family work initiatives. The opposition's Proyecto Varela has called for a government referendum on several crucial human-rights and civic freedoms, including "that necessary legal changes be made to guarantee citizens the right to establish and operate private businesses, as individual businesses as well as cooperatives, to conduct economic activities related to the production of goods or services." In September 2003, a pastoral letter issued by all Cuban Catholic bishops criticized the "economic involution and ideological return to the 1960s" that have increased the burden of licenses, taxes, and sanctions on private workers ("La presencia social" 2003).

Real Salary

The average real salary decreased by 43% between 1989 and 1996 as increases in prices in agricultural markets more than offset increases in wages, thereby decreasing workers' purchasing power. The latter acted as a disincentive to worker productivity, which fell from 5.4% in 1999 to 2.3% in 2001, slower than GDP growth (Triana 2000, 2002). Average real salary recovered somewhat after 1996 and grew modestly through 2002. In 2002 the real salary of Cuban workers was still 32% below its level in 1989.

Strikes are banned in Cuba, and unions cannot engage in real collective bargaining to negotiate over wages or other labor conditions. In November 2003, a report by the International Labor Organization's (ILO) Committee on Freedom of Association cited Cuba for its prohibition of independent trade unions, the harassment and detention of members of independent trade union organizations, and the imposition of extremely harsh sentences (ranging from 15 to 26 years) on seven officials of fledgling independent trade unions. According to the report, Cuban authorities recognize only a single trade union controlled by the state and the PCC and prohibit independent unions, which are forced to conduct their activities in a hostile environment. There is also absence of collective bargaining, lack of the right to strike, infiltration of the trade union movement by government spies, illegal house searches, and confiscation of union property. The committee urged Cuba to correct such violations of trade union freedoms, lamented that the regime rejected the possibility of sending an ILO mission to investigate them, and requested that imprisoned trade union leaders be freed (ILO 2004, 103–25).

Social Security

The cost of providing social security (encompassing pensions, health care, and social assistance) has been climbing as a result of several factors: nearly universal free coverage, very low retirement ages coupled with very high life expectancy, and the rapid aging of the population. In 2002, Cuba's population growth rate of 0.6% was the lowest in Latin America;[13] by 2025, Cuba will have the oldest population in the region, with only two persons of working age for each pensioner. Since 1998 social security expenditures have grown at a faster rate than overall economic growth, reaching 15.4% of GDP in 2003, and they should continue growing in the future (see chapter 3).

Economic and Social Targets and Performance

This section compares economic and social targets and actual performance during the five years from 1998 to 2002, as well as in 2001, 2002, and 2003. It also presents and analyzes the prospects for the targets set for 2004 (see table 7).

1998–2003 Quinquennium

The Fifth Congress of the PCC, held in October 1997, set relatively few but very ambitious economic and social targets for 1998–2002, none of which were achieved. This section reports the targets and actual results. (Targets are

Table 7. Planned Targets and Actual Performance in Cuba, 1998–2004

	1998–2002		2001	
	Planned	Actual	Planned	Actual
GDP growth rate (%)	4–6[b]	3.5[b]	5.0	3.0
Investment/GDP (%)	n/a	n/a	14.0[d]	4.4
Monetary overhang (%)	n/a	n/a	n/a	n/a
Budget deficit/GDP (%)			2.2	2.7
Sugar output (MT)	7.0[b]	3.6[b]	4.0	3.7
Nickel output (TT)	100.0	75.1[c]	75.0	76.5
Oil output (MT)	n/a	n/a	3.4	2.8
Tobacco output (TT)	50.0	34.5[c]	n/a	n/a
Cigar production (M)	n/a	n/a	328	339
Number of tourists (M)	2.0	1.7[c]	2.0	1.8
Tourism gross revenue (B$)	2.6	1.8[c]	2.2	1.8
Agricultural output[a] (%)	n/a	n/a	10.0[d]	2.4
Industrial output[a] (%)	n/a	n/a	7.4[d]	−1.7
Exports (%)	n/a	n/a	20.0[d]	−3.2
Imports (%)	n/a	n/a	4.0[d]	0.0[f]
Trade balance goods (%)	n/a	n/a	−4.5[e]	−0.9
Open unemployment (%)	n/a	n/a	n/a	n/a
Dwellings built (T)	50.0[b]	38.4[b]	n/a	n/a

Sources: Targets from "Resolución económica" 1998; BCC 2001, 2002; Ferradaz 2002; Lage 2002, 2003b; Rodríguez 2000, 2001, 2003; Triana 2001, 2002. Performance from ONE 1999 to 2003; BCC 2001, 2002; ECLAC, *Cuba* 2003; Rodríguez 2002.
MT = million tons.
TT = thousand tons.
M = millions.
T = thousands.
B$ = billion dollars.

from "Resolución económica" 1998. Results are from tables 2–6 in this chapter; ONE 1999–2003; BCC 1999–2002; Rodríguez 2002.)

  · To increase GDP at an average annual rate of 4% to 6%. The actual growth rate was 3.5%, 13% below the lower target and 42% below the upper target.

  · To average seven million tons in sugar production per annum. Sugar output actually averaged less than 3.7 million tons per annum, slightly more than half of the target value.

  · To reach 100,000 tons of nickel production. Nickel output was 75,116 tons in 2002, 25% under the target.

	2002		2003		2004
	Planned	Actual	Planned	Actual	Planned
	3.0	1.5	1.5	2.6	2.6
	n/a	n/a	n/a	n/a	n/a
	0.0[f]	8.6	n/a	n/a	n/a
	2.9	3.2	3.4	3.4	
	4.0	3.6	3.8	2.2	2.6
	>76.5	75.1	78.4	71.6	76.8
	4.1	3.5	3.6	3.6	6.3[d]
	n/a	n/a	n/a	n/a	n/a
	n/a	n/a	n/a	n/a	n/a
	1.8	1.7	1.9	1.9	2.1
	1.8	1.8	n/a	n/a	n/a
	n/a	n/a	3.0[d]	2.3[d]	3.7[d]
	n/a	n/a	4.6[d]	−2.1	2.5[d]
	n/a	n/a	n/a	n/a	7.5[d]
	n/a	n/a	n/a	n/a	[g]
	n/a	n/a	n/a	n/a	[g]
	4.5	3.3	<3.3	2.3	<3.0
	20.0	28.4	n/a	n/a	n/a

a. Non-sugar sector.

b. Annual average.

c. Year 2002.

d. Percentage increase over previous year.

e. Percentage decrease over the previous year.

f. No change over previous year.

g. Decrease of unspecified amount planned.

· To increase tobacco leaf output to 50,000 tons. Output in 2002 was 34,494 tons, 31% below the target.

· To attract two million tourists and increase gross tourism revenue to $2.6 billion. A total of 1,686,162 tourists visited Cuba in 2002, and gross revenue from tourism was $1.79 billion. Hence these targets fell short by 16% and 31%, respectively.

· To meet domestic oil needs through a combination of higher domestic production, energy conservation, and cuts in consumption. Although oil production expanded over the period, the share of oil needs met by domestic production increased only modestly to 33% in 2001 and 40% in 2002.

- To reduce income inequalities through taxation. A progressive general income tax has not been implemented and inequalities have expanded significantly (see chapter 3).
- To construct 50,000 dwelling units per annum. An annual average of 38,400 housing units was built during the period, 25% below the target.

The Sixth Congress of the PCC was scheduled for October 2002. It was cancelled and as of the first quarter of 2005 has not been rescheduled. The significant failure to meet the 1998–2002 economic and social targets may have been one of the contributing factors in the postponement of the Sixth Congress.

Year 2001

Out of 13 economic targets set for the year 2001, 12 went unfulfilled. No targets were set for inflation, monetary liquidity, and social services. (Targets are from Rodríguez 2000; BCC 2001; and Triana 2001. Performance figures are from tables 2–6 in this chapter; ONE 2001–2; BCC 2002; ECLAC, *Cuba*, 2002.)

- To expand GDP by 5%. Actual GDP growth was 3%, 40% below the target.
- To reduce the fiscal deficit to 2.2% of GDP. The actual deficit was 2.7% of GDP, 23% above the target.
- To produce four million tons of sugar. Actual production was 3.7 million tons, 8% under the target.
- To produce 75,000 tons of nickel. Actual production was 76,529 tons, 2% above the target, but the decline in world market nickel prices resulted in a decline in export value.
- To produce 3.4 million tons of oil. Actual production was 2.77 million tons, 18% under the target. World market oil prices declined, a favorable development for Cuba, and Cuba entered into an agreement with Venezuela that further reduced the cost of oil imports.
- To increase the production of cigars by 36%. The target was surpassed by 3%.
- To increase non-sugar industrial output by 7.4%. There was an actual reduction of 1.7%.
- To increase non-sugar agricultural output by 10%. Actual growth was 2.4%, about one-quarter of the target.
- To attract two million tourists and $2.2 billion in gross tourism revenue. Actual performance was 1.77 million tourists (12% under the target) and $1.85 billion in gross revenue (16% below the target).
- To increase exports by 20%. The value of exports actually declined by 3.2%.

- To increase imports by no more than 4%. Imports were essentially stagnant between 2000 and 2001.
- To reduce the merchandise trade deficit by 4.5%. The deficit decreased by only 0.9%.
- To achieve full implementation of the new enterprise management system, *perfeccionamiento empresarial*. Only 321 out of 3,000 enterprises (11%) had the system in operation by mid-2002.

Year 2002

Although the Economic and Social Plan for 2002 was not published, several official targets were released, some of them vague. (Targets are from BCC 2002; Ferradaz 2002; Lage 2002; Rodríguez 2001; Triana 2002. Performance figures are from tables 2–6 in this chapter; ONE 2003; BCC 2002; ECLAC, *Statistical yearbook*, 2002; Martínez 2002; Rodríguez 2002.)

- To achieve GDP growth of 3%. Actual growth was only 1.5%, one-half of the target but higher than the 1.1% reported by Cuban officials at the close of the year. An independent Cuban economist—who was condemned to 20 years in jail in 2003—cast doubt on the official figure of 1.1% growth reported at the end of 2002, arguing that there was actually a decline in GDP (Espinosa Chepe 2002b).
- To prevent an increase in monetary liquidity. Monetary liquidity rose by 8.6% and inflation grew by 5% for reasons noted later.
- To limit the budget deficit to 2.9% of GDP. The actual deficit was 3.2% of GDP because of increases in expenditures necessary to maintain the salary of 100,000 dismissed sugar workers, repair the damage caused by two hurricanes, and meet increases in pension and health-care expenditures.
- To produce four million tons of sugar. Actual sugar production was 3.6 million tons, 10% below the target. Sugar world market prices strengthened in 2002, however, a favorable development for Cuba.
- To produce more nickel than in 2001. There was actually a decline in production of 1.8% compared with 2001 (75,116 tons versus 76,529 tons). The very high energy consumption of this industry has led the government to consider shutting down some of the plants. There was an increase in output from the Moa plant (a joint venture with Sherritt International) and decreases in the other two.
- To produce 4.1 million tons of oil. In May 2002, the target was reduced to 3.56 million tons, and at the end of the year production of 3.53 million tons was reported, nearly 15% below the original target.
- To maintain the number of tourists and gross income from tourism. Tourist arrivals in 2002 totaled 1.686 million, 5% lower than the 1.775 million tourist arrivals in 2001. Meanwhile gross income from tourism

in 2002 was 1.769 billion pesos, about 4% below the 1.840 billion pesos recorded in 2002.
· To maintain unemployment at the 2001 level. Cuba officially reported that unemployment in 2002 was 3.3%, compared to 4.5% a year earlier. As has been discussed previously, this feat was accomplished by counting as employed the 64,000 dismissed sugar workers who were enrolled in education and training in that year as well as 326,000 persons engaged in urban agriculture. If these two groups were not counted as employed, the unemployment rate would have been about 12%.
· To build 20,000 new housing units. In 2002, 28,400 housing units were reportedly built, 40% above the target but fewer than the number of units destroyed by the hurricanes.

Year 2003

Coming on the heels of two years when the majority of targets had not been met, the targets set by the Economic and Social Plan for 2003 were modest (Rodríguez 2002; Martínez 2002; Lage 2003b). The targets, available information, and commentaries on their fulfillment follow (Madruga 2003; "Sherritt Eyes" 2003; Triana 2004; Ramos Lauzurique 2003; Rodríguez 2003; Martínez 2003; Barreiro 2003; "Crecimiento del PIB" 2003; ECLAC, *Cuba,* 2003).

· To achieve GDP growth of 1.5%, half of the target for 2002 and slightly above the 1.1% rate of growth in 2002. According to Minister of the Economy and Planning Rodríguez (2003), actual GDP growth in 2003 was 2.6%, 73% above the target. Writing from prison, independent economist Arnaldo Ramos Lauzurique (2003) questioned the veracity of the official figures, arguing that they were inconsistent with the poor sugar harvest, the consequent reduction in sugar exports, the uneven performance of the non-sugar industrial sector (only 10 of 21 branches of the sector met or exceeded their targets), and the unimpressive performance of the non-sugar agricultural sector. Targets and performance in some of these key sectors are discussed in more detail later.
· To limit the fiscal deficit to 3.4% of GDP. Deputy Osvaldo Martínez (2003) informed the National Assembly in December 2003 that the budget deficit had remained within the limits established in the budget law, suggesting that the target was met. On the other hand, Finance Minister Barreiro stated that government expenditures in 2003 were 20.661 billion pesos while revenues were 19.512 billion, for a deficit of 1.149 billion pesos, equivalent to 3.5% of GDP (3.4% according to ECLAC, *Cuba,* 2004). Among the significant expenses reported by Minister

Barreiro were 832 million pesos in subsidies to unprofitable state enterprises (primarily in the sugar industry) and 592 million pesos in transfers to the sugar and coffee sectors.

· To increase sugar output by 4.4% to 3.76 million tons. Sugar production in 2003 was 2.2 million tons, nearly 42% below the target. As indicated earlier, this figure represents the lowest level of production since 1933, when about two million tons were produced.

· To increase nickel output by 4.4%, or to about 78.4 thousand tons. Actual output was 4.7% below the 2002 level, or about 71.6 thousand tons, although Cuban officials point out that overall export revenue from nickel was higher than in 2002 because of strong world market nickel prices.

· To increase oil and gas output by 3%. Output of oil rose by nearly 4.5%, and oil and gas output combined by 4%.

· To increase the number of tourists to 1.9 million, 11.3% over the 1.7 million tourists in 2002. Reportedly the number of tourists rose by 12.7%, exceeding the target.

· To increase non-sugar industrial output by 4.6%. The actual increase was 2.1%, less than half of the projected rate.

· To increase non-sugar agricultural output by 3%. Minister Rodríguez (2003) reported a 72% increase in citrus production, severely affected in 2002 by the hurricanes, as well as recovery in the production of tubers, vegetables, bananas, and other crops, as well as strong growth in urban agriculture. Overall, however, ECLAC (*Cuba*, 2003) reported a 2.3% rate of growth for the agricultural sector, below the target.

· To further decrease the unemployment rate to under 3.0%. The reported 2002 rate of 3.3% was the lowest since the earliest 1970s, and clearly fabricated. For 2003, the Cuban government has claimed a further decrease to 2.3%, a figure as unbelievable as the one for the previous year. Explaining the apparent high levels of employment are several "study as employment" and compensation programs involving 16% of the labor force. Alternative estimates of the unemployment rate range from 9% to 25%.

Year 2004

As in recent years, the full Economic and Social Plan for 2004 has not been published. However, government officials with economic portfolios made presentations about the plan before the National Assembly in December 2003 that contain a scattering of targets in some areas of the economy. The targets for 2004 from those statements (Rodríguez 2003; Martínez 2003) are summarized as follows:

- To achieve GDP growth of 2.6%, the rate the government reported for 2003. This is a more ambitious growth target than the 1.5% rate planned for 2003 but still a lowering of expectations from 1998–2002 (projected rate of growth of 4% to 6%), 2001 (5%) and 2002 (3%). Government reports argued that the target had been surpassed in the first half of 2004 but damage inflicted by Hurricane Charley combined with the electricity system breakdown in the second half of the year might reduce the actual rate.

- To increase sugar production over the previous harvest to 2.6 million tons (Frank 2004d). Considering that the 2003 output of 2.2 million tons was abysmally low and that it occurred at a time of considerable turmoil in the sugar industry because of the shutting down of mills, achieving this target seemed feasible. In the spring of 2004 various problems were reported: insufficient sugarcane for the mills; a low industrial yield, averaging 10.5%; broken mills and equipment; substantial lost time in four provinces; and a drought in the eastern provinces (Frank 2004d; Varela Pérez 2004b). In June, Vice President Lage announced that the 2004 harvest had concluded and production was about 2.5 million tons, 74,600 tons (2.9%) short of the target (Varela Pérez 2004b; Grogg 2004).

- To increase nickel production to 76,800 tons, with higher revenues based on higher world market prices in 2004 compared with 2003. Minister Rodríguez (2003) reported that the three nickel plants operated at full capacity in 2003 and that an expansion of 40,000 tons is planned in the next five years, but it is questionable whether a 7.7% increase (a historical record of almost 77,000 tons) can be achieved within one year.

- To increase oil and gas production by 6.3%, to 4.6 million tons. The lack of commercial success of the high-profile Repsol YPF drilling efforts conducted in the summer of 2004 was a disappointment to foreign oil companies and to Cuba, but foreign interest in drilling in Cuba remains strong. Reportedly, the Brazilian state oil company Petrobras is again considering exploratory drilling in Cuba ("Brasil tras" 2004).

- To increase electricity generation by 1.6% and to generate 100% of electricity using domestic fuels. The breakdown of Cuba's most important thermoelectric plant and problems in other plants in mid-2004, extending into the fall of that year, suggest that this target may not be met.

- To increase the number of tourists by 10.5%, surpassing for the first time the 2 million mark and actually reaching 2.1 million tourists. Also projected is an unspecified increase in revenue generated by the tourism industry. These targets probably will be fulfilled, in spite of a reduction in U.S. tourists due to travel restrictions imposed by the Bush administration.

- To increase non-sugar agricultural output by 3.7%, through expected increases in production of tubers, vegetables, beans, coffee, and pork, among other products. Contributing to the projected increase in non-sugar agriculture is the conversion of land formerly devoted to sugarcane to other agricultural uses as part of an overall restructuring of the sugar industry.

• To increase non-sugar industrial output by 2.5%. Sectors of the non-sugar industrial sector expected to expand strongly in 2004 include manufactured foods, medicines, metalworking, and basic and light industries, but the electricity blackout may affect such plans.

• To increase merchandise exports by 7.5% over 2003 levels, while reducing imports from 2003 levels, with a consequent improvement in the merchandise trade deficit.

• To continue employment generation programs so as to maintain current levels of employment. We have interpreted this target as seeking to maintain the unemployment rate unchanged from the previous year.

Views of Cuban Economists on the Current Situation

In the first half of the 1990s there was a lively debate in Cuba on alternatives for economic reform, but the discussion was abruptly halted by the government in mid-1996 with the dismissal from their jobs of three of the principal participants. Since 2000, Cuban economists have again begun to write about the economic problems of the island and suggest reforms to address them. Limitations of time and space do not allow us to examine thoroughly all points of view expressed on these topics. To illustrate the breadth and depth of the analysis, we have chosen to focus on the writings of five well-known Cuban scholars: Julio Carranza (2001), Alfredo González Gutiérrez (2001), Hiram Marquetti (2000), Pedro Monreal (2001), and Juan Triana (2000, 2003). All recognize the economic progress that has been achieved since the depth of the economic crisis in the 1990s, some explicitly reject neoliberalism, and virtually all express the need to work for change within a socialist framework. Although there are differences among them, their identification of current problems is markedly similar. In what follows we summarize their views, many of which we share, at some points adding to their analysis or updating information. We bracket our comments to distinguish our views from those of the Cuban academics.

• The 1997–98 economic slowdown was an indicator that the economic recovery was not firmly anchored and therefore returning to pre-crisis economic conditions would be difficult. Another view is that the slowdown resulted from the "relative paralysis" of economic reform (Marquetti).

· The partial economic restructuring carried out in the 1990s was not capable of transforming the economy to the degree necessary to promote growth within the current international environment (Carranza). The progress that has been made lacks a solid foundation that would guarantee sustainable recovery. By 2000, the economy had not yet fully recovered and remained below 1989 levels (Marquetti). [In 2003, per-capita GDP was still significantly below 1989 levels.]

· Cuba has been unable to generate internal resources for investment to enable a full recovery. The former Soviet Union and other socialist countries contributed high levels of capital prior to the 1990s, but returning to those favorable conditions is impossible. New investments have been insufficient to support long-term growth. It is impossible to restrict consumption further to divert resources to investment, as consumption is already very depressed, so the only way out is to increase domestic efficiency and enterprise competitiveness (Marquetti).

· Tourism, foreign investment, remittances from abroad, fuels, and a few export lines contributed to the economic recovery of the 1990s, but their multiplier effects are insufficient to sustain dynamic growth and reduce external dependency (Carranza, Marquetti). Fuels are the only engine of growth that has not been depleted; the rest demand new conditions to recover their dynamism (Triana).

· Macroeconomic adjustment is still insufficient and continues to give rise to economic and social tensions. The process of change generates an internal conflict between economic objectives and political effects (Carranza, González). [The paralysis of reforms in 1996 resulted from leadership concerns about perceived negative political and social effects of the reform process, such as decentralization of decision making, increased independence and power of the private sector, and inequality. In the decision to halt the reform process, political objectives (survival of the regime and maintenance of control) took precedence over economic objectives (growth and financial stability).]

· The sugar industry is in a depression, which has a dampening effect on economic recovery. The sharp fall in sugar output has harmed the manufacturing sector and the economy overall and made it difficult to obtain international credit. The decline in the sugar share of total exports is not a result of growth in other exports but rather of a sharp decline in sugar exports (Marquetti, Monreal). [The situation of the sugar industry worsened in 2002–3 with the closing of about half of the mills in 2002 and a very poor sugar harvest in 2003.]

· The bulk (83%) of Cuban exports (sugar, nickel, tobacco, and fish) are traditional, primary products, typical of underdeveloped countries. Manufactured or semi-manufactured products represent a tiny minority

(7%) of exports (the biotechnology industry has not had a significant effect on international markets). The result has been excessive dependency on low-value-added activities and stagnant exports of high-value-added, high-technology products (Monreal, Carranza).

• Tourism services do not result in industrial upgrading, are typical of underdeveloped countries, are not indicators of progress toward higher modes of international insertion, and do not necessarily contribute to development. There is a very high imported component in the activities that generate hard currency, such as tourism (Monreal, González).

• The very high and growing dependency on imports of essential food products, as well as of fuel, curtails the importation of intermediate and capital goods, which are crucial for economic growth (Carranza). [In 2002, food and oil imports represented 19% and 21%, respectively, of total imports, for a combined 40%; in contrast, machinery and chemical imports represented 24% and 10%, respectively, of total imports, for a combined 34%.]

• The overvaluation of the peso at the official exchange rate creates disincentives to exportation. The dual monetary system and the two exchange rates are problems that must be corrected (Triana, González). [In 2002–4, the official exchange rate was one peso for one dollar but the government-run CADECAs exchanged 26 pesos for one U.S. dollar in 2002–3 and 27 pesos per dollar in 2004. Until there is currency convertibility, the competitiveness of Cuba's exports cannot be determined.]

• Economic growth has not reduced the deficit in the balance of payments, an obstacle to further growth. There is very limited access to external credits, which are only short term and very costly and hence difficult to pay back (Carranza, Marquetti). [We discussed this issue in more detail earlier in this chapter. The external-sector problems deepened in 2002–4.]

• Monetary liquidity significantly increased in 2000 (by 6%); 79 months after the inception of a program to reduce cash in the hands of the population (*desmonetización*), its effectiveness in extracting money from circulation was decreasing (Carranza). [The increases in monetary liquidity in 2001 (by 19%) and 2002 (by 9%) clearly support this analysis.]

• Prices in agricultural markets have not diminished in six years (1994–2000), feeding inflation and limiting the population's food consumption (Carranza). [Prices in agricultural markets rose in 2002, as did prices in dollar stores in 2002–4, with an adverse effect on population purchasing power and consumption.]

• There is a disconnection between wages, denominated in pesos, and prices of goods in free markets, denominated in U.S. dollars or responding to the unofficial peso–U.S. dollar exchange rate. This has negative effects: distortions in agricultural production due to differential returns between the price-regulated and unregulated sectors, obstacles to reestablishing formal sector work as the fundamental source of family income, disincentives to increase labor productivity, and obstacles to raising consumption by the population (Carranza, Triana).

· The enterprise management reform process (*perfeccionamiento empresarial*) is new and slow in its application. At present, there is "verticalism" and a trend toward enterprise concentration. The management reform process is bound to generate surplus labor (either open or hidden unemployment) that will be difficult to place elsewhere (Carranza, González, Triana). [In April 2003, *perfeccionamiento empresarial* was operational in only 15% of state enterprises (*Granma*, April 20, 2003). The dismissal of more than 120,000 sugar industry workers in 2002 must have worsened unemployment, despite official figures to the contrary.]

· Real wages have declined, and there is disguised unemployment, income stratification, and significant concentration of bank deposits in the hands of a minority of the population (Triana, Carranza).

The Economic Slowdown and Its Causes

In 2001 (particularly in the last quarter) and in 2002, several external events affected the Cuban economy negatively:

· The terrorist attacks of September 11, 2001, in the United States and the war in Afghanistan created an atmosphere of fear that significantly decreased international travel and tourism, which already had been adversely affected by the global recession of 2001 and the sluggish 2002 recovery.

· International market prices of nickel fell in 2001 (especially in the second half). Because of the recession, international market prices of sugar continued to decline in 2001–2, and international market prices of oil fell in 2001 but rose in 2002.

· Hurricane Michelle battered the central region of the island in 2001, causing damage estimated at 1,866 million pesos; in 2002, Hurricanes Isidore and Lili struck the western part of the island, causing 713 million pesos in damage.

· The political situation in Venezuela deteriorated in 2002, and deliveries of Venezuelan oil were suspended for several months.

· Hard currency credit became more difficult and more costly to obtain.

The official Cuban government position is that the economic slowdown of 2001–2 resulted exclusively from these external factors (BCC 2002). Yet the Cuban economists whose views we summarized previously (views that were written before the external events occurred) argued that (1) the structural problems of the Cuban economy were not corrected by the economic reforms of 1993–96; (2) the halting of the reforms had adverse economic effects; and (3) absent reforms, a recovery would be difficult to sustain. In 2003, one of these economists rhetorically asked, "Have the means [*resortes*] that made the economy grow over the last seven years been exhausted?" After analyzing different factors contributing to economic growth, he concluded that with the exception of the energy sector, those means had indeed been exhausted and new approaches were needed to revitalize the economy (Triana 2003). Thus, the external shocks of 2001–2 aggravated an already troubled economic situation but did not cause it. The same view is shared by economists outside the island; as one of us has said, for example (Pérez-López 2002: 517), "The disappointing performance of the economy in 2001 can be attributed to the inefficiency of Cuba's socialist economy [and the paralysis of essential structural reforms], compounded by a severely worsened external economic environment."

Furthermore, Cuban officials have exaggerated or distorted the influence of some external factors on the economic slowdown. For instance, the world market price of nickel did decline in 2001 (especially in the second half), but it remained at the 1999 level and above the 1998 level; the external shock argument is not applicable to 2002–3, when nickel prices rose above their 1998–99 average. The world price of sugar began to fall in 1996, when the Cuban economy was recovering; prices did fall sharply in the first half of 2001 but recovered in the second half of 2002. World oil prices rose in 2000, a year when Cuba recorded a reasonable growth rate, fell in 2001 (particularly in the last quarter) when growth slowed down, and increased significantly in 2002 and 2003 (prices from IMF 2001–3). Finally, the merchandise trade deficit reached a historical high in 2000—before the negative external factors took their toll—remained unchanged in 2001, and decreased in 2002. Cuban officials also conveniently ignored or minimized several positive external factors: a very favorable oil deal with Venezuela that guaranteed access to supplies at a discounted price, a reported 21% increase in remittances from Cubans abroad in 2001, and a 156% increase in foreign investment in 2002, according to a Cuban scholar.

Conclusion

Despite the recovery that began in 1994, Cuban GDP decreased at an average annual rate of 1.2% from 1991 through 2000, the worst performance in Latin America and the Caribbean. GDP growth slowed from 5.6% in 2000 to 3.0% in 2001 and 1.5% in 2002; in the latter year, per-capita GDP was still well below the 1989 level. GDP reportedly grew by 2.6% in 2003, but that estimate uses the new GDP series based on 1997 prices that increased GDP values by 60% over the previous series based on 1981 prices. Top Cuban leaders have criticized the international methodology used to calculate GDP and estimated an even higher Cuban growth rate of 3.8% in 2003, by adding the value of free social services and price subsidies, hence rendering Cuban GDP not comparable with that of other countries. At the average annual growth recorded in 1994–2003, it would take at least until 2010 for per-capita GDP to return to its 1989 level. According to official statistics, there was deflation (that is, negative growth in price levels) in 1999–2001; over this period, however, monetary liquidity (overhang) rose by 26%. In 2002, inflation rose by 7% and the monetary overhang by 10%. The budget deficit rose steadily from 2.4% of GDP in 2000 to 3.4% in 2003.

Sugar output averaged 3.7 million tons for 1993–2003, less than half the level of the 1980s. Forty-five percent of the sugar mills were shut down in 2002, and sugar production in 2003 was 2.2 million tons, the lowest since 1933. Output in 2004 was roughly 2.5 million tons, an improvement over 2003 but still 2.9% below the 2.6 million ton target. The main impediment to the attainment of the target in 2004 was sugarcane availability. Ministry of the Sugar Industry officials reported at the end of August 2004 that the sugarcane planting plan—part of the sugarcane destined for the 2005 harvest—was significantly behind schedule, with only 51% of the target met (Delgado 2004a, 2004b). The very low level of sugarcane reserves (uncut cane) from the previous harvest and the difficulty in meeting planting targets do not augur well for the 2005 harvest. To make things worse, in November 2004, the minister of the sugar industry announced that the 2005 harvest would start in January 2005, rather than in December 2004, thereby shortening its length ("Aplazan" 2004).

Oil and nickel production remains relatively strong. Output of oil continued to rise and set new production records. While the lack of commercial viability of the drilling efforts conducted in the summer of 2004 was a disappointment to foreign oil companies and to Cuba, foreign interest in drilling on the island appears to remain strong. Nickel output fell 6.4% between 2001 and 2003; with three plants operating at full capacity, reportedly there is a plan to expand production capacity in the next five years but concrete details are not available.

Production of other key industrial and agricultural goods (cement, textiles, fertilizers, citrus, fish, milk) sharply declined in 2000–2. Only the output of cigars and rice rose, but in 2003, output of both fell from 2002 levels, in the case of cigars by 5.2% and in the case of rice by 11.4%. Agricultural output in 2004 and 2005 is likely to be adversely affected by weather. The western part of the island was battered by two hurricanes in 2004: Hurricane Charley, which crossed the island over the city and province of Havana in mid-August, and Hurricane Ivan, which crossed Pinar del Río province in mid-September, bringing winds and heavy rains, and causing flooding in agricultural areas. At the same time, the eastern provinces continued to face a very serious drought, with the principal dams in the provinces of Camagüey, Holguín, Las Tunas, and Guantánamo holding less than 20% of capacity (Pagés 2004b). Despite the two hurricanes, overall precipitation in the country through the end of September 2004 was approximately 79% of the historic average, while the eastern provinces fared even worse: Las Tunas, 45% of the historic average; Camagüey, 59%; Granma, 63%; and Santiago de Cuba, 68% (Peláez 2004).

Overall exports decreased by 3% in 2001 (because of the fall in the volume of sugar exports and of world market prices for sugar and nickel), while imports were stagnant, resulting in a historical high in the merchandise trade deficit of 3.2 billion pesos. Despite a rise in world market prices of nickel and sugar in 2002, overall exports decreased by a further 14% in that year due to declining or stagnating output of main exports. Because imports were reduced by 14%, the merchandise trade deficit actually declined slightly to 2.7 billion, the first decrease since 1993. In 2003, exports rose to 1.6 billion pesos, but imports rose even faster to 4.6 billion pesos, so that the deficit rose again to 3.0 billion in 2003. Merchandise trade deficits equivalent to 9% to 10% of GDP, compounded by the lack of access to credits from international financial markets, present a formidable challenge. Unless merchandise exports increase, Cuba will have to cut imports further, harming economic activity and provoking a vicious cycle in the economy. The merchandise trade deficit has been partly offset by earnings from the services sector, mostly from tourism, by significant flows of remittances from Cuban Americans living abroad, and by foreign investment. However, tourism earnings decreased in 2001–2 (although they recovered in 2003), and foreign investment has been stagnant since 2000. The current account deficit rose to 2% of GDP in 2002.

Cuba's dreary record in repaying its debts to foreign creditors has severely affected its access to international financial markets. Cuba has had to resort to costly short-term loans to obtain sorely needed financing of its current account deficit. The hard currency foreign debt contracted slightly from $11.0 billion in 2000 to $10.9 billion in 2001 because two of the currencies in which the debt was contracted depreciated vis-à-vis the dollar, but it rose back to $11 billion in 2002 and remained at roughly this level in 2003. Cuba has stopped payments on its debts to Japan, France, Spain, Mexico, and several other countries and has requested restructuring; debt negotiations with the Paris Club broke down in 2001. Venezuela (currently Cuba's principal trading partner) suspended oil deliveries at subsidized prices for five months in 2002 because the island owed $142 million on fuel deliveries, and Cuba fell $750 million in arrears by the end of 2003. Incoming foreign investment, which was reported at $448 million in 2000, fell to $39 million in 2001, and has been estimated at $100 million for 2002. Cuba's entrance into the Cotonou Accord was indefinitely postponed by the EU in 2003. As a result of changes to the U.S. embargo that permitted cash sales of U.S. agricultural products to Cuba, the island bought in cash close to $1 billion of food products from the United States in 2001–4, while reducing food imports from Europe and Canada. The number of tourists visiting Cuba stagnated in 2001, declined by 5% in 2002, and reportedly increased by 12.7% in 2003; meanwhile, gross revenue from tourism decreased by 5% in 2001 and by an additional 3% in 2002, but rebounded strongly in 2003 with a 16% increase.

Open unemployment fell from 5.5% in 2000 to a reported 3.3% in 2002 and to 2.3% in 2003, but these statistics are highly questionable and there are no data on underemployment or hidden unemployment. Real wages fell by 32% between 1989 and 2002; increases in prices in dollar shops and agricultural markets, combined with the devaluation of the peso (from 21 to 26 for one dollar), led to a decline in consumer purchasing power. Social security expenditures jumped to 15.4% of GDP, the highest in Latin America, and will continue to grow as the Cuban population rapidly ages to become the oldest in the region.

All economic targets set by the Fifth Party Congress for 1998–2002 were unfulfilled. Of 14 targets set for 2001, 12 were not met. Out of nine targets set for 2002, seven were not fulfilled (GDP growth; inflation; monetary overhang; oil, nickel and sugar output; number of tourists; and tourist revenue), whereas two were reportedly met (unemployment rate and housing, the former dubious and the latter still below the number of dwellings destroyed by hurricanes in that year). The nine targets set for 2003 were quite modest compared with those for 2001–2. Yet four of them were not fulfilled (sugar production, the lowest harvest in 70 years, nickel production, and non-sugar industrial and agricultural output). Three other targets were met (budget deficit, number of tourists, and oil output), and fulfillment of two others was dubious (GDP growth and unemployment). The decline in overall industrial and agricultural output, as well as in the two most important products, combined with the questionable new GDP series, raises serious doubts about the alleged 73% overfulfillment of the 2003 economic growth target. In the same vein, the reported continuing reduction in open unemployment in 2003 appears to be the result of data manipulation.

There is a remarkable consensus among five Cuban economists whose work we have reviewed with regard to the economic problems that face the island. Writing before the 2001–2 economic slowdown, they agreed that the 1993–96 reforms would not generate sustainable growth and identified significant structural problems in the economy, among them inadequate capital investment (domestic and foreign); very high levels of monetary liquidity and of actual or repressed inflation; monetary dualism; overvaluation of the peso at the official rate; excessive centralization of economic management; a deteriorating sugar industry; generalized inefficiency of state enterprises; continuing dependence on merchandise exports of basic commodities; high concentrations of food and fuel imports, to the detriment of imports of capital goods; continuing expansion of the merchandise trade deficit; a high import component to the tourism industry; a fall in real wages and lack of consumer purchasing power to buy products sold in the agricultural markets and dollar stores; rampant hidden unemployment; and growing income inequality. The five economists supported an open debate on these problems and how to solve them.

The work of these five Cuban economists substantiates that the structural problems of the Cuban economy were not corrected by the partial and insufficient reforms carried out from 1993 to 1996. It further suggests that the "relative paralysis" of reforms may have contributed to the growth slowdown in 1997–98. In our view, the paralysis of reforms played a similar role in the 2001–2 slowdown. Thus, we conclude that the external-sector shocks in the second half of 2001 and in 2002 worsened but did not cause the underlying structural problems of the economy.

The Cuban government has blamed fluctuations in world commodity market prices for the slowdown, but a careful analysis of the data does not support that contention. For example, international prices of sugar had been declining since 1996 and actually rose in 2002. International prices for nickel declined in the second half of 2001 but stabilized at the 1999 level and rebounded in 2002. The merchandise trade deficit reached a historical peak in 2000, was virtually unchanged in 2001, and actually declined in 2002. The effect on the Cuban economy of the high world market oil prices in 2002 was partly offset by a highly favorable bilateral agreement with Venezuela that provided Cuba with oil on very advantageous terms. The suspension of oil shipments from Venezuela during this period was the result of Cuba's failure to pay for oil shipments received. The difficulties that Cuba faced in 2001–3—and continues to face today—in gaining access to international credit is the direct result of its failure to make scheduled repayments on its debt. Similarly, the decrease in foreign investment is the result of government policies that create disincentives to investors.

At the beginning of 2005, Cuba's economic situation continued to be critical. Despite a slight rebound in 2003, the standard of living of Cuban citizens continues to be substantially lower than in 1989. Rather than confronting the difficult economic situation with a coordinated set of reforms, the Cuban government has turned to increasing economic recentralization, repression against dissidents, and human-rights violations, policies that have provoked criticism and censure from the international community and have increased the isolation of the island.[14]

3

Social Welfare and Growing Inequalities

Until the end of the 1980s Cuba had one of the most egalitarian economies and societies in Latin America. Policies in pursuit of that goal have been implemented fairly continuously since the revolution, although the emphasis on egalitarianism peaked during two idealist cycles: the implementation of the Guevara-Castro model (1966–70) and the Rectification process (1986–90). The excessive emphasis on equality eroded the value of money, created disincentives to work, fostered labor absenteeism, and resulted in declining labor productivity. More moderate policies were applied during pragmatist cycles, such as during the implementation of the Soviet reform model (1971–85) and the economic reforms of 1991–96.

The economic reforms of the 1990s brought about significant increases in income inequality and in disparities in other social and economic indicators, reversing many of the gains that had been made in earlier years. In 1993, when the reforms started, Castro stated,

> One of the things about which the Revolution can be criticized is that it created too much equality, too much egalitarianism. This has to be rectified, because it was not working and it works even less in a poverty environment. The more poverty there is, the less well egalitarianism can work. . . . The changes we are making [that is, the reforms] were inevitable, and we have to make a few more that will promote individualism, selfishness, will enhance the importance of money. These changes will alienate people. (Castro 1993b: 4)

It is extremely difficult to quantify economic and social inequalities in Cuba because the revolutionary government has never published income distribution statistics and has been reluctant to make public information that might put into question one of the most vaunted accomplishments of the revolution.[1] The statistical yearbook published since the mid-1960s does not contain statistics on economic and social inequalities.

In the last 45 years, Cuba has conducted only three population censuses, in 1970, 1981, and 2002. Published statistics on income, housing, and other relevant variables from the 1970 and 1981 censuses are insufficient to support an adequate analysis of inequalities. (Statistics on respondents' race were collected in the 1970 census but were not published.) Two years after the 2002 census was conducted, statistics from it were not yet available. Because of these data limitations, in this chapter we rely on proxy variables and qualitative evaluations based on public documents, surveys, articles by experts published in Cuba and elsewhere, and interviews conducted by Mesa-Lago of recent visitors and émigrés from the island. The chapter focuses on the growing economic and social inequalities resulting from the economic reforms of the 1990s.

Growing Inequalities and Their Effects

In this section we review socioeconomic disparities and their effects from 1993 to the present, examining income and wealth, taxation, and social services. We also review disparities across races and geographic regions and between Cuban citizens and foreigners.

Income

The Cuban revolutionary government has not published statistics on income distribution. The only available information for selected years between 1962 and 1986 are rough estimates by two foreign scholars (Brundenius 1979, 1984; Zimbalist and Brundenius 1989). More recently, foreign and Cuban scholars have published estimates of income distribution, although measurements differ. The Gini coefficient in Cuba rose from 0.22 in 1986 to 0.55 in 1995, "a shocking increase by 33 Gini points." The share of total income earned by the top 5% of the population was 31% in 1995, an increase of 20 percentage points compared to 1986 (Fabienke 2001: 104). The Gini in 1995 was higher in Cuba than in 14 countries of Latin America (based on ECLAC, *Balance preliminar,* 2001). According to a Cuban economist, the national Gini coefficient was 0.25 in 1989; the poorest decile of the population received 3.7% of total income whereas the richest decile received 30% of total income (the national and urban Ginis were similar); by 1996–98, however, the Gini had risen to 0.38 in urban areas (Ferriol 2001a).[2] Another Cuban economist estimated Gini coefficients of 0.40 in 1996 and 0.41 in 1999 (Añé

2000). Despite the scarce and contradictory Gini data, ECLAC has stated that "Cuba has maintained the most equitable income distribution in Latin America and the Caribbean, despite the tensions generated by the economic crisis"; yet this assertion is not supported by a comparison of the Gini in Cuba versus 13 other countries (ECLAC 2000b: 37–38).[3]

Real wages in the state sector sharply decreased in 1989–2000. Using the official consumer price index (CPI), a Cuban scholar deflated nominal wages for 1989–98 and estimated that the average real wage declined by 44.4% during this period, from 131 to 73 pesos per month (Togores 1999: 88), equivalent to a decline from about $19 to less than $4 per month at the unofficial exchange rate.[4] Meanwhile, ECLAC estimated that average real wages declined by 45.2% between 1989 and 1998 (ECLAC 2000a; for a comparison of the two estimates see Mesa-Lago 2001a). More recent studies by Cuban economists show that the average real wage declined by 37% between 1989 and 2000, from 131 to 83 pesos per month ($4 at the CADECA exchange rate prevailing in 2000). The 5% increase in nominal salaries in 2002 did not significantly improve the situation because of the faster rate of increase of prices in dollar stores and in agricultural free markets (Togores and García 2003a; Triana 2003).[5]

Whereas real wages in the state sector fell sharply, the incomes of participants in the small but growing private sector increased significantly. Internationally known artists and musicians, private farmers, owners of *paladares*, private taxi drivers, self-employed workers, employees of tourist facilities, and black market speculators, among others, saw dramatic increases in income. Meanwhile, as discussed previously, employees in the state sector (nearly 77% of the civilian labor force in 2002) suffered a dramatic decline in their real salaries. Carranza, Gutiérrez, and Monreal (1995) have estimated that in 1994, the lowest-income worker in the informal sector earned in one day the equivalent of the average monthly wage of a state worker.

Based on interviews with Cuban visitors and immigrants from Cuba to the United States, and converting the Cuban peso into U.S. dollars at the CADECA exchange rate, Mesa-Lago (1998) estimated monthly incomes in dollars in the city of Havana in 1995 for several occupations as follows: average wage earner, $6; teacher, $8–$9; physician or university professor, $11–$12; taxi driver for tourists, $100–$467; private farmer, $187–$311; and owner of a small restaurant, $2,500–$5,000. Income inequality grew significantly in the 1990s: In 1989 the ratio of the highest to the lowest wage was 4.5 to 1, while in 1995 it was 829 to 1. Mesa-Lago updated his estimates of income inequality in Havana to March–April of 2002, based on interviews he conducted in Miami and Madrid with recent visitors and immigrants from Cuba.[6] He converted pesos to dollars using the CADECA exchange rate for

2002, namely 26 pesos for US$1. Table 8 presents the estimates of monthly salaries distinguishing between (1) occupations in the public sector, where incomes ranged from $4 for those earning the lowest salary/pension, to $23 for a cabinet minister (however, the best-paid police officers in the special corps providing security to tourists earned $31 per month); and (2) occupations in the private sector, where incomes ranged from $40 for a domestic servant in an exclusive neighborhood to $50,000 for the owner of a *paladar*. Although the 1995 and 2002 estimates are not technically comparable, they suggest a significant jump in income inequality: The ratio of highest to lowest income jumped from 829 to 1 in 1995 to 12,500 to 1 in 2002. Not included in table 8 are rates charged, usually in dollars, by self-employed workers (electricians, plumbers, auto repairmen, and so forth) who perform work at their clients' locations and whose rates vary greatly.

Two studies by Cuban analysts conducted in the city of Havana found significant income disparities among households in 1995 and 2001. In 1995, average household income per capita across ten income brackets ranged from 40 to 6,000 pesos, an extreme difference of 150 times; in 2001, the difference had become more extreme, with household income per capita ranging from 37 pesos to 7,266 pesos, a difference of almost 200 times (Quintana et al. 1995; Espina 2003). Although these disparities are not as pronounced as those found by Mesa-Lago (recall that Mesa-Lago estimated income for individual occupations, whereas the Cuban analysts relied on average household income), they nevertheless support that there has been a significant widening of income inequality in the 1990s. A household survey in the city of Havana in 2000 found that the average monthly income per capita was 198 pesos ($9.42 at the unofficial exchange rate); that 53% of households had per-capita monthly incomes of between 50 and 150 pesos ($2.38 to $7.14); that 14% of the households had per-capita monthly incomes of less than 50 pesos; and that 77% of the households considered their income level insufficient to meet their needs (cited by Pérez Villanueva 2001).

In an attempt to secure needed skilled labor in strategic sectors, in 1994 the government started to pay bonuses in dollars (in addition to regular pay in pesos) to workers in the tourism, mining, electricity, ports, and tobacco sectors. In 2000, about 1.2 million workers (about 30 percent of the labor force) received such bonuses, estimated at an average of $19 per month, while 1.5 million workers received in-kind rewards such as food or clothing (Rodríguez 2000; Triana 2000). Even with these incentives, it is clear that the state cannot compete with the private sector in terms of remuneration. For this reason, the state has stepped up its effort to check the growth of the private sector, trying to sap its vitality through a combination of higher taxes and fees and increased inspections. Members of the armed forces receive

Table 8. Monthly Income in the City of Havana, March–April 2002 (ranges in pesos and U.S. dollars)

Occupation	Pesos	U.S. Dollars[a]
State Sector		
Minimum pension	100	4
Minimum salary	100	4
Teacher (elementary and secondary)	200–400	8–15
University professor	300–560	12–22
Engineer, physician	300–650[b]	12–25
Garbage collector	300–500	12–19
Police officer (regular)	200–500	8–19
Police officer (security guard for tourists)	700–800	27–31
Officer in the armed forces	350–700	13–23
Cabinet minister	450–600	17–23
Private Sector		
Domestic servant	520–1,040[c]	20–40
Private farmer	2,000–50,000[d]	77–1,923
Transportation vehicle operator (20–60 seats)	10,000–20,000	385–770
Prostitute (*jinetera*)	[e]	240–1,400
Renter of room, apartment, or home	[e]	250–4,000[f]
Artist or musician (known abroad)	[e]	600–6,000[g]
Owner of *paladar*	[e]	12,500–50,000[h]

Source: Interviews conducted by Mesa-Lago in Miami and Madrid with visitors and immigrants from Cuba.

a. Converted at the rate of 26 pesos per $1 and rounded to the nearest dollar.

b. Physicians who were practicing in the 1960s may have signed an agreement with the government allowing them to maintain a private practice; such private practice would allow them to earn 10 to 20 times the earnings of a physician in a public sector job.

c. Those working in exclusive neighborhoods such as Miramar are paid at the top of the range; in addition, they receive room and board.

d. Earnings depend on the size of plot and how the land is used; those with crops in high demand or raising hogs earn the highest incomes.

e. Not applicable because they normally charge in U.S. dollars.

f. Monthly estimate based on room rates of $10 to $50 per night, that is, $70 to $350 per week.

g. Artists who are not well known earn $10–$13 monthly; the now-defunct Compay Segundo (Buena Vista Social Club) charged $6,000 net for one night's performance; Silvio Rodríguez, Jorge Perugorría, and Los Van-Van (musical group) have contracts paying as much as $200,000, with a percentage of the income going to the government.

h. Based on $500 to $2,000 daily; very few currently earn at the high end of the range.

extra monthly allotments of food and are also allowed to buy clothing and other goods at low prices.

Workers employed in foreign-operated enterprises or joint ventures receive considerably higher incentives than workers in the state sector: reportedly 15 to 20 convertible pesos[7] per month plus a basket (*jaba*) consisting of food, toiletries, and other consumer goods. For example, production workers at Canadian corporation Sherritt International's joint venture nickel processing plant in Moa (Pedro Sotto Alba) reportedly received incentives ranging from $30 to $35 monthly, and managers received $50. Many foreign firms and joint ventures also pay additional monthly sums under the table to retain good workers: $20 to $25 to production workers, $100 to $150 to secretaries, $200 to $300 to salespersons, and $600 to $800 to managers. Salespersons and managers also earn commissions on sales and often have the use of a company car and an allocation of 200 liters of gasoline per month. High-level employees of the state-owned conglomerate export-import enterprise Cimex S.A. are reportedly paid their entire salary in dollars (interviews conducted by Mesa-Lago in Miami and Madrid, March–April 2000).

These wide income inequalities between the non-state and state sectors, coupled with the lack of comparable incentives in the state sector, have given rise to several negative trends: skewed income distribution, low labor stability, declining labor productivity,[8] and falling school enrollment, particularly in higher education (discussed later).

Rising inequalities coupled with the massive influx of tourists have caused an increase in crime, while the opening of the economy to foreign investment has resulted in increased opportunities for fraud and corruption among public officials (Díaz-Briquets and Pérez-López 2002). Managers and workers at state enterprises steal goods for their own use, to sell on the black market, or for use as inputs by the self-employed. Stealing from agricultural enterprises is also common. In 1997–99, 6,000 police officers were added in the city of Havana alone; the penal code was revised to make drug trafficking and procurement of persons for sexual purposes punishable by death; and a major campaign to eradicate prostitution was launched. A number of bribery scandals involving high-level government officials have been reported in the press. Among the most notorious are the dismissals in March 2001 of the minister of the fishing industry, in December 2003 of the president of tourism corporation Cubanacán S.A., and in February 2004 of the minister of tourism and of key officials of Cimex S.A. in charge of duty-free stores serving tourists, but these are likely to be only the tip of the iceberg (Trumbull 2000; Frank 2001; Alfonso 2003; Cancio Isla 2004a, 2004b; San Martin 2004).

Remittances

In 1993 the government authorized receipt, possession, and circulation of foreign currency (essentially dollars) and later authorized the opening of dollar-denominated savings accounts earning interest payable in the same currency.[9] These measures resulted in a dual monetary system, where the Cuban peso and the dollar both circulate freely. With Cuba enveloped in a deep economic crisis, in the 1990s Cubans living abroad (mainly in the United States) sent larger remittance flows to relatives on the island through three different channels: (1) direct delivery of cash to relatives visiting the United States or to relatives on the island via Cuban-Americans traveling there; (2) delivery through individuals who travel to Cuba and carry dollars, either as a favor for a friend or relative or for a fee (*mulas*); and (3) transfers by wire or by other established means for a fee. The first two channels cannot easily be restricted because of their informal nature; the third can be limited, and in fact the U.S. government has instituted a maximum of $300 quarterly or $1,200 per year per U.S. resident. The conventional wisdom is that the bulk of remittances are sent through the first two channels, although there is no accurate information to confirm this.

The amount of remittances sent to Cuba cannot be precisely calculated for many reasons, among them because of the informality of channels and the lack of statistics from Cuban monetary authorities. Reportedly, Cuba estimates the value of remittances through an indirect method that relies on the value of (1) sales at state dollar shops (*tiendas de recaudación de divisas,* TRDs) that sell merchandise to Cubans and to foreign visitors; and (2) dollars traded at the CADECA houses. According to a Cuban scholar, "official Cuban statistics on the value of remittances do not originate from actual records of transactions but are merely an estimate subject to a significant margin of error"; according to this analyst, the value of remittances ranged from $300 to $500 million per annum in 1995–98 (Monreal 1999: 50, 53) and was $500 million in 2002 (Monreal 2003). Estimates by other Cuban analysts set the level of remittances in 2002 at between $800 million and $1.1 billion (Marquetti, cited by Togores and García 2003a).

ECLAC has also published a series of remittance estimates that obviously suffer from the same limitations as the Cuban estimates. The ECLAC estimates (in U.S. dollars) are $573 million in 1995, $630 million in 1996, $670 million in 1997, $690 million in 1998, $700 million in 1999, $720 million in 2000, $813 million in 2001, $820 million in 2002, and $915 million in 2003 (ECLAC, *Cuba,* 2001, 2002, *Balance preliminar,* 2003, *Estudio económico,* 2003). Other estimates based on surveys or analysis by scholars range from $100 to $400 million per year.[10] The ECLAC remittance series follows very closely the series on current transfers reported by Cuba in its balance of payments statistics. The official Cuban statistics do not break out remittances in the current transfer series, and therefore they are higher than ECLAC's remittance estimates. The most recent balance of payments statistics available for Cuba are from 2001 (ONE 2003).

If ECLAC estimates are accepted as accurate, remittances are Cuba's second major source of hard currency, after gross revenue from tourism, surpassing in recent years the value of nickel and sugar exports (ONE 2002, 2003). In 1999, dollar store sales were reported at $1 billion, $300 million more than the level of remittances estimated by ECLAC for that year; the difference between the two figures was attributed to bonuses paid in dollars to Cuban workers and earnings from *paladares*, house rentals, black market operations, and so forth (Trumbull 2000). Also tentative are estimates on the percentage of the Cuban population that receives remittances, variously estimated as between 32% and 49.5% in 1997, between 56.3% and 65% in 1998, and around 62% in 1999 and 2000 (ECLAC 2000a; Togores 1999; Pérez Villanueva 2002b).

Assuming 2002 remittances of $820 million and that 60% of the population (6.7 out of 11.2 million) is receiving money, then the average transfer per recipient for that year would be $122. This remittances level is higher than the average annual earnings of state workers in 2002, estimated at about $120.[11] This would mean that the recipient of the average remittance amount could be out of the labor force and still have the same income as the average state worker, or could keep the state job and double his or her income, potentially gaining a higher standard of living. Because the $122 figure is an average, there are Cubans who receive more than the average annual remittances, others who receive less, and about 40% who receive no remittances at all. Clearly, the existence and unequal distribution of remittances significantly affect income distribution and diminish productivity in the state sector.

The question of how remittances are distributed within the island is difficult to answer. A team of Cuban analysts estimated that although 35% of total households received remittances in 2001, that share was 63% for the highest income bracket but only 5% for the lowest income bracket (Iñiguez et al. 2001, cited by Espina 2003). Cuban economist Viviana Togores set the range of remittance recipients at 30% to 60% of the population in 2002, but warned that the population "segment was not homogenous as there was a high concentration and polarization in terms of both access and geographic areas," in addition, "the growing remittances have not solved the income deficiency of the majority of Cuban households and the situation has become quite tense" (Togores 2004: 125, 133). A reasonable hypothesis is the majority of remittances recipients live in Havana city and are white. Information gathered by Mesa-Lago in interviews with recent visitors and immigrants from Cuba consistently indicated that the farther from the capital city, the lower the level of remittances received; this seemed to hold true even for Santiago de Cuba, the second largest city, in the easternmost part of the island.

According to the 1990 U.S. census of population, 83.5% of Cuban immigrants living in the United States were white, and virtually all the rest (16.5%) were black. According to the Cuban census of 1981, the latest for which data have been published, 66% of the island's population was white and 34% nonwhite (basically black). Assuming that the relative prevalence of the two racial groups in the U.S. and Cuban censuses was accurate and remained unchanged through 2002, and further assuming that remittances were evenly distributed throughout the entire population, Cuban whites would have received $685 million in remittances (out of a total of $820 million) or $93 per capita, and Cuban blacks would have received $135 million ($35 per capita). If the same calculation were made only with respect to the 60% of the population estimated to receive remittances, the average size of receipts per capita would have been $154 for whites and $59 for blacks. If the proportion of blacks within the Cuban population is higher than the 34% in the 1981 census, the gap in remittances per capita between the two groups would be even wider.[12]

Shortly after the Cuban government authorized the receipt of remittances from abroad, Fidel Castro criticized the inequalities and privileges that this policy would generate but justified it anyway: "We need to understand, and not be ashamed. That would never be the correct attitude for a revolutionary . . . revolutionaries make sacrifices throughout their lives" (Castro 1993a). A decade later, even though remittances recipients are probably a majority of the population and the "ashamed revolutionaries" a minority, the disparities caused by remittances continue to irritate the true believers. In order to compensate for the differences in remittances receipts across the population, in 2001 the Union of Communist Youth proposed that recipients of remittances be denied access to free health care and education as well as to goods sold at subsidized prices through the rationing system. The proposal was rejected, probably because of difficulties in implementation, including a lack of information about who receives such remittances (León 2002).

Wealth

No data are available on wealth distribution in Cuba, but according to a Cuban economist, "the structure of bank accounts shows a widening gap between various groups of savers, which in turn is a reflection of differences in income distribution. . . . This implies inequalities in taking advantage of opportunities, which five years ago were not a function of income differences but rather of the just economic and social opportunities that individuals had [such as education]. . . . During the crisis, factors such as income and wealth have also shaped outcomes, diminishing the impact of equal opportunity policies" (Togores 1999: 92). We have already analyzed income inequalities. An indirect measure of wealth is savings account balances in branches of the state-owned Banco Popular de Ahorro. In 1994, 54% of the population held deposits of 6.3 billion pesos in those accounts, but by 2000, the share of savers had declined to 37% of the population and holdings to 5.2 billion pesos (based on ONE 2001; Pérez Villanueva 2002a), and the concentration of deposits had increased considerably.

Table 9 presents the distribution of savings accounts by the value of deposits, revealing the drift of deposits to larger accounts. In 1994, 61.7% of the accounts were small, holding up to 200 pesos and accounting for 4.4% of total savings; meanwhile, 2.2% were large, holding deposits of more than 10,000 pesos and accounting for 36% of total savings. By 1997, the share of small accounts had increased to 65.9%, accounting for only 2.4% of total savings, while that of large accounts increased to 3.0% but accounted for 46.4% of total savings. Rough estimates indicate that by 2002, small accounts had further decreased to 2% of total savings, while large accounts had increased to 48% of total savings. In 1994 there were no accounts with a balance of more than 50,000 pesos; in 1997, 0.1% of the accounts, holding 5.3% of total savings, were in this category (see also Pérez Villanueva 2002a).[13]

Table 9. Personal Savings by Amount of Deposits, 1994–2002

| | Percentage Distribution of Amount of Deposits | | | | |
	≤200 pesos	201–2,000 pesos	2,001–10,000 pesos	>10,000 pesos	Total
1994					
Percent of accounts	61.7	24.2	11.9	2.2	100.0
Amount of total savings	4.4	17.8	41.8	36.0	100.0
1997					
Percent of accounts	65.9	20.9	10.2	3.0	100.0
Amount of total savings	2.4	12.6	38.6	46.4	100.0
2002[a]					
Percent of accounts	63.0	22.0	12.0	3.0	100.0
Amount of total savings	2.0	12.0	38.0	48.0	100.0

Source: Togores 1999, 2004.

a. Approximate percentages based on bar graph.

Approximately 700 million pesos in savings were held in certificates of deposit (CDs) in 2000. For CDs denominated in pesos, Cuban banking institutions paid interest rates ranging from 3.5% for 3 months to 7.5% for 36 months, rather high rates in view of the low official inflation rate of the Cuban economy (BCC 2001; ECLAC, *Cuba*, 2002). These rates were increased by 0.5% across the board in 2003. High interest rates contributed to the increasing concentration of deposits into large accounts and CDs (Triana 2000).

In addition to savings in pesos, reportedly there are significant savings in dollars as well. Conventional wisdom has it that part of the population hoards a large amount of dollars at home; moreover, an estimated $200 million is held in dollar-denominated savings accounts in Cuban savings institutions (Ritter 2002). Interest rates for dollar-denominated CDs held by individuals ranged from 1.5% for 6 months to 2.75% for 36 months in 2003 (Pérez Soto et al. 2003).

Regressive Taxes

Prior to the crisis of the 1990s, the main source of government revenue was transfers into the state budget of profits of state enterprises, complemented by indirect turnover taxes ("circulation" taxes) levied on the sales of state enterprises, payroll contributions for social security and labor benefits, and import duties; only 1.7% of revenue originated from direct taxation on the population (for example, taxes on utilities, collected by the service provider). With the economic crisis, many state enterprises shut down and others significantly reduced their activities, so the volume of revenue they contributed to the state budget declined significantly. To cope with a huge fiscal deficit, a tax reform law was enacted in 1994 that changed the sources of government revenue. A general sales tax replaced the turnover tax, and other taxes and levies were imposed, including excise taxes on the consumption of certain goods (such as alcohol and tobacco); taxes on profits of all enterprises; payroll taxes for labor and social security (paid by enterprises); natural resource use taxes (for example, on mining activities); taxes on hard currency earnings from abroad (but excluding remittances); and real estate, inheritance, and public utility taxes. Although the imposition of social security contributions on workers was included in the law, its implementation was suspended for social and political reasons. Subsequently, other taxes and fees were imposed on self-employment, *paladares*, room rentals to tourists, and other private activities (Mesa-Lago 2000).

The essential outcome of the tax reform was a heavier emphasis on indirect taxation. Thus, in 2003 the distribution of government tax revenue was 59.6% from indirect taxes, out of which 53.9% was from sales taxes and

5.7% from public utilities (electricity, water, telephone); and 40.4% was from direct taxes, of which 10.5% originated from social security contributions, 13.7% from enterprise profits,[14] 5% from various other fees, and 2.4% from taxes on personal income (see table 10). Between 2001 and 2003, the percentage of total tax revenue raised by indirect taxes rose 4 percentage points (based on ONE 2003 and ECLAC, *Cuba,* 2004). Indirect taxes are regressive because their incidence is proportionally heavier on those segments of the population with lower incomes (Pérez Villanueva 2002a).

Among personal income taxpayers in 2000 were 107,000 self-employed workers, 33,830 private transportation workers, 16,250 artists, 12,000 landowners who leased their farms, 7,740 small sugarcane producers, and 1,730 sellers in agricultural free markets (ECLAC, *Cuba,* 2001). These combined 178,550 private-sector workers who paid taxes represented less than 4% of the labor force but contributed 2.6% of total tax revenue. Because of the onerous taxes and fees, the numbers of self-employed workers and owners of *paladares* have gradually declined, as have their contribution to government revenue. The self-employed workforce declined from 208,500 in November 1995 to 149,990 in 2003, and their contribution to net revenue dropped from 207 million pesos in 1995 to 135 million pesos in 2000 (Espinosa Chepe 2001a). Recall that workers who are paid in dollars or receive bonuses in dollars do not pay taxes on such income, and neither do illegally self-employed workers (probably the large majority of self-employed workers fall into this category) as well as black market operators.

Table 10. Tax Revenue by Source, 2003

Tax	Percentage
Indirect	**59.6**
General sales	53.9
Public utilities	5.7
Direct	**40.4**
Profits	13.7
Social security	10.5
Payroll[a]	8.8
Fees (airports, highways, other)	5.0
Personal income	2.4
Total	100.0

Source: Based on ECLAC, *Cuba* 2004.

a. Sickness and maternity leave, occupational safety, and health.

Deterioration of and Inequalities in Social Services

Cuban policies on social services (except housing) from the revolution until the end of the 1980s were characterized by continuous expansion in coverage, free delivery, and rising costs. ECLAC (2000a: 275–76) explains, "To some extent, the viability of the social policy was facilitated by the special and privileged relationship that Cuba had during [three] decades with the socialist countries, particularly with the USSR. . . . [The socialist bloc] contributed resources that raised the welfare of the Cuban population above the level of economies with similar or even higher income levels. . . . [In addition] there was the political decision to build an egalitarian society." This policy was not free from errors that had negative welfare effects, however, among them the imposition and expansion of commodity rationing, deterioration of the basic infrastructure, a significant housing deficit, and inefficiencies that did little to stop the steady expansion of free services. Mesa-Lago (2000) has estimated that between 1960 and 1990, Cuba received from the USSR alone $65 billion in resources, 40% in the form of non-repayable price subsidies and 60% in loans that should have been repaid but were not.[15] The collapse of the USSR, the socialist community, and the CMEA provoked a deep economic crisis with severe repercussions for the social services system, although the government has attempted to maintain it. The deterioration in social services and the effect of such deterioration on inequality and other aspects of Cuban society are analyzed next.

Health Care

It is widely recognized that, in the revolutionary period, Cuba significantly improved its health-care services and levels of health, but not as well known is that in 1958 Cuba led Latin America in most of the same health indicators. In the 1960s, the government established a National Health System (Sistema Nacional de Salud, hereafter NHS) that rapidly instituted universal health care, providing free services for everything except medicines for outpatients. In the 1980s, Cuba introduced a family doctor program that expanded primary health-care services considerably and made them more accessible by locating physicians and other health-care providers in the neighborhoods where their patients live. From 1959 through the end of the 1980s, virtually all health indicators steadily improved (Mesa-Lago 2000):

- The number of physicians rose from 9.2 to 33.1 per 10,000 inhabitants, hospital beds from 4.2 to 5.4 per 1,000 inhabitants, and the hospitalization rate from 12.6% to 15.5%.
- The infant mortality rate fell from 33.4 to 11.1 per 1,000 live births, the maternal mortality rate from 125.3 to 26.1 per 100,000 live births,

and the mortality rate of the population ages 65 and above from 52.9 to 46.3 per 1,000 inhabitants.

• Most contagious diseases (diphtheria, malaria, measles, rubella, scarlet fever, tetanus, tuberculosis, typhoid fever, and polio) were eradicated, became insignificant, or were dramatically reduced, although others (acute diarrhea and respiratory diseases, venereal diseases, hepatitis, and chicken pox) increased.

• There was a significant reduction in the gap between urban and rural areas in terms of access to health-care facilities and personnel, as well as in health standards.

The performance of several indicators demonstrates the adverse effect of the economic crisis of the 1990s on health care. Between 1990 and 2002 the number of physicians relative to the size of the population continued to increase (from 33.1 to 59.6 physicians per 10,000 inhabitants) and the infant mortality rate to decline (from 11.1 to 6.5 per 1,000 live births),[16] but other indicators deteriorated. Most of these indicators fell sharply in 1993–95 and later recovered, although not to pre-crisis levels: The number of hospital beds per 1,000 inhabitants fell from 5.4 to 4.3 and the hospitalization rate from 15.5% to 11.9%; the maternal mortality rate rose from 26.1 to 65.2 per 100,000 live births and then decreased to 41.7;[17] the mortality rate of the population ages 65 and over jumped from 48.4 to 55.7 per 1,000 inhabitants, and later dropped to 49.7 (see table 11). Although the majority of diseases continued to be under control, all the contagious diseases that exhibited a rising trend before the crisis continued to rise, tuberculosis reappeared, and the rate of HIV/AIDS infection rose. Between 1989 and 1996 the rates of illness per 100,000 inhabitants rose and reached historical peaks for nine diseases (acute diarrhea, acute respiratory infection, chicken pox, hepatitis, scarlet fever, syphilis, gonorrhea, tuberculosis, and typhoid). From 1997 through 2002, however, the rates of most of those diseases declined dramatically to below the 1989 level (a suspicious development discussed later), with the exception of acute respiratory diseases and tuberculosis (MINSAP 2000, 2001; ONE 2003). The percentage of the population immunized against contagious diseases in 2002 was between 25% and 90% lower than in 1989 for the five main vaccines, and Cuba ranked eighth in the region in mortality from contagious diseases (CEE 1991; ONE 2003; PAHO 2004a). Between 1970 and 1997, the daily per-capita consumption of calories declined by 6%, of protein by 24%, and of fats by 28% (UNDP 2000). The proportion of Cuba's population that was undernourished increased from 5% in 1990–92 to 13% in 1998–2000, leaving Cuba ranked ninth in the region with respect to this indicator (FAO 2002).

Table 11. Cuban Health-Care Indicators, Selected Years, 1988–2002

Indicator	1988–89	1993–94	2001–2
Infant mortality (x 1,000 live births)	11.1	9.9	6.5
Maternal mortality (x 100,000 live births)	26.1	65.2	41.7
Population mortality 65+ (x 1,000 inhabitants)	48.4	55.7	49.7
Physicians (x 10,000 inhabitants)	33.1	46.7	59.6
Hospital real beds (x 1,000 inhabitants)	5.4	5.2	4.3
Hospitalization rate (%)	15.5	12.7	11.9
Hospital occupancy rate (%)	83.9	71.3	69.8

Sources: CEE 1991; ONE 2002, 2003; Mesa-Lago 2000, 2003a; Sixto 2003.

Causes of the deterioration in health standards have been a severe scarcity of medicine, spare parts for equipment, materials for laboratory tests, anesthetic drugs, and other basic inputs; a breakdown of the basic infrastructure for delivery of potable water and sewage services, which had been neglected even before the crisis; the lack of prophylactics; a drop in vaccinations; and serious nutritional deficiencies (more on this follows). Among others, these problems resulted in long waiting periods for surgery and lack of essential medicines to treat patients. In addition, while health-care expenditures per capita in real terms increased by 162% from 1976 to 1989, they fell by 75% from 1989 to 1993; in spite of some improvement since then, in 1999 they still were 21% below their 1989 level.

Inefficiency of the health-care system became worse, as hospital occupancy dropped from 83.9% to 69.8% and the average hospital stay rose from 9.9 to 10.4 days, although it declined to 9.4 days in 2000 (table 11; Mesa-Lago 2000, 2003a). According to a Cuban journal, the efficiency and quality of health-care services have deteriorated for several reasons: (1) structural damage and broken equipment in health centers, attributable not only to natural wear and tear but also to general indolence and widespread stealing by employees at all levels; (2) lack of coordination in consultation, referral, and hospitalization due to poor treatment and abuse by institutions; (3) priority given to enforcement of impersonal rules that impede access, obstruct service, and delay care with requirements unrelated to strict medical considerations; (4) difficulty of access to complex tests and equipment, which are scarce, prompting reliance on contacts (*sociolismo*) and bribes; and (5) lack of humane treatment and relations between patients and medical personnel ("La salud pública" 2004).

In light of the preceding analysis, recent official morbidity statistics that show eradication or dramatic reduction in several contagious diseases appear suspicious. For instance, reported cases of hepatitis reached a historical peak of 323 in 1991 and there were still 223 cases in 1997, but no cases were reported in 2002 (ONE 1998, 2003). The government argues that water chlorination, suspended in the early 1990s, has been partially restored since 1996, but both potable water and sanitation infrastructures have continued to deteriorate: The daily average of water service was 12 hours in 2002 and it was unstable due to electricity interruptions, forcing the population to store water in tanks and other vessels and reducing its potability (ECLAC 2004a); half of the city of Havana currently relies on a sewer system built almost a century ago; 46% of the main polluting sources in the country released untreated wastewater into inland and marine waters in 1998; the volume of water evacuated by sewage decreased 15% from 1998 to 2002; only 17 or 18% of urban sewage received any treatment before it was discharged in 1998; and state control and inspection of food have worsened. Despite the alleged improvement in chlorination, outbreaks of waterborne diseases were significantly higher in 1996–2000 than in 1993–95 (Driggs 2004a). According to a Cuban expert, $180 million is needed for the rehabilitation of the infrastructure (Alonso Tejada 2003).

In the same vein, venereal diseases have steadily risen since the late 1960s, and cases of gonorrhea and syphilis peaked in 1995–96, with 412 and 144 reported cases, respectively. In 2002, however, 114 cases of syphilis and 41 of gonorrhea were reported, a drop of 72% in both diseases, dramatically reversing the rising trends of the three previous decades (Mesa-Lago 2000; ONE 1998, 2003). In view of increasing prostitution in Cuba and severe shortages of prophylactics and antibiotics, those rates are not credible and suggest statistical manipulation.[18]

In addition to the NHS for the population at large, Cuba has a separate health-care scheme for members of the armed forces, the state security system, and the top hierarchy of the government and the Communist Party. This system provides better services and care than the NHS does. Finally, the pressure to obtain badly needed foreign exchange prompted the government to create a health-care system available only to foreigners ("health tourism"), who pay for services in hard currency. Unlike the NHS, the two latter schemes have not been affected by the economic crisis. Prior to the crisis, public resentment about these two exclusive programs was mild because of the universal, free, and high-quality services provided by the NHS, but with the severe scarcity of medicines and deterioration of the NHS, the preferential public health programs have become a symbol of inequality and an irritant.

At present, there is a surplus of physicians in Cuba and 16,000 are working abroad (Castro 2004), thereby reducing the number of physicians per 10,000 inhabitants to 45.4. Moreover, on the island, thousands of physicians work as taxi drivers, as waiters in tourist facilities, and in other occupations in which they can earn significantly higher salaries than they can in their learned profession. University graduates, including physicians and other health-care specialists, are prohibited from practicing their professions as self-employment (although they can work in other authorized occupations). This policy is absurd in view of the surplus of physicians and health-care workers, the dramatic decline in the salaries they earn in the state sector, and the need for more personalized care. Some physicians who had a private practice before the revolution have been allowed to keep it (most of the members of this cohort have retired or died) and others who completed their training after 1959 have illegal private practices. As a result, those persons who receive dollars as remittances or earn dollars have access to private health care and to medicines sold in the dollar shops, whereas those who have access only to pesos have no choice other than to rely on the NHS and endure the health-care inequality.

Education

The educational budget in real terms contracted by 38% from 1989 through 1997, resulting in shortages of educational materials (paper, pencils, books), a freeze on new school construction and building maintenance, deterioration of equipment and laboratories, lack of spare parts, cutbacks in transportation and school meals, and an overall decline in the quality of services (ECLAC 2000a). Enrollment in primary education decreased slightly, from 100% to 99%, between 1989 and 1999. Enrollment in secondary education fell from 90.2% to 74.5% between 1989 and 1994, but rose to 79.4% in 1998, still about 11 percentage points below 1989 (see chapter 4). The children of the elite are largely shielded from the deterioration in the educational system, as they attend exclusive schools (for instance the Lenin School in Havana) that have been protected from drastic budget cuts. In addition, high-income families within the elite have the means to purchase private educational services (such as private tutors) to educate their children.

Cuba's income pyramid has been inverted: Prior to the crisis, physicians, engineers, and university professors were at the top of the pyramid, but they have been replaced by owners of *paladares*, prostitutes, domestic servants, and private transportation operators, whose income is several times more. Many professionals have abandoned their careers and shifted to well-paying occupations (for example, those in tourism) in either the private sector or the state sector, therefore not using their human capital to the full extent.

As a percentage of the population of university age, higher education enrollment decreased from 23% in 1987 to 12% in 1997 (Mesa-Lago 2000; UNESCO 2001). The share of the population in the higher education age cohort fell from 21% in the 1989/90 academic year to 12% in 1998/99. Whereas during the 1989/90 academic year 33,199 students graduated with degrees from higher education institutions, the number decreased to 18,093 in 2001/2 (ONE 2001, 2003; Orrio 2001; ECLAC, *Statistical Yearbook*, 2002). Three principal reasons explain this decline: (1) it is not cost-effective to invest six years in studying medicine or five years in studying education if no jobs are available after graduation; (2) university graduates earn very low wages in the state sector and are not allowed to practice their professions as self-employment, creating income disincentives to pursue higher education; and (3) the number of students admitted to higher education was cut back during the crisis. The effect of these declines will not be felt immediately, because there is a glut in certain professions (such as medicine and education), but in the long run they will create a shortage of professionals and adversely affect economic growth.

Table 12 presents university enrollment by discipline for the following academic years: 1989/90 (prior to the crisis), the 1995/96–1999/2000 period (when the lowest enrollment occurred), 2000/1, and 2002/3. The last two academic years are shown to expose an important change in Cuban statistical series introduced in 2002 that increased higher education enrollment significantly.

Table 12. University Enrollment, Selected Academic Years, 1989/90–2002/3

Discipline	1989/90	Lowest enrollment in 1995–2000	1995–2000 over 1989/90 (%)	2000/1	2000/1 over 1989/90 (%)	2002/3[a]	2002/3 over 1989/90 (%)
Humanities and social sciences	5,095	5,366	+5.3	6,358	+25.3	33,898	+565.3
Natural sciences and math	6,399	4,019	−37.2	3,828	−40.2	3,934	−38.5
Agriculture	11,606	4,680	−59.7	5,125	−55.8	5,039	−56.6
Education	115,529	35,068	−69.6	38,892	−66.3	68,782	+342.9
Economics	18,789	4,893	−74.0	11,061	−41.1	20,307	+8.0
Technical	29,819	13,020	−56.3	14,514	−51.3	20,134	−32.4
Medicine	37,305	23,457	−37.1	24,606	−34.0	27,702	−25.7
Total enrollment[b]	242,366	102,598	−57.7	116,734	−51.8	192,864	−20.4

Sources: Based on CEE 1991; ONE 1998, 2001, 2003.

a. In 2002, enrollment in humanities and social sciences, as well as economics, was raised for the period 1996/97 to 2001/02, with increases from 10% to 14%, without explanation, thus resulting in increases in total enrollment.

b. Excludes physical education and art.

According to the data in table 12, overall university enrollment shrank 58% between 1989/90 and the lowest enrollment year during the 1995–2000 period; in 2000/1, enrollment was still 52% below the 1989/90 level. In economics and education, enrollment fell by as much as 74% and 70%, respectively, between 1989/90 and the lowest enrollment year in the 1995/2000 period; in 2000/1 it was still 41% and 66%, respectively, below 1989/90 levels.

In the 2002 statistical yearbook (ONE 2003), however, enrollment series from 1996/97 to 2000/1 were revised upward, increasing significantly the enrollment figures for selected disciplines: For the humanities and social sciences the increase was as much as three times, and for economics as much as 46%. This unexplained change leads to an upward adjustment of overall higher education enrollment by 10% to 14% for the 1996/97–2000/1 period, suggesting statistical manipulation (ONE 2001, 2003). Furthermore, in 2002/3 enrollment in the humanities and social sciences jumped 433% compared to 2000/1, while in a like period enrollment in education increased 77% (although Cuba already has the lowest ratio of students per teacher in the region). Conversely, 2002/3 enrollment in agriculture, natural sciences, math, and other technical careers was 26% to 57% below their 1989/90 level (see table 12). In spite of huge jumps in certain disciplines, overall higher education enrollment in 2002/3 was still 20% below the 1989/90 level. The priorities reflected in these statistics reveal a misallocation of very scarce resources and the threat of a future shortage of technicians needed for development.

In 2003/4, Cuban officials reported another big jump in higher education enrollment, although some of the presented data are contradictory. In September 2003, at the opening of the 2003/4 academic year, President Castro announced that 128,377 workers would enter higher education: 38,103 unemployed persons whose job is to study, 85,488 who combine work and study, and 4,786 as professors (Castro 2003). In December, Minister of Economics and Planning Rodríguez (2003) gave the figure for new enrollment in higher education as 146,913. In a December 2003 interview, Minister of Higher Education Fernando Vecino Alegret reported that more than 300,000 persons would be enrolled in higher education, an increase of 107,000 over the 192,864 enrolled in the 2002/3 academic year, for a 56% leap in a single year. He explained that the 17 then-existing universities had been "multiplied" by the creation of 732 higher education centers in municipalities, while the number of professors had been increased by 83%, most of them "adjunct." Said Minister Vecino, Cuba is experiencing a true "university explosion," the "universalization of higher education," as part of the "Battle of Ideas" launched by Castro. About 150,000 persons would be enrolled in nontraditional courses: regular and long-distance learning (*a distancia*) courses; new programs such as sociocultural studies, social work, and tourism; agricultural sciences for dislocated sugar workers who are studying at the closed sugar mills; and "popular universities" programs for retired workers and pensioners. The journalist conducting the interview cautiously asked the minister, "As higher education becomes massive, isn't there a risk that youngsters won't work diligently?" The minister answered, "There is always a danger, but we have faith in the soundness of our educational system, our values, and the student's own interest" (Vecino Alegret, interview in *Granma*, December 16, 2003).

The higher education explosion is probably part of a strategy to avoid open unemployment and to delay young people's entrance into the labor market. But other crucial questions could have been posed to the minister: (1) How was it possible in a single year to expand the number of higher education institutions by 43 times, the number of professors by 83%, and enrollment by 56%? (2) What kind of training have the 44,000 new professors received? (3) What is the quality of the new programs? and (4) Where are the hundreds of thousands of eventual graduates of the new programs going to find jobs, and doing what? A Cuban economist warns that the new massive higher education programs "will create social tensions, because the demand for university graduates is limited, such programs could increase emigration [and] create a challenge to the Cuban model, because their massive application requires an efficient utilization . . . and their large-scale results cannot be evaluated yet" (Victoria Pérez Izquierdo in ECLAC 2004b: 96, 116).

Social Security Pensions

The state consolidated and standardized entitlement conditions, and centralized the administration of 54 social insurance pension funds (old-age, disability, and survivors) that existed prior to the revolution. Pension coverage expanded from 63% to 91% of the labor force between 1958 and 1989. Excluded from mandatory coverage were the self-employed, private farmers, and unpaid family workers, but these workers could join voluntarily. By the end of the 1980s the Cuban pension system was probably the broadest, most generous, and costliest in Latin America. Retirement ages currently are 55 years of age for females and 60 for males, among the lowest in the region. Salaried workers do not contribute to social security and employers pay only 12% of payroll, less than one-half of the total contribution in Latin American countries similar to Cuba, such as Argentina and Uruguay. Although the pensions were low, they were supplemented by a broad safety net consisting of subsidized prices for consumer goods, free health care, free or cheap housing, low-cost transportation, and other free or low-cost public services (Mesa-Lago 2000).

The economic crisis and the aging of the population combined to turn the positive features of the pension system into liabilities. The non-state sector grew from 5.9% of the civilian labor force to 23.3% between 1989 and 2002 (CEE 1991; ONE 2003). Only a small segment of these workers is covered by the pension system, and as the non-state sector grows, the overall coverage of the pension system diminishes. Self-employed workers can join the system by contributing 12% of their income, but state salaried workers do not make any contributions. The low retirement ages, combined with a steady rise in life expectancy, result in Cuba having the longest average period of collecting pensions in Latin America: 20 years for men and 26 for women. According to projections by the Latin American and Caribbean Demographic Center (Centro Latinoamericano y Caribeño de Demografía, CELADE), by 2025 Cuba will have the oldest population in the region: one senior citizen per every four persons in the population.

Because of the rising cost of living and the very small increases in nominal pensions, the average real pension shrank by 42% from 1989 to 1998. To make matters worse, the social safety net is tattered and has largely disappeared as a result of the reduction in rationed goods (it is estimated that they last only one week per month), price increases, public transportation cutbacks, and the deterioration in health care. The cost of social security pensions in relation to GDP rose from 4.6% in 1986 to 6.6% in 2003. Insufficient contributions resulted in growing deficits in that period (from 26% to 33.1% of total expenditures) that must be financed by the state and have taken from 1.3% to 2.3% of GDP. In the year 2003, to balance contributions and payouts, employer contributions would have had to be raised from 12% to 18%, and to actuarially balance the system in the long run, the contribution would have had to be raised to between 39% and 86% based on various scenarios. The ratio of active workers per pensioner has dwindled from 3.6 in 1989 to 2.8 in 2002 and is projected to decrease further to approximately 1.5 by 2025 (see table 13; Mesa-Lago 2003a).

To cope with the financial problems of the pension system, the government has been discussing for several years a draft bill to reform it. The features of the original proposal were a gradual rise in the retirement age over 20 years, to 60 years for women and 65 for men; mandatory worker contributions (approved by law in 1994 but applied only to workers employed in state enterprises already under the system of *perfeccionamiento empresarial*, which accounts for only 15% of total enterprises; these workers contribute 5%); and an increase in the nominal pension (Peñate and Gutiérrez 2000). A recent proposal is even more modest: Current retirement ages are not changed for "regular" work but are reduced in five years for hard or hazardous types of work; an incentive is provided for all workers to work past the retirement age by increasing the pension for each year after the 25 years required for

Table 13. Financing of Social Security Pensions in Cuba, 1986 and 2003

Indicator	1986	2003
Income (million pesos)	664	1,405
Expenditures (million pesos)	897	2,101
Deficit (million pesos)	233	696
Deficit covered by the state (% of expenditure)	26.0	33.1
Deficit (% of GDP)	1.3	2.3
Cost of social security (% GDP)	4.6	6.6
Current wage contribution (%)	10.0	12.0
Contribution needed to eliminate deficit (%)[a]	13.5	17.9
Number of pensioners	1,072	1,424
Ratio of active workers per pensioner	3.6[c]	2.8[d]
Average monthly pension (pesos)	56	108[d]
Average monthly pension (U.S.dollars)[b]	8	4.15[d]

Sources: Mesa-Lago 2003a, updated with ONE 2003, ECLAC, *Cuba* 2004, 2004b.

a. In a given year, to actuarially balance the scheme in the long run a contribution from 39% to 86% would be needed based on various scenarios.

b. At the black market exchange rate in 1986 and at the CADECA exchange rate in 2002.

c. 1989.

d. 2002.

retirement, as well as for each year until five after the minimum retirement age; and monthly pensions of 250 pesos are maintained but any amount exceeding that sum is reduced by 50% (Sandó 2003). These proposed measures are grossly insufficient to cope with the pension system's financial problems.

As with health care, there is a parallel pension scheme for members of the armed forces and the internal security agencies, which is much more generous and costlier per person than the general system. For instance, a man who enters the armed forces at age 17 and accumulates 25 years of military service can retire at age 43, 17 years sooner than under the social security system. The average period over which members of the military draw pensions is 37 years, 12 years longer than the 25 years of typical military service. The pension they draw is 100% of their salary during their last year of service, and once pensioned, they can work in the state civilian sector and still collect their full pension. In contrast, under the general social security system, the pension amount is based on an average of the last five years' salary, and pensioners cannot collect their full pension if they perform salaried work in the state sector. It has been estimated that in 1995, the retirement system for members of the military cost as much as the deficit of the entire general pension system. To finance it adequately, a salary contribution of 118% would be needed (actually, the state finances all expenses of this scheme; Donate 1995).

In 2002, 1.4 million pensioners under the general social security system were paid an average monthly pension of 108 pesos, equivalent to $4.15 at the CADECA exchange rate (a 48% decline since 1986, see table 13). Estimates of how much an average pensioner would need monthly to meet his or her needs range from 190 pesos to buy essential foodstuffs to 432 pesos to cover all basic needs. Thus, the average pension provides only 25% of what is required to meet all basic needs. Pensioners—particularly those receiving the minimum pension of 60 pesos (equivalent to $2.30 at the CADECA exchange rate)—cannot make ends meet unless they receive help from their families or remittances from abroad (Mesa-Lago 2003a). Says a Cuban scholar, "Pension payments are insufficient by themselves to cover basic needs" (Espina 2003: 10). Pensioners are probably the group enduring the most difficult conditions in Cuba today. In contrast, the pension scheme of the armed forces/internal security agencies constitutes a costly privilege enjoyed by a tiny minority.

Housing

As a Cuban economist has stated, "Housing is the most serious social problem afflicting the nation . . . the accumulated needs are substantially higher [than new housing construction] because, among other reasons, of the deterioration of the existing housing stock" (Triana 2000: 10). Another Cuban expert asserts that the increase in housing construction in the 1980s did not reduce significantly the cumulative deficit, which is aggravated by poor maintenance; since 1990, housing construction decreased sharply, and only toward the end of the decade was there some increase, although still below the level of the 1980s (Alonso Tejada 2003). Official statistics on housing have been changed several times, which makes it difficult to estimate annual construction of housing units.[19] In addition, data on the size and characteristics of the units built have not been published.

Even before the crisis, in 1981 the cumulative housing deficit was estimated at 877,000 units (Mesa-Lago 2000). Table 14 shows that the estimated average annual number of dwellings built in 1981–89 was 61,198; this figure decreased by more than half to 28,638 in 1990–94 and recovered to 41,604 in 1995–2003, still 33% below the 1980s level. In 2002 housing construction was 27,460 and in 2003 it was 25,000, below the average level even during the worst of the economic crisis. Units built per 1,000 inhabitants decreased from 6.1 in 1981–89 to 2.8 in 1990–94, increased to 4.5 in 1995–2003 (still below the level of the 1980s), and was 2.2 in 2003, below the lowest level recorded during the crisis (see table 14). Because of population growth and deterioration of the housing stock, the number of units built has not only failed to reduce the cumulative deficit but actually added to it. The economic development plan for 1980–2000 estimated that an annual average of 60,000 dwellings would have to be constructed merely to replace those that collapsed, but the actual number built was only 48,000 (Mesa-Lago 2005).[20] In 2001, Hurricane Michelle destroyed 18,243 dwellings and damaged 179,814 others, while in 2002 Hurricanes Isidore and Lili destroyed 17,481 dwellings and damaged 92,291 others. In 2001, 35,805 housing units were built, and in 2002 a further 27,460, for a net increase of only 27,541 units after replacing the 35,724 units destroyed by the hurricanes, not taking into account the ones that were damaged (Rodríguez 2000, 2002; ONE 2003). In 2004, Hurricane Charley destroyed between 14,000 and 16,000 dwellings and damaged between 40,000 and 70,000. In view of all this, the housing deficit probably surpassed the one million mark in 2004; this estimate does not take into account the condition of the housing stock, which on average is very poor.[21] It has been estimated that currently 100,000 new dwellings per year are required just to keep up with demand (Bauzá and Collie 2002).

Reportedly 40% of all housing is in "mediocre" (*regular*) or "bad" condition and 60% in "good" condition (ECLAC 2004a), but there are significant differences in the condition of housing across the country and within cities. For instance, in Havana's high-income neighborhoods such as Miramar, Nuevo Vedado, and sections of Vedado, the housing stock is generally in good condition and well maintained; but in low- and middle-income neighborhoods such as Habana Vieja, Centro Habana, Cerro, or La Víbora, which have high population densities, housing units are in deteriorated condition, often propped up with wooden beams and surrounded by collapsed dwellings. In 1999, 57% of dwellings in the city of Havana were rated in good condition and the remaining 43% in mediocre or bad condition, but in

Table 14. Housing Construction in Cuba, 1981–2003

	1981–89	1990–94	1995–2003	2002	2003
Annual average dwellings built[a]	61,198	28,638	41,604	27,460	25,000
Dwellings built per 1,000 inhabitants	6.1	2.8	4.5	2.4	2.2

Sources: Authors' estimates based on Mesa-Lago 2000; ONE 1998–2003, ECLAC, *Cuba* 2004.

a. Based on total housing units built 1981–87, including those without occupancy permit; in 1988–2002 the latter were not reported.

Habana Vieja, 75% were in mediocre or bad condition. Moreover, 59% of the housing units reported structural problems and although 98% were equipped to receive running water, only half received such service daily (Pérez Villanueva 2001; regional disparities are discussed further later). In a survey taken in Havana in 2002, 22% of interviewees classified themselves as "poor" in housing and 19% as "almost poor" (Ferriol 2003).

Those with access to dollars can buy construction materials, paint, and other supplies needed to maintain and repair their homes and can hire self-employed workers to do the labor. (The state agency in charge of home repairs is virtually useless.) They can also move up to better or larger housing by swapping with other owners, often paying considerable sums under the table. Those who do not have access to dollars, however, cannot afford construction materials and repairs, and their dwellings gradually deteriorate and sometimes even collapse. Because of the government's failure to build new housing and restrictions on private home construction, relatively little change has occurred in the prerevolutionary distribution of housing units according to race. The majority of blacks continue to live in poor neighborhoods, such as Habana Vieja, in deteriorated and overcrowded dwellings (de la Fuente 2001).

Regional Inequalities

Disparities in economic and social conditions among Cuba's 14 provinces have narrowed in the last 45 years, but several indicators in table 15 show that three of the five eastern provinces (Las Tunas, Granma, and Guantánamo) consistently perform below the national average with respect to most indicators, while the city of Havana performs above the national average and, in fact, ranks at the top in most categories.

According to a study on poverty carried out in Cuba, in 1996 about 11.5% of Havana's population was deemed "at risk," compared to 21.7% of the population of the eastern provinces. An index that measures the homogeneity of the nation's 14 provinces with regard to several socioeconomic indicators places Havana as the most homogenous and Granma as the least, with Las Tunas and Guantánamo falling fairly close to Granma. While Havana's population was 100% urban in 2002, urbanization in the three eastern provinces was less than 60%. Investment per capita in Havana in 1997 was three times the level of Las Tunas and five times the levels of Guantánamo and Granma.[22] Whereas 56% of the housing units in Havana were in good condition in 1999, only 44% met this standard in Las Tunas, 38% in Granma, and 34% in Guantánamo. Connection with public water was available in 99% of homes in Havana in 1997, compared to 66% in Granma, and 48% in Las Tunas and Guantánamo. Public sewer systems were available to 64%

of homes in Havana, compared to 38% in Guantánamo, 26% in Granma, and 18% in Las Tunas. In Havana, there were 91 physicians per 10,000 inhabitants in 2000 but only 41 to 44 in the three eastern provinces, substantially lower than the nationwide average of 58 physicians per 10,000 population. There were 9.2 hospital beds per 1,000 inhabitants in Havana, compared to 4.0 to 4.4 in the three eastern provinces and 5.2 nationwide (see table 15).

Moreover, whereas in 1997 Havana had the highest income per capita, the three eastern provinces had the lowest. In 2000, the three eastern provinces had the lowest elementary school enrollment rates in the nation, as well as the highest infant mortality and mortality of children under age five rates per 1,000 live births. Granma also had the highest mortality for the population ages 65 and older and the highest open unemployment rate (14%), 2.5 times the national average. Guantánamo had the highest proportion of infants born underweight (ONE 2001; MINSAP 2001). In 2001, the average diet in the five eastern provinces provided less than 80% of the minimum recommended daily intake of proteins, less than 50% of fats, and insufficient vitamin E and mineral intake for sustained growth (United Nations WFP 2001).

Given the severe disparities in economic and social conditions across regions of the country, it is not surprising that the three eastern provinces of Las Tunas, Granma, and Guantánamo have net outflows of population, while Havana has a net inflow, as Cubans move from the eastern provinces to improve their economic and social lot. In 2001, Havana had one of the highest rates of internal immigration (2.4%), whereas Guantánamo and Granma had the two highest rates of emigration (4.7% and 3.9% respectively; see table 15).

Migration from the interior of the country to Havana intensified during the economic crisis of the 1990s because migrants (particularly those from eastern provinces) believed that economic and living conditions were better in Havana and that it was easier to gain access to hard currency in the capital city. Some 45,000 internal migrants reportedly moved to Havana in 1993–95 and in 1996 alone it is estimated that 55,000 migrants settled in the city, putting tremendous pressure on Havana's physical infrastructure and social services, particularly housing. Such internal migration resulted in significant overcrowding of housing units and shanty towns sprang up surrounding the city. In response to the internal migration crisis, the government in 1997 tightened administrative rules determining who was permitted to live in Havana[23] and even forcibly returned unauthorized migrants to their home communities (Díaz-Briquets and Pérez-López 2000).

Table 15. Socioeconomic Indicators of Cuba's Least Developed Provinces Compared with the City of Havana and the National Average, Selected Years, 1996–2002

Indicator and year	City of Havana	Las Tunas	Guantánamo	Granma	National Average
Urban population at risk, 1996 (%)	11.5	21.7c	21.7c	21.7c	14.7
Human Development Index, 1996a	0.7278	0.4348	0.3724	0.4641	0.7260
Index of homogeneity, 1997b	1.000	0.282	0.000	0.034	n/a
Urban population, 2002 (% of total)	100.0	58.9	59.8	57.7	75.2
Investment per capita, 1997 (pesos)	435	130	87	89	n/a
Housing in good condition, 1999 (% of total)	56.1	44.3	33.8	38.0	n/a
Homes with access to public water connection, 1997 (% of total)	98.6	48.0	48.1	65.5	93.8
Homes with access to public sewer system, 1997 (% of total)	63.7	18.1	38.4	25.7	36.0
Physicians, 2000 (per 10,000 inhabitants)	90.7	43.3	41.3	44.0	58.2
Hospital beds, 2000 (per 1,000 inhabitants)	9.2	4.0	4.4	4.3	5.2
Net internal migration, 2001 (%)	2.4	–0.9	–4.7	–3.9	n/a

Sources: Based on "Informe de Cuba" 1997; CIEM 1997, 2000; ONE 2001–3.
a. Estimated by the Cuban government following the methodology of the Human Development Index.
b. Homogeneity of provinces based on multiple socioeconomic indicators: most homogeneous = 1 and the least homogeneous = 0.
c. Aggregate percentage for all eastern provinces.

Racial Inequalities

While the revolutionary government has not enacted legislation that specifically proscribes racial discrimination, it has implemented certain policies that favor the poor and therefore tend to benefit Cuba's blacks because of their overrepresentation among the poor. These measures include job creation (blacks face higher unemployment rates than whites), expansion of free health care, and reduction of illiteracy combined with significant expansion of free education at the primary, secondary, and higher education levels. (Blacks had higher illiteracy rates and lower school enrollment rates than whites.) The Cuban government also eliminated some institutions in which participation by blacks was very low, such as private beaches and social clubs and private education (de la Fuente 2001).

In 1962, the government proclaimed that racial discrimination had disappeared with the eradication of "privileged classes" and therefore declared the "racial problem" solved. Thereafter, public discussion of race-related issues became taboo and the government took actions to discourage or ban black organizations and separatist black activities. Black societies and clubs were closed down and some Afro-Cuban religious sects were banned, allegedly for being socially dangerous and linked with a culture of criminality. (They were later reauthorized but under tight restrictions.)

By the 1980s, although their situation had improved, blacks continued to lag behind whites in many respects: The concentration of blacks in rundown housing in poor neighborhoods was virtually unchanged; blacks remained underrepresented in managerial positions but overrepresented in menial jobs and in the prison population; there were few black actors and directors in television and cinema; and folk humor continued to focus on negative images of blacks. As de la Fuente (2001: 295) states, "The lack of a public debate about race and racism facilitated the survival and reproduction of the very racist stereotypes the revolutionary leadership claimed to oppose."

The severe economic crisis of the 1990s reversed some of the gains previously made by blacks and created new inequalities. Although foreign remittances are crucial for survival on the island, blacks receive proportionately lower levels of remittances than whites. An estimated 84% of Cuban émigrés residing abroad are white, while at least 34% of the island's residents are black. Because of this imbalance, blacks receive an estimated one-third of the level of remittances received by whites. Blacks' access to jobs in tourism is limited because of domestic racial prejudices exacerbated by discrimination by foreign companies that manage or comanage tourism facilities. Because blacks concentrate in poor neighborhoods, and their homes are in poor condition and overcrowded, they are unable to open *paladares* or rent rooms to tourists. Relatively few blacks own private farms. The expansion of the private sector, where the government does not control hiring decisions, contributes to racial discrimination in employment. For example, black women reportedly make up a high percentage of prostitutes.

There are some signs of dissatisfaction with Cuban government policies among blacks. For example, most of the participants in anti-government riots in the summer of 1994 in Havana were Afro-Cubans. Surveys also show that young blacks desire to organize all-black societies to protect the rights they have acquired and to prevent backsliding. A Fraternity of Blackness (Cofradía de la Negritud) was created in 1999 to make the government fully aware of the growing racial inequality (de la Fuente 2001: 332).

Inequalities vis-à-vis Foreigners

Foreigners have certain privileges in Cuba that the average Cuban citizen does not. We have already discussed how the higher quality health-care services available to foreigners in special facilities dedicated to health tourism contrasts with the sharply deteriorated health-care system available to average Cubans. Furthermore, Cubans are prohibited from entering or patronizing hotels, restaurants, and other outlets reserved for foreign tourists. Cuban-American visitors are not even allowed to rent (and pay for in hard currency) hotel accommodations for use by a Cuban relative or friend. Such discrimination has been labeled by some observers as "tourist apartheid."

Last but not least, although the 1995 Cuban foreign investment law allowed foreigners to own businesses on the island (in some cases with 100% foreign ownership), Cuban citizens are prohibited from investing in, owning, or operating even small family businesses (except for *paladares*). It is ironic that technically the 1995 foreign investment law does not preclude Cuban-Americans (U.S. citizens or residents) from investing in the island and owning or operating businesses (U.S. law does, however), but denies those rights to Cuban citizens. In 1995, a draft bill was circulating on the island that would have granted Cuban citizens the right to establish and operate small businesses, but it was not formally considered by the National Assembly and has not been mentioned in the last five years (Mesa-Lago 2000), an issue raised among others by the opposition's Proyecto Varela (see chapter 2).

Deterioration and Inequalities in the Satisfaction of Basic Needs

The reforms have differentially affected the satisfaction of basic needs of two groups of Cubans. Those who earn dollars or are paid bonuses in dollars or in convertible pesos, receive dollar remittances from abroad, or have substantial bank savings are able to meet their basic needs. As shown in table 9, savers have withdrawn funds from their bank accounts in recent years to make ends meet, so that 87% of savers have lowered their balances, while 3% have increased them significantly. In contrast, those whose income is limited to a state-sector salary or a pension in pesos and/or who lack savings cannot satisfy even their basic food needs.

Six factors contributed to the deterioration of the ability to satisfy basic needs during the crisis:

· a decrease of at least 37% in the average real salary and pension and, consequently, in consumers' purchasing power;

· a 700,000–person increase in population while the supply of food and basic consumer goods has remained the same or contracted, even when considering both domestic production and imports (Fernández Mayo 2003);

· an expansion of the rationing system to virtually all consumer goods, coupled with a reduction in the size of monthly rations or quotas (goods sold at subsidized prices), to the point where such goods cover only one week per month of consumption, forcing the population to buy essential foodstuffs and supplies in state-owned dollar shops, in agricultural free markets, or on the black market, using dollars;

· the very high prices for food and other consumer goods in TRDs as a result of taxes as high as 240% (Spadoni 2003);

· the very high prices in agricultural free markets; although there were some price reductions in 1995–2001, prices rose again in 2002 and 2004; and

· the reduction in personal consumption by 22% to 25% below the 1989 level (Togores and García 2003b), as well as in social consumption or free social goods.

Through the end of the 1980s, the rationing system provided barely enough goods to cover consumers' minimum monthly consumption needs. The rationing system was inconvenient and uncertain: Consumers had to wait in long lines because goods were sold on a first-come, first-served basis, and availability was not guaranteed.

During the economic crisis, the government tightened the rationing system so that it became less important to Cuban consumers because the quantities offered were so low. Table 16 illustrates the significant decreases in ration quotas for consumer goods between 1979 and 2002. Out of 13 products for which comparable data are available, there were cuts in the quota (ranging from 29% to 89%) for seven and quotas were established for three others that were formerly freely supplied. Only quotas of rice and beans (as well as milk for children younger than seven years of age) were unchanged. Some monthly quotas in 2002 were sufficient only to support about one week's consumption for more than a week: 2.7 pounds of beef, fish, and chicken combined, eight eggs, and 1 pound of pasta and 1¼ of beans. Finally, Cubans were allotted only half a bar of soap per month.

The very high prices of agricultural products outside of the rationing systems are attributable to three factors. First, the very low prices the state pays for agricultural products from private farmers and UBPCs creates disincentives to increase production. Second, state farms and UBPCs are required to

Table 16. Monthly Ration Quotas per Person in Havana, 1979 and 2002

Commodity	Ration Quota (pounds) 1979	Ration Quota (pounds) 2002
Lard and oil	1.5	0.5
Rice	6.0	6.0
Beans	1.25	1.25
Sugar	7.0	5.0
Fish (fresh)	Free	0.7
Tubers	n/a	15.0
Beef	2.5	0.5
Ground beef and soy	n/a	0.5
Chicken	1.5[a]	1.0
Plantain	n/a	3.0
Pasta	n/a	1.0
Milk (liter, daily)[b]	1.0	1.0
Eggs (units)	Free	8.0
Bread (roll, daily)	Free	1.0
Bath soap (bar)	1.5	0.5
Washing soap (bar)	1.5	0.5
Detergent (liter)	0.5	0.33

Sources: 1979 figures from Mesa-Lago 2000; 2002 figures from Togores and García 2003a; Roca 2004.
a. In 1991.
b. Only for children up to seven years.

sell nearly all of their agricultural production to the state. And third, collusion among sellers in agricultural markets ensures high enough prices that they can earn profits of about 20%, but these are not passed on to the producers and therefore do not stimulate production (Togores 1999; Pérez Villanueva 2002a).

Table 17 compares prices of goods sold through the rationing system and through other markets (agricultural free markets and the government parallel market) during the period from December 2001 to February 2002. As is clear from the rightmost column, there are significant price differences between the two outlets, with the ratio of prices outside of the rationing system to those within it ranging from 4 to 49, depending on the product.[24]

For example, in the 1980s bread was distributed under the rationing system but could be purchased in unlimited quantities; under the economic crisis the quota of bread has been set at one small roll per person daily, at five centavos per unit; additional rolls may be purchased at 66 centavos each in

Table 17. Peso Prices under the Rationing System and in Havana Markets, December 2001–February 2002

Commodity	Rationing System	Markets (Nonrationed)[a]	Price Ratio (Market to Rationing System)
Milk (1 liter)	0.25	3.57	14.3
Bread (small roll)	0.05	0.66	13.2
Eggs (one)	0.15	3.00	20.0
Rice (1 pound)	0.24	4.26	17.8
Beans (1 pound)	0.30	7.09	23.6
Cooking oil (1 liter)	0.40	19.45	48.6
Lard (1 pound)	0.30	22.60	75.3
Pork (1 pound)	6.00	28.00	4.7
Lamb (1 pound)	4.50	20.00	4.4
Fish (1 pound, low quality)	0.50	9.20	18.4
Sugar (1 pound, refined)	0.14	2.44	17.4
Salt (1 pound)	0.10	2.00	20.0
Potatoes (1 pound)	0.30	n/a	n/a
Taro (*malanga*) (1 pound)	n/a[b]	2.00	n/a
Plantain (one)	n/a	1.00	n/a
Pumpkin (one, medium sized)	n/a	7.00	n/a
Guava (1 pound)	n/a	2.50	n/a
Soap (one bar)	0.25	7.30	29.2
Chinese-made TV	n/a	4,000.00	n/a

Sources: Pérez Villanueva 2002a; Espinosa Chepe 2001a, 2002a; and Mesa-Lago interviews in Miami with Cuban visitors and immigrants.

a. Includes goods sold in government stores, free agricultural markets, and state agricultural markets.

b. Available only for children.

market outlets, 13 times the rationed price. Fish, available "free" outside of the rationing system during the 1980s, has been brought under quota; the quota of half a pound per person per month can be purchased at 50 centavos per pound, whereas the price in market outlets is 9.20 pesos per pound, 18 times higher than the rationed price. Finally, eggs were plentiful in the 1980s, when grain feed could be imported from the USSR; as a result, eggs were removed from the rationing system and became a staple commodity of the Cuban population. In 1993–94, with egg production way down as a result of cuts in grain feed imports, they were again brought under the rationing system. The price of rationed eggs has been held at 15 centavos per unit, but the non-rationed price in December 2001 was 1.74 pesos and by February 2002 it had jumped to 3 pesos.

Furthermore, many goods are available only in the dollar shops (TRDs) and must be purchased with dollars. When converted to pesos at the CADECA exchange rates, TRD prices are as much as 100 times higher than rationed prices. The average monthly salary of 261 pesos in 2002 (equivalent to about $10 at the CADECA exchange rate) could be nearly used up at a TRD buying one bar of soap, half a liter of oil, and a pound of taro (*malanga*). Some food products are luxuries not affordable to the average Cuban: For instance, one pound of shrimp costs about 60 pesos, one-fourth of the average salary in 2002 (Céspedes 2004). At the beginning of 2002, Panda brand TV sets made in China sold for 4,000 pesos each in the state non-rationed market, equivalent to 1.3 times the average annual salary of a state worker; sets were also sold in the TRDs at $470 (equivalent to 12,200 pesos). The price of these sets in China was reportedly $100, hence Cuba made profits of 50% or 370%, depending on the market in which they were sold (Maseda 2002a). In May 2004, in reaction to Bush administration measures restricting remittances and travel to the island, the Cuban government raised prices in the TRDs by the following percentages: food, 10% to 15%; toiletries and detergent, 10%; bath soap, 10% to 33%; clothing and shoes, 10% to 15%; consumer durables, 10% to 20%; and fuels, 10% to 22% (Circular Especial 5 of the Ministerio de Comercio Exterior, May 17, 2004). In November, the 10% charge imposed on all transactions in dollars resulted in an additional increase in TRD prices, for a combined increase ranging from 20% to 46%. The Conference of Cuban Catholic Bishops declared that the actions of the U.S. and Cuban governments "directly and indirectly harm the poorest families of our nation" ("Nota" 2004).

According to Cuban economist Togores, "income is insufficient to meet even basic food needs. Other needs, such as toiletries and personal hygiene products, clothing, and consumption of certain services—such as transportation, electricity, cooking fuel—that are also essential [cannot be met]."[25] There has been a deterioration in the caloric intake of the Cuban population as well as a shift in the components of nutrition. Statistics show that the consumption of certain nutrients basic to a healthy diet is well below established parameters, thereby threatening food security" (Togores 1999: 94–96).

Daily per-capita consumption of calories decreased from 2,955 in 1984 to 1,863 in 1993, climbed to 1,993 in 1995, and reportedly reached 2,362 in 2002, still 21% lower than the 1984 level and slightly below the internationally recommended nutritional level. Protein consumption decreased from 78 grams in 1985 to 46 grams in 1993, rose to 50 grams in 1995, and reportedly was 70 grams in 2002, below the 1985 level but close to the internationally recommended level. Fat consumption was 44.5 grams in 2002, 41% below the recommended level (Togores 1999; Togores and García 2003b; Sixto

2003; ECLAC 2004a). These figures are averages and there are significant differences in nutritional intake across the population; furthermore, the statistics appear to be for the city of Havana where, according to a Cuban expert, the food situation is better than in the rest of the country (Fernández Mayo 2003). For 1995, Togores (1999) found that the diet of Cubans had serious deficiencies in consumption of fats and fatty acids, vitamin B, and niacin (important for the neurological system and obtained from fruits and meats), vitamin B12 (important for the generation of red blood cells), and vitamin A (important for growth, vision, and the immune system). In 1998, the intake of vitamin A was still 54% below the recommended level (Togores and García 2003b). In 1998–2000, 13% of the population was undernourished, and 40% of women in the third trimester of pregnancy and 50% of children younger than one year old suffered from anemia (PAHO 1998; United Nations WFP 2001; FAO 2002).

The average cost of the quantity of foods necessary to meet minimum nutrition needs increased from 73 pesos in 1989 to 189 pesos in 1995. The cost difference of 116 pesos (61.6%) was attributable to the need to buy some goods in dollar shops, in agricultural free markets, or on the black market.[26] But the real per-capita average income decreased from 131 pesos in 1989 to 66 pesos in 1995, 123 pesos short of the cost of the basic food requirement (Togores 1999). The situation has deteriorated since 1995; in a more recent article, Togores affirms that "a great percentage of the households do not cover their expenses with the income they receive, forcing them to resort to survival strategies to seek alternative sources of income or lose altogether access to goods and/or services" (Togores 2004: 133).

Poverty and Social Assistance

The first report on poverty in Cuba, published in 1997, referred to the "population at risk of not meeting some essential need" rather than to incidence of poverty. The report argued that Cuba was unique because its government guaranteed a minimum level of basic foodstuffs each month at subsidized prices, provided free health care and education, and granted social security or social assistance protection; in addition, most of its population either owned their home (80%) or paid very low rent or no rent at all. The urban population at risk was defined as persons with insufficient income to purchase a basic basket of foodstuffs that established the poverty line. Cuban analysts estimated the value of the free social services and added it to the average income of the population. The estimates of the cost of the food basket took into account subsidized prices of food bought through the rationing system; at the time, that system was estimated to supply 70% of foodstuffs, and agricultural free markets, the black market, and food grown for self-consumption the remaining 30%.

The study did not show the full calculations behind the estimates and the scattered data provided were unclear and at times contradictory. The average monthly income of the urban population was not reported, but the imputed value of social services was estimated at "between 110 and 160 pesos . . . the equivalent of 40% of average income." Taking the two end points of this range, the average monthly income can be calculated as between 275 and 400 pesos, a very high amount considering that the average monthly state salary was only 206 pesos in 1996. Adding the average income plus the imputed value of services would yield average monthly income estimates of 385 to 560 pesos, an obvious overestimation. Meanwhile, the value of the monthly food basket was calculated at 74 pesos, an underestimate. Based on these questionable estimates, the urban population at risk was calculated at 14.7% in 1996, compared to 6.3% in 1988. The urban population at risk included children below age 14; persons living in households with more than six members; women more often than men; persons with low levels of education (primary education only); and those who were unemployed or not economically active. Between 1988 and 1995, the percentage of the population at risk in the city of Havana rose from 4.3% to 20.1% because of growing inequalities, yet the report indicated that between 1995 and 1996 the population at risk shrank from 20.1% to 11.5% due to a "reduction in inequality" (Informe de Cuba 1997).[27] This finding is contradicted by the data we have presented in the first part of this chapter. In fact, a noted Cuban economist recently has estimated that the urban population at risk rose to 20% in 1999, and that preliminary estimates for 2001 confirmed the persistence of poverty (Ferriol 2003).[28]

The dubious 1997 study just discussed was followed by a much more sophisticated one authored by Togores (1999). Relying on the average cost of a person's food requirement, the gap between that cost and the average income per capita of the population, and the distribution of the population by income levels, Togores estimated an index of severity of poverty in Cuba for 1995, following a methodology developed by Nobel Laureate Amartya Sen. The severity of poverty index combines two variables: poverty incidence, or the percentage of the total population below the poverty line (based on the cost of a basket of minimum essential foodstuffs), and the Gini coefficient of the distribution of average income among the poor.[29] Based on two different variants of the index, Togores estimated Cuba's poverty index as 61% or 67% of total population, and the severity of poverty index at 39.7% or 41.8%.

Togores argued (along the same lines as the 1997 study cited previously) that the Sen index determined poverty based only on the insufficiency of income to acquire necessary foodstuffs, but excluded from consideration the value of free social services such as education, health care, social security, and social assistance. (She excludes housing from the state-provided services.) Taking these services into account would reduce measures of both income inequality and poverty incidence. Togores acknowledged that increasing prices of foodstuffs in recent years had had an adverse effect on consumer consumption, but argued that transfers of free social services partially compensated for those losses. (She did not consider state subsidies for consumer goods.) Finally, she stated that expenditures on social services rose by 26% during the economic crisis (1989–98), at an annual average growth rate of near 3% (Togores 1999: 97–100). However, this reported increase in social expenditures is in nominal terms, and not adjusted for inflation.

Table 18 shows that per-capita expenditures for social services in real terms declined by 78% from 1989 through 1993 and, although they increased from 1994 through 1998, in 1998 they were still 40% below their 1989 level. That is, not only did real income per capita plummet by about 45% between 1989 and 1998, but real social service expenditures shrank by 40% in the same period.

In this chapter we have also demonstrated that the quality of social services has severely deteriorated since the early 1990s. This means that free social services, the "missing factor" in estimating poverty incidence and severity of poverty, did not play a significant compensatory role in both measures, contrary to Togores' contention, and therefore her initial estimates are probably closer to reality. Furthermore, the expansion of income inequality since the 1990s has widened the gap between the poor and the still small but growing segment of the population that has accumulated substantial wealth.

The most recent poverty study is based on a survey to measure the "population at risk" conducted among households in the city of Havana in 2002. Interviewees were asked to classify themselves into one of three categories with respect to several indicators: poor, nearly poor, or not poor. Survey results showed that 41% to 54% of the population considered themselves poor or nearly poor as follows: with regard to income, 31% poor and 23% nearly poor; with regard to food, 21% poor and 24% nearly poor; with regard to housing, 22% poor and 19% nearly poor; and with regard to overall living conditions, 23% poor and 20% nearly poor (Ferriol 2003).

The reappearance of poor people in Cuban streets since the mid-1990s and the government struggle to eliminate beggars who harass tourists by panhandling for money or other gratuities, particularly in Havana, provides further evidence that income inequality and poverty have grown. Finally, as described already, the extent to which availability of foodstuffs at rationed prices compensates for income inequality (as alleged by the 1997 study) has

Table 18. Social Expenditures in Nominal and Real Terms, 1989–98 (in million pesos)

Expenditures	1989	1990	1991	1992	1993	1994	1995	1996	1997	1998
Nominal Terms										
Education	1,650	1,620	1,504	1,427	1,385	1,335	1,359	1,421	1,454	1,510
Health care	904	937	925	938	1,077	1,061	1,108	1,190	1,265	1,345
Social assistance	1,094	1,164	1,226	1,348	1,454	1,532	1,594	1,630	1,636	1,705
Housing[a]	406	383	281	248	260	315	411	462	488	566
Social welfare	101	96	88	96	94	94	119	128	135	145
Total	4,155	4,200	4,024	4,057	4,270	4,337	4,591	4,831	4,978	5,271
CPI	1.443	1.509	1.830	3.515	6.578	5.575	2.940	2.883	2.904	2.903
Real Terms	2,880	2,784	2,199	1,288	648	778	1,561	1,676	1,714	1,815
Per capita[b]	272	260	204	106	59	71	142	152	154	163
Index[c]	100.0	95.9	75.0	39.1	21.8	26.1	52.2	55.9	56.9	60.0

Source: Authors' calculations based on nominal expenditures from ONE 1998, 2000; CPI from Togores (1999); and population (to estimate per capita) from ONE 2001.

a. Togores excludes housing, but we have included it.

b. In pesos.

c. 1989 = 100.

shrunk by three-fourths since 1989. In conclusion, Togores' 1995 estimates of a poverty incidence of 61% to 67% and of a severity of poverty index of 40% to 42% seem to conform to our own analysis in the first part of this chapter and approximate reality more closely than the 14.7% population at risk rate calculated in the mentioned 1997 study on poverty in Cuba.

It should be also noted that free social services as well as price subsidies for rationed foodstuffs and state-provided transportation services are not targeted at the poor, but rather are distributed to the entire population, including workers who earn high incomes in the private sector, receive bonuses and awards in kind, or receive foreign remittances (Ferriol 2001b). In view of the increasing inequality and poverty in Cuba, this policy of universal price subsidies and free services is not only a waste of scarce resources but also an obstacle to providing more help to those who desperately need it.

Table 18 shows that social assistance expenditures aimed at those who are in severe need averaged only 2.4% of total social expenditures in nominal terms for 1989–98, by far the lowest share among all social services. Using the data in table 18 we estimate that social assistance expenditures in real terms shrank 29%, from 70 million pesos in 1989 to 50 million pesos in 1998, in spite of increasing poverty. There are no data on the number of beneficiaries of social assistance for 1989–96; between 1997 and 2000 the number allegedly declined by 14% and, despite an increase in 2001, it was still below the 1997 level. There was a significant increase in 2002 to 192,511 beneficiaries, equivalent to 1.7% of the total population, which contrasts with the estimate that 20% of the population is at risk (ECLAC 2004b; Mesa-Lago 2005). The maximum amount paid to single social assistance recipients in 2002 was 62 pesos ($2.38 at the CADECA exchange rate), and a family of five received a maximum of 105 pesos (ECLAC 2004a). That translates to 21 pesos per capita, an insufficient amount to buy even rationed foodstuffs and other essential goods for one week (see tables 16 and 17).

Conclusion

In this chapter we have documented the deterioration in social welfare and analyzed socioeconomic inequalities in Cuba over the 1990–2002 period, focusing on eight areas:

- Income and wealth: The real average salary in the state sector declined by 37% between 1989 and 2000. The ratio of highest to lowest income rose from 829 to 1 in 1995 to 12,500 to 1 in 2002. Between 50% and 65% of the population receives remittances from abroad, estimated at an average of $122 per capita per annum. Converted at the CADECA exchange rate, the annual average per-capita level of remittances in pesos was slightly higher than the average annual state-sector salary in that currency. In 2002, 3% of the savings accounts had balances exceeding 10,000 pesos and held 48% of all savings, while at the other extreme 63% of the savings accounts had balances of less than 200 pesos and held only 2% of the value of deposits.

· Regressive taxation: The 1994 tax reform shifted the tax system from reliance on direct to indirect taxes. Indirect taxes, primarily sales taxes, generated nearly 60% of tax revenue in 2003. Most taxes, therefore, are indirect and are regressive because their effect is proportionally heavier on those segments of the population with lower incomes. The Cuban government does not tax remittances. Incomes of those illegally employed are not taxed either.

· Social services: The deterioration in key health indicators (morbidity, maternal mortality, malnutrition) affects the vast majority of the population, but not the members of the armed forces, security services, and political leadership, who are shielded because they have their own health-care system. The health-care facilities that serve the latter have not experienced the shortages that afflict the general health-care service. Real expenditures on education fell by 38%, secondary school enrollment declined by 11%, and higher education enrollment by 20%. Children of the elite have been protected from the deterioration of the educational system because they have access to special schools or are able to afford private instruction. The real value of social security pensions fell by 42% and the complementary social safety net—foodstuffs at subsidized prices, free health care, low-priced services such as transportation, electricity, attendance at sports and cultural events—has deteriorated sharply. Because the retirement age is too low and workers do not currently contribute sufficient amounts to their pensions, the social security system has a huge deficit that is currently covered by the state. Private-sector workers are not covered by the social security system. Members of the armed forces and state security personnel have a special pension system that is more generous than the general system, and these individuals may also have special access to certain goods and services in special outlets. The number of dwellings built in 2003 was 60% lower than the annual average in the 1980s and 13% lower than the annual average during the worst period of the crisis. The cumulative housing deficit probably surpasses the one million mark and 40% of the existing housing units are in either bad or mediocre shape. The condition of housing units varies substantially across Havana neighborhoods and between Havana and other provinces.

· Regional inequalities: The city of Havana scores substantially higher than three eastern provinces (Las Tunas, Granma, and Guantánamo) with regard to most socioeconomic indicators. Compared to Havana, these three eastern provinces had higher levels of poverty and unemployment; worse housing; lower access to piped water and municipal sewer services; and lower rates of health-care access, such as number of physicians per 10,000 inhabitants and of hospital beds per 1,000 inhabitants.

· Racial inequalities: Black Cubans receive an estimated one-third of the level of remittances that whites receive. Blacks tend to be concentrated in poor neighborhoods, where the housing stock is severely deteriorated, and they face discrimination in securing employment in tourist facilities.

· Discrimination vis-à-vis foreigners: Cuban citizens do not have access to the same high-quality health-care system available to foreigners who pay in dollars. Similarly, they are barred from tourist facilities, hotels, and restaurants reserved for foreigners. Cuban citizens are not allowed to operate their own businesses or to make investments in the island, whereas foreigners can do so. Foreigners have taken advantage of Cuba's openness to foreign investment and have established a large number of joint ventures on the island.

· Satisfaction of basic needs: The decline in real salaries and pensions; the cutbacks in the supply of goods under the monthly rationing system to the point where they cover only one week's consumption; and the high prices of goods in TRDs, other dollar outlets, and agricultural markets have decreased the degree to which the population can satisfy its basic needs. The cost of a basket of basic commodities per person rose by 113%; and daily consumption of calories, protein, and fat fell below internationally recommended levels.

· Poverty and social assistance: Estimates by Cuban analysts of the percentage of the urban population "at risk" (a euphemism for being in poverty) show a rising trend: from 6% in 1988 to 14.7% in 1996 and to 20% in 1999–2001. The poverty incidence was estimated at 61% or 67% in 1995, and from 41% to 54% of the population of Havana considered themselves poor or nearly poor in 2002. Social service expenditures per capita in real terms have declined by 40%. Free social services and subsidized foodstuffs are not targeted at the poor but are supplied to the entire population regardless of income. Social assistance expenditures constitute only 2.4% of social expenditures and have been declining in real terms despite increasing poverty. In 2002 only 1.7% of the population received social assistance but 20% was estimated as being at risk of poverty. Widening disparities in income and wealth have exacerbated socioeconomic inequalities.

4

Cuba and the Human Development Index

In chapters 2 and 3 we have shown that Cuba suffered a severe economic crisis between 1991 and 1993, and that a decade later, the recovery process that began in 1994 had not returned the island to pre-crisis levels, with a few exceptions. But the previous two chapters lacked a systematic comparison of Cuba with other countries in the world and Latin America. In this chapter we evaluate how Cuba's performance has been portrayed by one of the leading international measures of economic development, the Human Development Index (HDI), published annually since the late 1980s by the United Nations Development Programme (UNDP) in its *Human Development Report* (hereafter the *Report*). The HDI has ranked as many as 174 countries in the world, including Cuba, on the basis of their performance with respect to selected socioeconomic indicators.

In two earlier publications, Mesa-Lago has argued that it is not technically possible to estimate the HDI for Cuba because of the lack of basic statistics to estimate the critical economic component of the HDI. This concern has not deterred the UNDP from calculating and publishing the HDI for Cuba, however. The results of the exercise are quite unsettling: They do not seem to coincide with trends in Cuban socioeconomic development, the underlying data sometimes contradict official Cuban data, and the methodology for some of the estimates is not properly explained. As a result, the estimated HDI for Cuba and Cuba's ranking with respect to the world and Latin American countries have been subject to questionable changes in index levels and leaps in rankings that defy explanation.

In this chapter we trace Cuba's performance in the HDI. We begin with a brief description of the concepts behind the index and its measurement, then trace the HDI values and rankings for Cuba over the years, identify inconsistencies in the social indicators and deeper concerns regarding the economic indicator, and explain the source of Cuba's miraculous jump in ranking in 1997 and very strong performance since then.

Concepts and Background

The indicator most frequently used to measure the development level of a country is its gross domestic product (GDP), which estimates the value of all goods and services generated by the economy within a given time period, typically a year. To take into account the effect of price increases (inflation), GDP is normally adjusted by an index constructed from individual changes in prices of a basket of commodities and services. For purposes of international comparison, GDP is divided by the population, to account for the size of the country and obtain GDP per capita (GDP p/c). Finally, because GDP is usually calculated on the basis of the national currency of each nation, GDPs in national currencies are converted to a common currency (typically U.S. dollars, US$). Two conversion factors, or exchange rates, are generally used for this purpose: (1) the official exchange rate of the foreign currency for the U.S. dollar, or (2) a purchasing power parity (PPP) exchange rate, calculated by comparing the domestic currency and dollar prices of a large number of goods and services in the foreign country and in the United States, respectively.

In its *World Development Report*, the World Bank annually ranks countries of the world on the basis of their GDP per capita, adjusted for inflation and converted to U.S. dollars using the PPP exchange rate (hereafter GDP p/c PPP US$). Countries are classified in three groups according to their level of national income: high, medium, and low (World Bank 2002b).

In the 1960s and 1970s, the World Bank included Cuba in its *World Development Report*. At that time, Cuba computed its national accounts by means of the material product system (MPS), the national accounts methodology used by the USSR and the socialist countries. The rest of the world used a different methodology, the system of national accounts (SNA). The two national income accounting methodologies are not comparable for two main reasons. First, to compute the global social product (GSP; the closest macroeconomic aggregate to GDP under the MPS), the MPS double-counted the value of a product as it moved through different stages of processing, instead of counting only the "value added" at each stage of production or transformation, as is done when using the SNA to compute GDP. For instance, as raw cotton is successively converted into yarn, fabric, and clothing, the MPS adds up the value of each of these outputs to calculate the value of production, whereas the SNA would start with the value of raw cotton and add to it only the value created at each stage of processing. Second, as a legacy of Karl Marx's thought, the MPS excluded the value of all "nonproductive" services (that is, services not directly related to material production), such as education, health care, social security, and defense, which are included in the SNA. Whereas the first difference in methodology tends to overstate the value of the GSP, the second tends to understate it—particularly in the Cuban case since social services and defense are such important areas of Cuba's economic activity.

Cuba officially used the MPS system from 1962 to 1989, although a few Cuban economists provided GSP data until 1993. Starting in 1995, Cuba shifted to the SNA system and published a GDP series extending back to 1985. The MPS and SNA series cannot be connected (Mesa-Lago 2000). To compound the problem, between 1961 and 1989 Cuba changed its methodology for calculating the GSP and other MPS aggregates four times, yielding four series that could not be connected either. Moreover, Cuban statisticians have never made public how they measure inflation and estimate GSP or GDP at constant prices. And, of course, a lingering issue is how to convert the value aggregates from the Cuban peso to dollars. World Bank analysts seem to have used the official exchange rate of one peso for one dollar, even though the black market rate was several pesos for one dollar. Cuba did not then—and does not now—publish the necessary information about goods and services prices, as well as about many other variables that are needed to estimate PPP exchange rates. Therefore, equating GSP in Cuba with GDP in the rest of Latin America and other capitalist countries is tantamount to comparing elephants to peanuts.[1]

Cuba's HDI Scores and Methodology

The ranking of countries based solely on their GDP p/c presupposes that development can be measured using only that single indicator. Consider however a country with a highly unequal income distribution, where the top 10% of the population receives 40% of GDP and the bottom 40%, just 10%. That country's GDP p/c would be a deceptive indicator of average income, because the income of a minority of the population would be considerably above the national average, and the income of a majority would be considerably below the average. There are also countries like Costa Rica, Cuba, and Uruguay that have reached higher standards in their social indicators (health care, education, social security) than in their GDP p/c levels, while the opposite is true in other countries that have neglected their social services despite significant growth in overall and per-capita GDP.

The HDI Methodology

In order to address this problem, the UNDP constructed the HDI, a measure that combines three indicators, one economic and two social. The economic indicator is GDP p/c PPP US$, based on estimates by the International Comparisons Project of the United Nations. The two social indicators are (1) life expectancy at birth (to capture health standards); and (2) a combination of the adult literacy rate and the joint primary, secondary, and tertiary education enrollment rates (to capture educational levels).

The values of the three indicators cannot be combined directly because they are expressed in different units: PPP in dollars, life expectancy in years, and literacy and educational enrollment in percentages. To overcome this difficulty, an index is estimated for each of the three indicators, with maximum and minimum values obtained from ranking all of the countries under consideration. The indices range from 1, for the country with the best performance, to 0 for the worst. Each index contributes one-third (equal weights) to the HDI value, which is calculated by adding the three indices for a given country and dividing the result by three. Based on HDI scores, countries are grouped into three categories, high, medium, and low, and are numerically ranked from the best performer (1) to the worst (currently 174).

The HDI methodology favors Cuba because it assigns double weight to social areas in which Cuba has performed quite well (health care and education), compared to the single weight assigned to the economic indicator, an area where Cuba's performance has been lackluster. Of course, the same situation occurs with respect to other countries in the region, like Costa Rica and Uruguay, that have invested considerable resources in developing their social services. As we have seen in chapters 2 and 3, the crisis of the 1990s not only caused a sharp decline in Cuba's GDP but also adversely affected most social indicators.

The Fall and Surprising Jump of Cuba's HDI Rankings

Table 19 shows Cuba's ranking on the HDI with respect to all countries in the world and to Latin America, for the 1989–2000 period. The first column of the table indicates the year of publication of the *Report* (1992–2002), and the second column the year on which data for the HDI is based (1989–2000).[2]

In 1989, before the economic crisis, Cuba was ranked 61st among 160 countries in the world for which the HDI is calculated and 9th among 20 Latin American countries. In 1991, when the economic crisis began, Cuba fell to 89th place in the world (among 173 countries) and to 12th place in the region. Even though the economic crisis worsened in 1992 and 1993, in those years Cuba climbed, according to the HDI, to the 72nd and 79th places in the

Table 19. Ranking of Cuba in the World and within Latin America, 1989–2000[a]

Human Development Index (Years)[b]		Number of countries in the world	Ranking[c]	
Publication	Data		World	Latin America
1992	1989	160	61	9
1993	1990	173	75	10
1994	1991	173	89	12
1995	1992	174	72	11
1996	1993	174	79	11
1997	1994	175	86	11
1998	1995	174	85	11
1999	1997	174	58	9
2000	1998	174	56	6
2001	1999	162	[d]	[d]
2002	2000	173	55	6

Sources: UNDP 1991–2002, 2001b.

a. Years refer to HDI data.

b. The ranking for the data years 1989–1995 and 1997–2000 are not technically comparable due to a change in methodology in the 1999 *Report*.

c. The lower the rank, the better the country's performance.

d. The indirect rank was between 50th and 51st in the world and 5th in Latin America (HDI website).

world and to 11th rank in the region. In 1994, the decline of Cuba's GDP stopped and a slight economic recovery began in 1995, spurred by the modest market-oriented reforms initiated in 1993. The HDI for 1994 and 1995 had Cuba dropping to the 86th then 85th places overall and remaining in 11th place for Latin America during those two years.

Cuba's GDP growth rate during the 1990s peaked in 1996, but no HDI was computed for that year.[3] In 1997–98 Cuban economic growth slowed, but nevertheless, its HDI for 1997 jumped to 58th place in the world and 9th place in the region, and for 1998 to 56th place and 6th place, respectively. (Note, however, that HDI values and rankings before and after 1997 are not technically comparable due to a change in methodology, as will be explained in detail later.) Cuba's HDI ranking in 1998 was significantly higher than in 1989, even though the country's GDP in 1998 was still 33% below the 1989 level (see chapter 2). How did this surprising result occur? To explain this phenomenon, it is necessary to look behind the HDI to analyze the three indicators that compose it and the calculation methodology.

Why the Jump: Questions about the Social Indicators

Health care, measured by life expectancy at birth, contributes a third to the value of the HDI. Within Latin America, Cuba has traditionally—both before and since the revolution—ranked among the two or three leaders for this indicator and, in the 1990s, held second place (after Costa Rica). Life expectancy tends to change very slowly over time, which has been the experience in Cuba (see ECLAC, *Statistical Yearbook*, 2001). Therefore, this indicator cannot explain Cuba's HDI jump in 1997.

Moreover, the series on Cuban life expectancy reported in the HDI raises serious questions: (1) For 1990, it was given as 75.4 years in three consecutive editions. (2) For 1992, two different figures, 75.6 years and 75.3 years, were reported in various editions. Based on the first figure, life expectancy increased compared to 1990, but based on the second figure it declined. (3) For 1993, life expectancy was reported as 75.4 years, which suggests that it stagnated at the 1990 level. (4) For 1994, it was reported as 75.6 years, which can be interpreted either as no change or an improvement in relation to 1992, depending on which 1992 figure is used. (5) For 1995–99, life expectancy showed a slight increase from 75.7 years to 75.8 years. For 1995 and 1997, the life expectancy figure was unchanged (75.7 years)[4] and the index value for this indicator (Cuba in relation to all countries being examined) remained unchanged at 0.84 (UNDP 1991–2000). Thus, the life expectancy indicator cannot explain Cuba's miraculous jump in HDI in 1997.

The United Nations Human Development Report Office (UNHDRO) in New York did not agree with our conclusion. In correspondence with one of the authors, UNHDRO officials argued that (1) "it is not correct to compare data estimated with different methodologies"; (2) "lack of data for Cuba didn't allow enough adjustment through the years"; and (3) "fluctuation is not a sign of data contradiction neither of doubt upon their accuracy" (letter to Mesa-Lago, May 22, 2002). We do agree with the last point, but our analysis shows that two different estimates of life expectancy were used in the 1992 HDI. Moreover, the most important point, not addressed by the UNHDRO, is that since there was no increase in Cuba's life expectancy in 1995–97, this indicator could not explain the jump in Cuba's HDI value for 1997. Actually, a comparison of life expectancy used in the 1999 *Report* shows a *decline* of two points for Cuba between 1995 and 1997 (UNDP 1999: 165).

Education also contributes one-third to the value of the HDI. This indicator combines two variables: (1) the adult literacy rate (for the population older than 15 years), assigned a weight of two-thirds of the education indicator; and (2) the combined percentage of the school-age population enrolled in primary, secondary, and higher education, assigned a weight of one-third.

In the 1990s, Cuba ranked third in the region (after Uruguay and Argentina) with regard to adult literacy. Because only about 4% of Cuba's adult population is illiterate, it is very difficult to raise the literacy level significantly, particularly in a short time period; therefore, the illiteracy rate cannot be responsible for the miraculous jump in HDI. For 1985, the HDI reported Cuba's adult literacy rate at both 96% and 92.4%. Based on the first figure, adult literacy stagnated until 1998 (96.4%), but based on the second figure there was an improvement of 4 percentage points from 1985 to 1998. In 1990, the adult literacy rate was reported at 94% and there was some improvement subsequently, but the increase in 1995–97 was only 0.2 of a percentage point (from 95.7% to 95.9%), which does not seem to explain Cuba's great leap forward in 1997 (UNDP 1990–99). In its 2002 letter to Mesa-Lago the UNHDRO repeated with regard to the literacy rate the first argument it gave regarding the life expectancy indicator, but once again, did not address the major point: The very small increase in the adult literacy rate in 1995–97 cannot explain Cuba's jump in the HDI in 1997. (In fact, the UNDP comparison of literacy levels between 1995 and 1997 showed no change over these years; UNDP 1999: 165.)

The second variable within the education indicator is the combined percentage of the school-age population enrolled in primary, secondary, and higher education (see the first three columns of table 20). Elementary education was already available in Cuba to the whole population by the end of the 1960s and, based on official data, the gross enrollment rate was 100% in 1989.[5] Since 1990–91, however, that rate has begun to decrease, reaching 99.3% in 1992 and 99.1% in 1999 (ONE 1998, 2000).

According to UNESCO (2001), Cuba reached its highest secondary education enrollment rate in 1989 at 90.2%; subsequently this rate decreased to 74.5% in 1994, rose to 80.8% in 1996, fell to 79.4% in 1998, and increased to 81.9% in 1999, still 8.3 percentage points below the 1989 level.[6] Figures about actual enrollment in higher education—242,366 in 1989 and 106,787 in 1999—show a decline of 56% (CEE 1991, ONE 2000); the gross enrollment rate was 20.5% in 1989 (21.8% in 1987 according to UNESCO 2001), declined to 12.4% in 1996–97 (this decline is acknowledged by CIEM 2000), and rose to 18.9% in 1998 and 20.8% in 1999, recovering almost to the 1990 level. Since primary and higher education gross enrollment rates fell almost uninterruptedly from 1989 to 1997, while the secondary enrollment rate in 1997 was well below the 1989 level, it stands to reason that the combined enrollment rate at the three levels must have fallen in that period.

Unfortunately, the HDI does not use consistent series for the three combined educational levels for 1989–99: In the first three years, it used average years of schooling, but in 1992 it shifted to school enrollment rate, and the two series cannot be connected.[7] The last column of table 20 shows the decline in the HDI estimates of combined gross enrollment rate for the three levels of education from 65% in 1992 to 63% in 1994, which agrees with the figures from Cuba and UNESCO. The combined gross enrollment rate in the HDI, however, shows an enormous jump from 66% in 1995 to 73% in 1998. This does not agree with official Cuban data on primary education enrollment, which show a decrease from 99.7% to 99.3% in that period and, because of its weight relative to the others, trends in primary education enrollment largely determine the trend of the combined enrollment variable. There is also a contradiction between the increase in the HDI combined enrollment rates from 1995 to 1998 and the decline in the secondary education enrollment rate, which fell from 79.8% to 79.4% in that period. With regard to higher education, there was an increase in the enrollment rate from 12.7% to 18.9% from 1995 to 1998, but the 1998 level was still 1.6 percentage points below the 1989 level. In 1999, the HDI combined enrollment at the three levels further increased from 73% to 76%, while primary enrollment decreased from 99.3% to 99.1%, although both secondary and higher enrollment rose to 81.9% and 20.8%, respectively; 1999 secondary enrollment was still below the 1989 level (table 20).

To summarize, the behavior of the health-care indicator (life expectancy)

Table 20. Educational Enrollment According to Cuba, UNESCO, and the HDI, 1989–99 (Percentage)

Year	Cuba Primary	UNESCO Secondary	UNESCO Higher	HDI (3 levels combined)
1989	100.0	90.2	20.5	a
1990	99.7	88.9	20.9	a
1991	99.8	85.7	19.8	a
1992	99.3	81.8	18.1	65
1993	99.5	76.7	16.7	65
1994	99.2	74.5	13.9	63
1995	99.7	79.8	12.7	66
1996	99.4	80.8	12.4	n/a
1997	99.3	80.0	12.4	72
1998	99.3	79.4	18.9	73
1999	99.1	81.9	20.8	76

Sources: HDI from UNDP 1992–2001. Cuba: Primary from ONE 1998–99; secondary and higher 1989–99 from UNESCO 1999, 2001; the year 1997 is an estimate by the authors (based on ONE 1998) to allow for a comparison with the same year from the HDI.

a. In these years, a different indicator was used (average years of schooling) that cannot be connected with the subsequent indicator.

used by the HDI raises questions about its reliability. Within the education indicator, the literacy variable is relatively consistent and cannot explain Cuba's miraculous jump in HDI ranking in 1997. Finally, the overall enrollment rate data used in the HDI (combining the three educational levels) do not agree with official Cuban figures or data from UNESCO. Next we examine the economic indicator of the HDI.

The Questionable Calculation of the Economic Indicator

The economic indicator, which contributes one-third to the HDI, is the GDP p/c PPP US$. For Cuba, this is an extremely complex indicator to construct and analyze. As explained in the first part of this chapter, Cuba used the MPS system from 1962 through 1993 and shifted to the SNA in 1995, when it began to publish GDP at current and at constant prices (adjusted for inflation, with 1981 as the price base year); Cuban statistical agencies also recomputed GDP for earlier years and produced a series that extends back to 1985. Thus, there is an official GDP series at constant prices covering the 1989–2000 period.[8] The shift to the SNA obviated some of the very serious problems that afflicted Cuban national accounts under the MPS (overcounting of output, underestimation of the contribution of services, impossibility of connecting diverse subseries), but did not solve the problems of proper adjustment to account for inflation and the conversion to PPP dollars.

Cuban statistical agencies have not provided information on how they have adjusted GDP for inflation. There is no published methodology for the consumer price index presumably used as the GDP deflator, nor is there information on the nature of the basket of goods and services included in the index, on the price relatives used to calculate overall price change, or on the relative importance assigned to each good or service in order to obtain a weighted average of price changes. There is also no information on how Cuban statisticians take into account price changes in the different markets that coexist in Cuba, such as the agricultural free markets, dollar shops, parallel official markets, and black market. According to a Cuban source, the price of a basket of commodities sold in the free markets rose by 1,552% from 1989 to 1993 (CIEM 2000), indicating that inflation was much higher in these markets than the overall inflation rate calculated for the Cuban economy.

With regard to the conversion from pesos to dollars, Cuba's official exchange rate continues to be one peso for one dollar. The exchange rate in the state-run CADECAs, established in 1995, was 95 pesos for one dollar in that year. The Cuban peso strengthened in value subsequently, so CADECA outlets paid about 21 pesos for one dollar in 1998 and 2000. Even more problematic would be how to calculate the purchasing power parity (PPP) exchange rate of the peso, since Cuba has not been part of the United Nations International Comparisons Project and does not publish the statistics necessary to replicate such estimates. It should be noted that *Investigación sobre el desarrollo humano y la equidad en Cuba, 1999,* a detailed and impressive study on human development by Cuban specialists associated with the Center for Research on the World Economy (Centro de Investigaciones de la Economía Mundial, CIEM) under UNDP sponsorship, simply reproduced the HDI figures for the economic variable and did not elaborate on how Cuba's GDP p/c PPP US$ was estimated (CIEM 2000).

To sum up, based on the preceding discussion and our accumulated experience studying and analyzing Cuban economic statistics for many decades (see, for example, Mesa-Lago 2001b), we believe that it is impossible to estimate Cuba's GDP p/c PPP US$. How did the HDI accomplish the impossible?

The first column of table 21 shows HDI estimates of Cuban GDP p/c PPP US$. The second column contains Cuban GDP p/c, adjusted for inflation and converted to dollars at the official exchange rate of one peso per one dollar. Admittedly, these two sets of data are not strictly comparable. As the UNHDRO official stated in the 2002 letter to Mesa-Lago: "It is not correct to present the progress of HDI by collecting data from different reports and to build a table to evaluate changes. Should a comparison be possible, it is by using Table 2 of the *Report* where the HDI is computed with the same methodology through the years." But this recommendation is unfeasible because the referenced table of the *Report,* which shows trends calculated using the same methodology in various years (1975, 1980, 1985, 1990, and 1998) does not contain any data on Cuba (UNDP, 1999: 151–58; 2000: 178–85; 2001: 145–48). Thus, the estimates provided in table 21 provide the only viable comparison.

The HDI shows a drop of 20% in Cuba's GDP p/c PPP US$ between 1989 and 1991, consistent with the Cuban economic crisis, but an increase of 71% in 1992, when the crisis was deepening, and a decrease of only 12% in 1993, when the crisis reached bottom. For 1989–93, then, GDP p/c PPP US$ as computed by the HDI shows an overall *improvement* of 20%, while the Cuban figures show a *decrease* of 41%. For 1993, GDP p/c based on Cuban statistics converted to dollars at the official exchange rate was 61% lower than the HDI figure. Between 1989 and 2000, according to the HDI, Cuba's GDP p/c PPP US$ *rose* by 81%, while Cuban data show a *decrease* of 25% in GDP p/c converted to dollars at the official exchange rate. Even with the faulty estimates of the HDI, Cuba's GDP p/c PPP US$ in 2000 ranked 12th among the 20 countries of Latin America, below Peru and the Dominican Republic, and only slightly ahead of El Salvador (UNDP 2002). In 2000, Cuba's GDP per capita converted to dollars at the official exchange rate was

Table 21. Estimates of GDP per Capita in Dollars from the HDI and from Cuba Official Data, 1989–2000

Information year	HDI[a]	Official[b]	Cuba Unofficial Exchange Rate[c]
1989	2,500	1,976	7
1990	2,200	1,787	7
1991	2,000	1,580	20
1992	3,412	1,386	35
1993	3,000	1,172	78
1994	3,000	1,175	95
1995	3,100	1,201	32
1997	3,100	1,317	23
1998	3,967	1,327	21
1999	4,224	1,405	20
2000	4,579	1,478	21

Sources: HDI from UNDP 1992–2001. Cuba official data from CCE 1991; ONE 1998, 2000; BCC 2001; unofficial exchange rate from ECLAC, *Balance preliminar* 2001.

a. GDP p/c PPP US$; the years before and since 1997 may not be comparable.

b. GDP p/c adjusted for inflation and converted to dollars at the official exchange rate of one peso per one dollar (not PPP).

c. Annual average; for 1990–94, black market exchange rates were used; for 1995–2000, CADECA rates were used.

about a third of the HDI's GDP p/c PPP US$. Although it is not technically sound to estimate Cuba's GDP based on the unofficial exchange rate, it is obvious that if such a conversion were made, GDP in dollars would be markedly lower than if it were based on the official exchange rate (one peso equal to one dollar). The last column of table 21 shows the unofficial exchange rate, which differs very significantly from the official rate.

Could the differences between the HDI and the Cuban data be explained by the use of two different exchange rates; that is, the official exchange rate versus the PPP exchange rate? Leaving aside that currently it is impossible to estimate Cuba's PPP exchange rates accurately, in our opinion the answer to that question is no for two reasons: (1) the very large gap between the two sets of figures; and (2) the depreciation of the peso vis-à-vis the dollar (at the CADECA unofficial exchange rate). The Cuban Central Bank did argue in 1996 that the value of the free social services provided to the population (health care, education, social security), combined with subsidized prices of rationed goods, was equivalent to 50% of the monetary value of GDP.[9] If we were to accept this argument, Cuban GDP would have been $2,217 in 2000 at the unofficial exchange rate, still half the HDI estimate.

The key question is, how did the HDI estimate GDP p/c PPP US$ without having the essential statistics from Cuba?[10] To try to answer that question it is necessary to undertake tedious detective work, scrutinizing the explanatory notes that appear in several editions of the *Report*, which document how the estimates were done. For example, in the 1995 edition (for the year 1992) a note reads with regard to Cuban GDP p/c PPP US$: "Preliminary update of the Penn World Tables using an expanded set of international comparisons, as described in Summers and Heston 1991."[11] Checking that source reveals three important problems: First, Cuba is not one of the 138 countries (including 19 Latin American countries) for which Summers and Heston estimated GDP p/c PPP US$ as part of the Penn World Tables. Second, to replicate the PPP methodology, information on prices of between 400 and 700 goods, services, and labor inputs, as well as expenses for 150 detailed GDP categories, is required. These data are not available in Cuba's statistical publications nor have foreign experts conducted fieldwork and surveys in Cuba to obtain such information. Third, during the relevant time period of the Summers and Heston estimates, Cuba used the MPS instead of the SNA, which would make the estimation even more challenging (these problems were noted in Mesa-Lago 1998).

In the 1996 edition, however, the explanatory footnote of the *Report* gave the source for the Cuban GDP p/c PPP US$ estimate as "*World Bank Atlas 1995* (Washington D.C., 1994: 18–19)." The cited source, however, does not contain an estimate of Cuban GDP p/c PPP US$ in the referenced table, although a footnote does indicate that Cuba's estimate was in the range between $696 and $2,785. How HDI estimated Cuba's GDP p/c PPP US$ at $3,000—a figure outside the range between $696 and $2,785—is not explained.[12] In the 1997 edition, the source given in the footnote was the same as in 1995.

The 1998 and 1999 HDI editions (for the years 1997 and 1998) give a general source for the economic indicator "calculated on the basis of estimates from World Bank." For Cuba, however, the estimate carried the following footnote: "Human Development Report Office estimates" (UNDP 1998: 129–30; 1999:135–37). Thus, for the 1998 and 1999 HDI estimates, the UNHDRO did not rely on an external source for Cuban GDP p/c PPP US$, and instead took responsibility for the estimates. However, the UNHDRO did not elaborate on the methodology it used to derive the estimates. A hint as to how this might have been done was revealed in the 2000 edition, where a specific note said, "As GDP per capita (PPP US$) is not available for Cuba, the subregional weighted average for the Caribbean was used" (UNDP 2000: 160).

Using an average of GDP p/c PPP US$ for the Caribbean region as a proxy for this variable in Cuba is absurd on its face given the wide differences between Cuba and the countries of the Caribbean region on many dimensions. Moreover, the HDI does not even state which countries in the Caribbean basin were used for the comparison.

In 1998, for example, five English-speaking Caribbean countries (Bahamas, Barbados, Saint Kitts and Nevis, Antigua and Barbuda, and Trinidad and Tobago) had GDP p/c PPP US$ figures that ranged from $7,500 to $12,000, which placed them in the top group of the HDI with respect to this indicator, much higher than the $3,967 estimated by the HDI for Cuba. Six other Caribbean countries (Suriname, Dominica, Grenada, Belize, Saint Vincent, and Saint Lucia) had GDP p/c PPP US$ estimates ranging from $4,566 to $5,161, 15% to 30% higher than the reported estimate for Cuba, and only three had a lower GDP p/c PPP US$: Guyana ($3,403) and Jamaica ($3,389) had a GDP p/c PPP US$ slightly lower than Cuba; and Haiti—the poorest country in the region—had a GDP p/c PPP US$ significantly lower than Cuba at an estimated $1,389. The Dominican Republic's GDP p/c PPP US$ was $4,589, 16% higher than Cuba's. The unweighted arithmetic average of GDP p/c PPP US$ for these 15 countries was $6,586, 66% higher than the estimate for Cuba. The HDI probably used some sort of a weighted average, perhaps based on the population of each of the Caribbean countries, to arrive at the estimate for Cuba, but the UNHDRO does not spell this out and leaves it to the imagination of the reader.[13]

To sum up, the questions about the two social indicators used in computing the HDI discussed in the previous section pale by comparison with the questions and concerns about the economic indicator discussed here. Taken together, they suggest that the HDI for Cuba has been calculated in a faulty manner and inferences about human development in Cuba based on HDI scores and rankings are questionable.

Cuba's Partial Exclusion from the HDI and Its Reappearance

Perhaps as a result of the shortcomings analyzed in the previous two sections, the 2001 edition of the *Report* excluded Cuba (and 11 other countries) from the HDI master table, as well as from other key tables, citing the "lack of reliable data." Table 28, "Basic Indicators for Other UN Member Countries," of this issue of the *Report* did contain information on Cuba not included in the master and other tables, and reported on ten social indicators but excluded GDP p/c PPP US$. The online version of the *Report* on the United Nations Development Programme website also provided, in an addendum table, socioeconomic statistics for Cuba and other countries excluded from the HDI, but warned that these data "may be of varying quality and may not be directly comparable to those presented in the Report" (UNDP 2001; this statement does not appear in the printed version).

Consistent with the printed version of the *Report*, the online addendum table does not show GDP p/c PPP US$ for Cuba either, but a footnote states that "the Human Development Report Office estimate of the sub-regional weighted average of the Caribbean of $2,224 (PPP US$) was used." Based on the social indicators plus this estimate of the economic indicator, the UNHDRO then calculated Cuba's HDI and indirectly ranked Cuba between the 50th and the 51st places in the world (UNDP 2001b), despite the fact that Cuba and its ranking were excluded from the master table. This performance meant a further advance in human development for Cuba in relation to 1998 and unofficially ranked it in fifth place within Latin America. Interestingly, this information did not appear in the printed version of the *Report*.

After more than a decade, the UNDP has acknowledged that Cuba's GDP p/c PPP US$ is not available and that its estimate is not comparable with data used to calculate the HDI for other countries. But this judgment was made for 1998–99, when Cuba for the first time in nearly four decades published GDP statistics conceptually comparable to those published by most other countries (although still insufficient to carry out the estimate appropriately). It follows, then, that previous HDI estimates of Cuba's economic indicator were even less valid, as they referred to time periods when there were no statistics or the existing ones were less reliable. In fact, the 1999 and 2000 *Reports* published a series of GDP p/c US$ for 1975–97 that included all Latin American countries except Cuba (UNDP 1999: 152; 2000: 179). Finally, using the average GDP p/c PPP US$ for the Caribbean as a proxy for Cuba is inappropriate, and even worse, the methodology for computing the average has not been specified. If Cuban data are not reliable, why did the UNDP persist in making inappropriate estimates of Cuba's GDP p/c PPP US$ and include Cuba in HDI world and regional rankings?

The 2001 *Report* stated the intention of the UNDP to "include [reinclude in the Cuban case] all UN member countries in the HDI exercise" and continue "to improve the statistics" (UNDP 2001: 136). The UNHDRO joined forces with the World Bank and the University of Pennsylvania to estimate Cuba's GDP p/c PPP US$, but admitted that it was an "extremely difficult" task (correspondence with Mesa-Lago, May 22, 2002). In 2002, however, the UNDP reported that for Cuba "we are again using our own estimate," which means continuing to use the inappropriate Caribbean average as a proxy. Surprisingly, the 2002 *Report* reincluded Cuba in the HDI master table and reported Cuba's GDP p/c PPP US$ in 2000 at $4,519 (table 21), with a footnote stating, "Pending the outcome of ongoing efforts to calculate GDP per capita (PPP US$) for Cuba, the Human Development Report Office estimate of the subregional weighted average . . . was used" (UNDP 2002: 152). That is, Cuba has returned to the HDI and its performance was ranked before a study of its GDP PPP US$ was completed. The 2002 HDI *Report* ranked

Cuba as 55th in the world in 2000, and 6th in Latin America (after Argentina, Chile, Uruguay, Costa Rica, and Mexico).

Effect of a Methodological Change

We have explained that Cuba's improvement in HDI rankings in 1997–2000 was in part the result of deficiencies in the measurement of the three basic indicators that underlie the index. More important, however, was a change in the methodology used to estimate the economic index.

For the entire 1989–99 period, Cuba was not one of the Latin American countries in the HDI high human development group: Argentina, Chile, Costa Rica, and Uruguay consistently ranked in this group, while Mexico, Venezuela, Colombia, Panama, and Brazil were in the medium group or sometimes broke into the high human development group.[14] At the other end, Haiti was consistently in the low human development group, while Bolivia, Guatemala, Honduras, El Salvador, and Nicaragua occasionally fell into that group or were otherwise in the medium human development group.[15] Cuba, Ecuador, Paraguay, Peru, and the Dominican Republic consistently ranked in the medium human development group. In 1989–95, Cuba ranked lower than Venezuela, Panama, Mexico, and Colombia and, in 1991–94, also lower than Ecuador within this group. Cuba miraculously jumped ahead of Ecuador and Brazil in 1997–99, and ahead of Panama, Venezuela, and Colombia in 1997–2000. According to 2000 HDI rankings, Cuba was at the top of the medium human development group, surpassed only by the five countries in the high human development group.

The estimation methodology used by the HDI for the GDP p/c PPP US$ indicator has been modified several times. In the 1994 to 1998 editions (with information up to 1995) this indicator was estimated by a formula that distinguished whether countries were below or above an income threshold that represented the world average. Beginning with the 1999 edition (with information for 1997), the estimation formula changed, a change that severely affected both the values of the HDI and the country rankings.[16] The 1999 *Report* stated in this regard, "Because of these changes, this year's HDI [1997] is not comparable with last year's [1995]. The improvements in methodology and data affect the HDI ranking of nearly all countries. . . . A drop or rise in rank may be attributed to the change in methodology or data" (UNDP 1999: 129).

Our objective here is not to pass judgment on the merits or shortcomings of the new HDI methodology for estimating GDP p/c PPP US$, but rather to examine how it affected estimates for Cuba. As a result of the methodological change, GDP p/c PPP US$ for the high-income countries fell, negatively affecting their HDI scores and rankings. GDP p/c PPP US$ also fell for countries in the medium-high income group. For medium-middle, medium-low, and low income groups, however, GDP p/c PPP US$ and HDI scores and rankings improved. The HDI study done in Cuba concluded, after analyzing in detail the methodological change, that "the new methodology for treating income in the HDI relatively favors the poorest countries, and penalizes the richest countries" (CIEM 2000: 128). Thus, Cuba benefited from this change, since in 1995 it was in the medium-middle income group and the new methodology caused a rise in its GDP p/c PPP US$ index, its HDI value, and its world and regional rankings in 1997.

Between 1995 and 1997, the *absolute value* of GDP p/c PPP US$, as estimated by the HDI, increased for all Latin American countries except Cuba, which stagnated. Nevertheless, Cuba ascended in relative terms in the economic index (which ranks all countries against each other), while ten Latin American countries descended in it. The four Latin American countries in the high group (Chile, Argentina, Uruguay, and Costa Rica) considerably increased their GDP p/c PPP US$, but fell in the economic index, their HDI values, and their world rank, even though most of those countries also improved or maintained the levels of their two social indicators.[17] The same occurred with regard to the four Latin American countries in the medium-high group (Venezuela, Panama, Mexico, and Colombia). In contrast, Cuba's life expectancy index fell slightly, its education index improved slightly (based on incorrect data, as we pointed out), and its GDP p/c PPP US$ in absolute terms was unchanged. Yet, Cuba's economic index experienced a *significant jump* that considerably improved its HDI value, vaulting it from 85th to 56th in world rank. As a result of this, Cuba overtook Brazil and Ecuador, whose GDP p/c PPP US$ in absolute terms increased but which nevertheless experienced a marked decline in their economic index.

Table 22 illustrates how the change in methodology affected Brazil and Cuba. The table compares—for 1995 and 1997—the behavior of the three component indices of the HDI: health care (life expectancy, first column), education (literacy rates and enrollment in the three educational levels, second column), and economic (GDP p/c PPP US$, third column). Recall that (1) the indices compare all countries against each other (the best performers score close to 1 and the worst close to 0); (2) each index contributes a third to the HDI value; and (3) the higher the HDI index, the better the performance of the country with regard to human development and the higher its rank. Although the *Report* warns that HDI scores and rankings for the years 1995 and 1997 should not be compared due to methodological changes in the economic index, it is important to do so precisely to isolate the effects of these methodological changes on index behavior.

With regard to the health index, between 1995 and 1997, Brazil showed a

Table 22. Impact of Methodology Change on the HDI Indices, Value, and Rankings of Brazil and Cuba, 1995 versus 1997

Country	Year	Indices			HDI	Rank		Absolute
		Health	Education	GDP p/c PPP US$		World	Latin America	GDP p/c PPP US$
Brazil	1995	0.69	0.80	0.94	0.809	62	9	5.928
	1997	0.70	0.83	0.70	0.739	79	11	6.480
Cuba	1995	0.85	0.86	0.48	0.729	85	11	3.100
	1997	0.84	0.88	0.57	0.765	58	9	3.100

Sources: UNDP 1998, 1999.

slight improvement (+0.01) while Cuba showed a slight decline (–0.01). With regard to education, both countries improved, Brazil slightly more (+0.03) than Cuba (+0.02). Thus, with regard to the two social indicators, Brazil performed ahead of Cuba. With regard to the economic indicator, however, Brazil declined markedly (–0.24) while Cuba improved (+0.09). Brazil's slide in the economic index and Cuba's rise are at odds with the behavior of their GDP p/c PPP US$ in *absolute* value, which is shown in the last column of table 22: Brazil's GDP p/c PPP US$ rose by 9% (from $5,928 to $6,480) between 1995 and 1997, while Cuba's was unchanged ($3,100 for both years). The change in methodology for estimating the economic index resulted in a decline in Brazil's HDI value (–0.07) and an increase in Cuba's (+0.04). This translated into a drop of 17 positions in Brazil's human development world ranking (from 62nd to 79th place) and a jump of 27 positions in Cuba's ranking (from 85th to 58th place). It also translated into a switch in ranking within Latin America for the two countries, with Brazil falling from 9th to 11th place and being replaced by Cuba, which leapt from 11th to 9th place.

The HDI study conducted by Cuban experts is the most comprehensive analysis we are aware of on the effect of the methodological change in the economic index on the HDI ranking of Latin American and Caribbean countries, as it disaggregates the effects of this change from the effect of changes in other factors. This study concludes, "Cuba experienced the largest positive difference (26 positions)[actually 27] in ranking, exclusively because of the change in the methodology to estimate income" (CIEM 2000: 128). In other words, Cuba's jump from 85th to 58th place was solely attributable to the methodological change in the economic index. In contrast, Brazil fell 17 positions in the HDI ranking. The Cuban study recognizes that Brazil's fall from 62nd to 79th place occurred despite improvements in social indicators and was attributable directly to the change in methodology (CIEM 2000: 134).[18] The 1999 *Report* acknowledges that Cuba's improvement in rankings and Brazil's decline for 1997 were "ranking changes due to the refined methodology" (UNDP 1999: 165).

In 1998, the financial crises in Asia, Russia, and other emerging economies negatively affected economic growth in Latin America, and most of the nations in the region experienced a decline in GDP p/c PPP US$, their economic indexes, their HDI scores, and their HDI rankings. This was the case, for example, in Panama, Venezuela, and Colombia, three countries that traditionally placed ahead of Cuba in the HDI. Cuba, however, was one of the few countries that, according to the 2000 edition of the *Report*, experienced robust growth of its GDP p/c PPP US$—28% growth—a veritable miracle, particularly taking into account that, according to official data, GDP p/c US$ converted at the official exchange rate increased by only 0.8% in that year (ONE 2001). Due to this anomaly, Cuba climbed in terms of economic index, HDI value, and world and regional ranking, overtaking Panama, Venezuela, and Colombia within the region. In the 2002 edition of the *Report*, Cuba's HDI ranking continued to climb, improving from 56th to 55th.[19]

Conclusion

In this chapter we have shown that HDI estimates for Cuba from 1989 through 2000, as well as Cuba's ranking in the world and within Latin America based on the HDI, have been flawed for the following reasons: (1) the health indicator is based on a life expectancy series that is afflicted with inconsistencies and contradictions; (2) the education indicator is based on rising school gross enrollment rates when in reality elementary and secondary school enrollments declined, and their rates in 1999 were still below those in 1989 (higher education enrollment was slightly higher than in 1990); (3) the economic indicator was estimated despite an absence of the essential statistics, using questionable sources and methods, and most recently based on an inappropriate Caribbean average (the HDI estimated a GDP p/c PPP US$ increase of 81% for 1989–2000, while Cuban official GDP p/c adjusted for inflation and converted to US$ based on the official exchange rate decreased by 25%); and (4) changes in methodology for estimating the economic index in 1997 were solely responsible for Cuba's improvement by 27 positions in HDI world ranking, even though in that year Cuba was the only Latin American country with a stagnant GDP p/c PPP US$ (for 1998, the HDI estimated a 28% growth in the GDP p/c PPP US$ even though the official GDP p/c adjusted for inflation and converted to US$ using the official exchange rate increased by only 0.8%).

The flawed data and methods result in indices that show Cuba's HDI ranking surpassing those of Panama, Venezuela, Colombia, and Brazil, countries that for many years were ahead of Cuba in world and regional HDI rankings. The 2001 *Report* excluded Cuba from the HDI, acknowledging the unreliability of data and unavailability of GDP p/c PPP US$. Nevertheless, the *Report* estimated Cuba's GDP p/c PPP US$ in 1999, based on a questionable Caribbean average, which led to another climb in Cuba's ranking.

The 2002 *Report* again included Cuba in the HDI—calculating GDP p/c PPP US$ preliminarily, pending a thorough study (which has not been completed)—and propelled Cuba to 55th rank in the world and 6th in Latin America, very near the upper boundary of the group of middle human development countries within Latin America and surpassed only by five countries in the high human development group. It is ironic that countries that produce reliable statistics on GDP p/c PPP US$ are penalized for doing so by the HDI, as they are overtaken by a country that does not produce such statistics and for which it is not possible to make reliable GDP p/c PPP US$ estimates.

The new official Cuban GDP series unveiled in 2002 shifted its base from 1981 to 1997 prices, resulting in a revaluation of GDP by about 60% for 1996–2001, the six years for which estimates on the two price bases are available (see chapter 2). Moreover, in 2002, President Fidel Castro, Minister of the Economy José Luis Rodríguez, and Chairman of the Economic Commission of the National Assembly of People's Power Osvaldo Martínez launched a coordinated, sharp attack on GDP, arguing that it is not an acceptable measure of development because it fails to account for social development. In the case of Cuba, which provides extensive social services, they argue that the conventional GDP would have to be adjusted upward to account for the value of these services.

In 2003, Minister Rodríguez reported that Cuban statisticians and economists had calculated the PPP of the peso and estimated that GDP p/c PPP US$ was $5,200, compared to a GDP p/c of 2,245 pesos, implying that the PPP exchange rate was 1 peso equivalent to $2.32. To date, Cuba has not published the methodology for the revised GDP, but Minister Rodríguez (2003) hinted at the nature of the modifications: (1) adjustment of salaries to account for goods and services that are offered for free or at subsidized prices and that tend to understate the purchasing power of salaries;[20] and (2) valuation of social services at more "realistic" prices. He also indicated that additional methodological adjustments were being made and that in the course of 2004, Cuban analysts would be working to adjust Cuban GDP to account for the fact that "GDP was designed for a market economy, where there are numerous superfluous activities" that are not relevant in a socialist economy such as Cuba's. Probably Minister Rodríguez has in mind activities such as advertising, public relations, lobbying, and work carried out by political parties and nongovernmental organizations. The last change will probably boost Cuban GDP and GDP p/c even higher. Will future HDI estimates of the Cuban economic indicator be based on these new figures and move Cuba even higher in HDI scores and rankings?

We hope that our analysis will sensitize UNDP staff to the problems with Cuba's social indicators and will result in technical assistance to the island to improve the measures. We also hope that the staff will understand more clearly the intractable problems in estimating Cuban GDP p/c PPP US$ and will cease making flawed estimates based on unreliable and incomplete statistics. Until credible and accurate statistics become available, the prudent approach is to exclude Cuba from the HDI and from world and Latin American rankings.

5

The Performance of Cuba's Economic and Social Model Compared with Those of Chile and Costa Rica

With the objective of providing a deeper look at Cuba's socioeconomic development within the context of Latin America, in this chapter we compare development models and performance in Cuba, Chile, and Costa Rica over the last 50 years. In this period, Cuba followed a socialist development model under an authoritarian, single-party political system (1959 to the present); Chile pursued a neoliberal economic model and shifted during the period under examination from a military, authoritarian regime to democratic pluralism (1973 to the present); and Costa Rica practiced throughout a mixed economic model and a pluralist political system (1953 to the present). Our question is, How well did these three countries provide for the economic and social needs of their citizens?

To answer this question, we first describe the three models and the main policies associated with each, examine the role of market and plan, and analyze economic organization and development strategy. In the second part of the chapter we assess the performance of the three models from 1980 to 2000 based on 20 economic and social indicators comparable across countries. In the third part we summarize our findings and explore the viability of the three models in the three countries at the turn of the twenty-first century.

The Three Models

The three economic models are completely different, as they represent the two extremes and an intermediate position within a continuum of world economic systems between two theoretical models: market and plan. At one extreme is the centrally planned, command economy, or socialist model, pursued by Cuba since 1959. At the other extreme is the neoliberal, monetarist, or competitive market, model adopted by Chile after 1973. Somewhere between these two extremes is the mixed economy model pursued by Costa Rica since 1953.

Each of the three countries has followed one basic model during the period under analysis. However, even the Cuban and Chilean models cannot be characterized as "pure" examples of centrally planned or competitive market economies, respectively. Cuba never had a perfect centrally planned economy; rather, it had a partially centralized system with significant deviations from the ideal at certain points in time. Chile has not had a perfectly competitive market either. There is no clear theoretical paradigm for Costa Rica; initially, the development model was based on the market with a relatively high dose of indicative planning, as well as involvement of the state in the production of goods and the delivery of services.

Moreover, the three countries have deviated from the ideal models in important ways. We have already seen in chapter 1 that the economic model applied in Cuba differed significantly from the orthodox Soviet central planning model. In 1966–70, for example, the central plan was supplanted by sectoral plans and miniplans. At two different times, Cuba experimented with moral incentives, and there was an attempt to create a "New Man" devoid of material concerns; both of these efforts had disastrous results. Until the economic crisis of the 1990s, Cuba placed a heavier emphasis on egalitarianism than did the Soviet Union, and at certain times Cuban policies were closer to the Maoist Great Leap Forward than to the conventional Soviet centrally planned model.

Even during the military regime, there were significant deviations from the neoliberal model in Chile. In the 1970s, wage determination was not left to the market but instead was carried out by the government in order to control inflation, to the detriment of workers, who endured the heaviest burden of the adjustment. The exchange rate was controlled and not allowed to float during this period, resulting in an overvalued currency and the first economic crisis. When unemployment rose to intolerable levels, the government did not wait for the market to adjust and eventually generate jobs, instead implementing massive public employment programs. And when the economic crisis of the early 1980s threatened the stability of the system, the state intervened in many enterprises and banks until there was an economic recovery.

Costa Rica's mixed economy model followed the example of other Latin American countries and pursued an import substitution industrialization (ISI) development strategy, combined with social welfare policies typical of the most socially advanced countries of the region (Argentina, Chile, and

Uruguay). The result was one of the most advanced welfare states of the region. The economic crisis of the early 1980s forced the adoption of a structural adjustment program, but it followed an approach of gradual change and included compensatory social programs to cushion the adverse effects of the adjustment on the most vulnerable populations.

Policy Stages in Economic Organization and Development Strategy

Even though each of the three countries followed one basic economic model, socioeconomic policies shifted at different stages during the period under analysis. Policy stages are examined with respect to two sets of policies: economic organization and development strategy.

As we discussed in chapter 1, during the Cuban revolutionary period there have been eight cycles and subcycles of economic organization:

1. Elimination of capitalism and erosion of the market (1959–60). Cuba appeared to create a mixed economy but in fact implemented rapid collectivization.
2. Introduction of orthodox Soviet (Stalinist) central planning (1961–63). This set of policies failed because of the lack of a foundation for their implementation.
3. Socialist debate and experimentation with two alternative models of organization (1964–66). The first model was supported by a pro-Soviet group that favored some market mechanism and the second by a radical, anti-market group led by Guevara.
4. Adoption of Guevara's anti-market model and its radicalization by Castro (1966–70). This cycle resulted in further collectivization and a more prominent role for the state in the management of the economy, suspension of central planning, and reduction in the use of material incentives, which led to economic chaos.
5. Timid pro-market economic reforms patterned after the Soviet (pre-Gorbachev) reform model (1971–85). A few market levers were incorporated.
6. The Rectification process (1986–90). This cycle suspended the use of market levers and returned to anti-market policies.
7. The Special Period (1991–96). This set of emergency policies implemented to deal with the severe economic crisis prompted by the collapse of the Soviet bloc included some market-oriented reforms.
8. The slowdown, eventual paralysis, and reversal of the market-oriented reforms (1997–present).

Some policies were applied consistently until the 1990s, among them collectivization of the means of production, concentration of decision making in a small elite, expansion of free social services, maintenance of full employment, and progressive income redistribution. Application of others fluctu-ated, depending on whether the leadership was espousing anti-market or pro-market policies; examples are labor mobilization and unpaid voluntary work versus work norms and differential wage scales, moral versus material incen-tives, elimination versus acceptance of agricultural free markets, and restric-tion/harassment versus promotion of self-employment.

There have been five changes in Cuba's development strategy that overlap the shifts in economic organization and, on three occasions (1963, 1970, and 1990), both sets of policies failed simultaneously, compounding the resulting crisis. The first four development strategies were (1) inward-oriented, based on ISI and agricultural diversification (1959–63); (2) outward-oriented, pur-suing giant sugar crops and exports (1964–70); (3) more balanced outward-oriented, still centered on sugar exports but combined with export diversifi-cation and tourism (1971–85); and (4) continuation of the preceding strategy with the addition of promotion of food self-sufficiency (1986–90). During the time when these four strategies were implemented, Cuba's economy was essentially closed, extremely dependent on the USSR and CMEA trade and aid, with very little interaction with market economies. When the Soviet bloc collapsed, Cuba launched its fifth development strategy: outward-oriented with a strong emphasis on increasing international tourism, attracting for-eign investment, and generating hard currency. Through this strategy, Cuba is confronting the challenging task of reintegrating its economy into the capi-talist world market—the only alternative left after the disappearance of the CMEA—after more than three decades of isolation, protectionism, lack of competitiveness of exports, and a lingering U.S. trade embargo.

General Augusto Pinochet governed Chile from 1973 until a democratic government was elected in 1990. There have been five stages of economic organization in Chile since 1973:

1. Monetarism, adjustment, privatization, and first economic crisis (1973–76). During this time the neoliberal strategy started and the first economic crisis—characterized by high inflation and fall in GDP—oc-curred.
2. Monetarism, open economy, economic growth, and indebtedness (1976–81). This stage was characterized by an accelerated opening to foreign trade and investment, a reduction of inflation, a rise in internal and external debt, and economic recovery.
3. Second crisis and state intervention (1981–83). The state intervened in the economy to address a severe economic crisis characterized by a sharp decrease in GDP and high unemployment.
4. Adjustment, expansion of privatization, recovery, and economic boom (1984–90). Inflation was controlled, the foreign debt was reduced,

and there was strong economic growth and a new surge of inflation.

5. Democracy, continued application of the model, and growth with equity (1990–present). Policy changes were made during this stage to bring inflation under control and stabilize the economy, sustained economic growth was achieved, and more progressive labor and social policies were implemented.

Key economic organization policies in Chile functioned uninterruptedly from 1974 through 1990: monetary policy, stabilization, and fiscal balance; privatization; structural adjustment; and increasing role of the market. Other policies were changed when they faltered or provoked a crisis. In the first stage, government leaders believed that inflation could be controlled by monetary and structural adjustments alone; when these policies proved ineffective, the exchange rate was also used as a key variable in stabilization. The establishment of a fixed exchange rate in 1979–81, however, led to the overvaluation of the peso, a fall in exports, and rising merchandise trade deficits. Deregulation of the financial market and the suspension of credit controls stimulated the growing indebtedness of the private sector. These policy errors contributed to the second crisis, which was more severe than the first. During the third stage, there were several devaluations, and the government temporarily took over some banks and enterprises to prevent their bankruptcy. In the fourth stage, the government regulated large economic entities, the financial system, and private pension funds to avoid a repetition of previous policy errors. In the fifth stage, the democratic government undertook fiscal reforms to improve income distribution and generate revenue to finance social programs aimed at correcting the problems created during the previous four stages.

Chile's development strategy was more stable and consistent than its economic organization policies. Government opposition to the inward-oriented strategy (ISI cum protectionism) began in the first stage. In the second stage, ISI was discarded and replaced with promotion of nontraditional exports and openness to foreign trade and investment. This outward-oriented strategy was continued thereafter and expanded by providing subsidies to producers and exporters of nontraditional agricultural products (fourth stage) and by involving the state in infrastructure development and modernization of production processes (fifth stage). The very sharp and quick reduction in import tariffs aimed at stimulating competition in the second stage provoked many bankruptcies in the manufacturing sector and stimulated imports of manufactured goods that, combined with easy access to credit, led to a significant increase in the foreign debt and contributed to the second crisis. Thereafter, the modified development strategy implemented in the fourth stage was successful.

Costa Rica experienced three stages of economic organization:
1. Establishment of the economic and social development model (1948–58).
2. Consolidation, expansion, and crisis of the model, divided into two sub-stages: (a) an expansion of the role of the state in the economy and integration of Costa Rica into the Central American Common Market (CACM) (1958–70); and (b) a more interventionist role of the state in the economy and eventual economic crisis (1970–82).
3. National debate on the economic and social development model and modification through structural adjustment (1982–present).

Most economic organization policies were applied consistently in Costa Rica until the structural reform in 1982: increasing public ownership of the means of production, protection of key sectors of the economy, indicative planning, taxation, domestic and international government borrowing to raise funds to finance public programs, exchange rate controls, dual import tariffs, increase of employment in the public sector, and expansion of social services. These growth-oriented policies often provoked fiscal deficits and inflation, and imports grew at a faster rate than exports, resulting in merchandise trade deficits. At the onset of the 1980s, the foreign debt peaked (boosted by two world energy crises) and a combination of high debt, internal and external imbalances, and an overvalued currency led to the suspension of debt service and an economic crisis. Structural adjustment policies introduced since 1982 and continued thereafter have included reduction in the size of the state; privatization of state enterprises; deregulation; price and interest rate liberalization; cuts in state subsidies, credits, and public expenditures; gradual adjustment of the exchange rate to market rates; decrease of import tariffs; and renegotiation of the foreign debt. But the structural adjustment program was implemented gradually; for example, import tariffs were not cut as drastically or rapidly as in Chile, and privatization proceeded at a slower pace.

Costa Rica's development strategy in the first stage was outward-oriented, focusing on exports of coffee and bananas, but also promoting industrialization and state support for diversification and modernization. In the second stage, the development strategy shifted to inward-oriented, based on ISI, with state support for industrialization as well as agricultural diversification for domestic consumption and export. Giving impetus to the strategy were the "state as entrepreneur" policy and the creation of the CACM, which promoted industrial exports. The economic crisis of 1981–83 prompted a return to an outward-oriented strategy that remains in place today, based on opening to foreign trade and investment, increase of nontraditional exports, reduction of subsidies to industry, and efforts to increase efficiency and improve competitiveness.

The Double Role of the State and Continuity versus Change in Policies

Of the three countries under examination, the Cuban state has been the most powerful both politically and economically. An authoritarian socialist government has ruled the country over the entire period, only one political party (the PCC) is authorized, opposition parties are banned, labor unions are tightly controlled, and the media is owned and operated by the state. Because of its enormous political power, the Cuban state has had a free hand in designing, implementing, and changing economic policies. The government has collectivized nearly all of the means of production, controls practically all economic activities, and delivers all social services. Until the end of the 1980s, Cuba's private sector was very small; it expanded in the 1990s but was still dwarfed by the state and heavily regulated; and in the early 2000s the private sector has been reduced again.

The Chilean state has been the second most powerful politically. For 17 years, the authoritarian military government of General Pinochet either banned or ruled with a heavy hand over political parties, labor unions, and the media. Without a legal opposition, the state had a great deal of discretion over designing and implementing policies (although markedly less than in Cuba). In contrast with its heavy-handed role in the political arena, under Pinochet the state played a subsidiary role in the socioeconomic arena, eschewing intervention in economic activities and social services, which were largely transferred to the private sector and the market. The return to democracy reduced significantly the political power of the state but expanded somewhat its regulatory economic and social functions.

The Costa Rican state has been the weakest of the three with respect to its capacity to implement policies, because it has been a pluralistic democracy whose citizens have enjoyed full civil liberties throughout the entire period under examination. Nevertheless, the Costa Rican government has intervened in the economy and has been considerably involved in economic activities and delivery of social services, although this power has declined since the mid-1980s and particularly in the 1990s.

Proponents of the Cuban and Chilean models justified their political systems and economic policies with similar arguments, although they reached diametrically opposite conclusions. Castro attributed all prerevolutionary ills to the market and promised that the state would correct them, while Pinochet blamed the state for the previous socioeconomic problems and promised that the market would solve them. Both leaders justified the authoritarian nature of their governments as necessary in order to implement drastic changes to the old order. (Interestingly, despite their ideological differences, they both referred to their programs as "revolutionary.") Costa Rican leaders also referred to their program as a revolution, but they implemented it through democratic means, blending the market and the state.

Continuity in economic policy has not always been positively correlated with political control. Costa Rica has had the most stable economic policies despite thirteen presidents and nine shifts in the political party in power. It was only when the "entrepreneurial state" began to compete with the private sector in the 1970s, and then when the economic crisis demanded structural adjustment policies in the 1980s, that the consensus began to splinter. This crisis provided the opening for the creation of an opposition party with a neoliberal program that controlled the executive and legislative branches during 1990–94 and intensified the implementation of neoliberal reforms.

Chile is second to Costa Rica with respect to the continuity of economic policies. Pinochet's government consistently applied pro-market policies during its tenure, except for a partial and brief reversal in 1983 (when the neoliberal model was in danger because of the economic crisis) and for minor corrections in 1976–81 and 1984–90. The military government was defeated in the 1990 elections by a coalition of opposition parties that through three consecutive administrations maintained the same economic model, although with some modifications in order to address the problems of the poor, promote more equity, and empower the state with more regulatory powers.

Surprisingly, although Cuba has been governed by Castro since 1959 (more than 46 years) and has maintained a socialist system since 1961, it has undergone the greatest number of economic policy changes: eight in economic organization and five in development strategy. Castro's strict political and economic control over the nation and his deeply rooted ideological distaste of the market have resulted in frequent political changes or cycles (analyzed in chapter 1). The deep economic crisis of the 1990s forced the Cuban leadership to undertake modest market-oriented reforms in the first half of the 1990s but these have been stalled since 1996 and reversed to a significant degree.

Continuity in economic policies should have a favorable effect on long-term economic performance, provided the policies are sound. It can be argued that the continuous and relatively stable policies pursued by Costa Rica and Chile have had a positive influence on their long-term economic performance. In Costa Rica, a pluralist democracy, frequent changes in the political party at the head of government, and the influence of the rank and file—particularly during election years—contributed to consensus seeking, moderation, and gradualism, cushioning errors in economic policy and their negative effects on the population. In Chile, the authoritarian government, unconstrained by opposition, applied drastic policies and committed serious errors that had negative effects on the economy and society. In Cuba, meanwhile, there were frequent and significant policy changes in economic organization and development strategy. This instability—the policy cycles lasted less than six years on average—did not permit sufficient time for a given policy to become established and yield results. The enormous concentration of political power in the hands of the leader, highly centralized decision making, absence of policy debate, and lack of feedback from the base or checks and balances on the actions of the leadership explain the frequency of such changes and the fact that they were implemented at the national level before they were tested on a smaller scale. As a result, policy errors had disastrous effects.

The Goals of the Models

The goals of the Cuban model were to create a collectivized society with full employment, egalitarianism, and universal free social services. Economic growth was also a goal, but it was subordinated to social goals. It was believed that the transformation of social values would spur economic growth, lower external economic dependence, and promote higher social welfare. Castro's vision of the future of Cuba came closer to Mao Zedong's vision than to Soviet leaders'. Reluctantly, Castro applied the conventional Soviet model during two stages, first when seduced by generous economic aid from the USSR and later when forced to shift gears by the termination of this aid.

The conflict between Castro's ideology and the reality of a small, insular economy dependent on a single export commodity and vulnerable to external economic shocks prompted fluctuations in both economic organization and development strategy. Castro's single-minded pursuit of chimerical goals—the highest level of industrialization per capita in the region, the production of 10 million tons of sugar, the creation of an unselfish "New Man," food self-sufficiency—caused gross misallocation of resources and adversely affected economic performance. Failing to achieve those goals and faced with economic deterioration, Castro shifted course, engaging in a tactical withdrawal from idealist policies and pursuing more pragmatist policies and moderate goals until he felt that his government was sufficiently strong to launch a new grandiose program, and so on, creating a vicious policy cycle. It is only because the current economic situation presents extraordinary challenges that Castro has not been able to completely turn back the reforms of the early 1990s and initiate a full anti-market cycle, although he has stopped the reform process and reversed some of its policies.

In contrast to the traditional interventionist role of Latin American military governments, Chile's military regime drastically reduced the role of the state in the economy. The objective of the military's coup d'etat was to stop Chile's road toward socialism, but Pinochet lacked an economic program and the "Chicago boys" filled the vacuum, resulting in an odd marriage of political authoritarianism and economic liberalization. The primary goals of the economic model were to increase foreign investment, expand capital markets, and promote economic growth, allowing as much competition as possible, based on private ownership of the means of production and private-sector delivery of social services. Once these goals were met, a "trickle down" effect was expected to generate more jobs, higher salaries, and enhanced social welfare. The role of the state was to create an environment conducive to the operation of market forces and to play a subsidiary role in the economy, intervening only when the market could not perform its proper functions. In the social arena, distribution would be determined by the market, with the state limited to redressing the worst cases of market failure. (According to the orthodox neoliberal view, some inequality is essential to generate wealth, and the emphasis on equality defeats the efforts of the most productive persons within society to better their lot.) Swift and radical reforms were undertaken to correct distortions created by excessive state intervention and to introduce the new model. Policy errors and the drastic structural adjustment program (shock therapy) caused two economic crises and forced some corrections with regard to the role of the state, thereby increasing the state's regulatory power and, since 1990, its involvement in the social arena.

Costa Rica's model has had as its main goal to create a mixed economy, in which the market predominated but the state maintained an important—and even growing—role in promoting economic growth with equity. Unlike in Chile and Cuba, Costa Rican leaders did not believe there was a conflict between the market and the state. The role of the state was to promote economic development by supporting the private sector, intervening as needed, and directing activities in certain strategic areas such as banking, insurance, public services, infrastructure, energy, and even some productive sectors. This mixed approach was posited to generate employment, higher wages, and overall social welfare. The state would correct for the negative effects of the market by providing free social services (especially for the poor), promoting income redistribution, and guaranteeing a minimal social safety net. The Costa Rican model was quite successful for three decades but faced a serious crisis in 1981–83 that required structural adjustments. These changes were implemented gradually within the context of a democratic system, minimizing social costs and preserving social accomplishments while reforming social programs to reduce costs.

Evaluation of Performance

To assess the performance of the three models, we examine 20 indicators (11 economic and 9 social) for which roughly comparable data are available for the three countries.[1] We have arranged the indicators into four clusters:

- Macroeconomic: The six indicators in this cluster are GDP growth rate, GDP per capita (p/c), gross domestic investment, inflation rate, fiscal balance, and composition of GDP.
- External sector: The five indicators in this cluster are export concentration in a single commodity, import composition, geographic concentration of trade, trade turnover and merchandise trade balance (both p/c), and foreign debt p/c.
- Employment and distribution: The three indicators in this cluster are real salary, composition of the labor force by sector, and open unemployment. This cluster has only three indicators because Cuban data are not available for other potential indicators.
- Social standards: The six indicators in this cluster are illiteracy rate, school enrollment in secondary and higher education, infant mortality, life expectancy, rate of contagious diseases, and change in housing stock (number of new housing units built) per 1,000 inhabitants.

For comparative purposes, we combined the first two clusters into an economic area, and the last two clusters into a social area.

The two most problematic indicators in the comparison are GDP growth rate and inflation rate for Cuba. As we discussed in chapter 4, for three decades Cuba followed the MPS used by socialist countries and constructed four series of macroeconomic indicators that could not be connected. In the early 1990s, Cuba scuttled the MPS methodology and began to calculate its GDP based on the SNA used by most countries in the world, but the new series cannot be connected with the previous ones. Therefore, GDP growth rates for Cuba cannot be strictly computed for the entire period under review and, moreover, are not comparable with growth rates for Chile and Costa Rica. The inflation estimates for Cuba are also suspect, as the Cuban government has not released information on how they are computed.

The 20 indicators in the three countries were evaluated by designating as the best performer the country that had (1) the highest GDP p/c growth rate; (2) the highest GDP p/c in U.S. dollars; (3) the highest gross investment-to-GDP ratio; (4) the lowest average inflation rate; (5) the most positive fiscal balance (highest fiscal surplus or lowest fiscal deficit) as a share of GDP; (6) the lowest share of agriculture and highest share of industry within GDP; (7) the lowest concentration of exports in a single commodity (highest export diversification); (8) the lowest share of food imports and the highest share of machinery and equipment imports; (9) the lowest geographic concentration of trade (highest diversification of trade partners); (10) the highest trade volume p/c and the most positive trade balance p/c; (11) the lowest foreign debt p/c; (12) the lowest share of the labor force in primary activities (agriculture) and the highest in secondary activities (manufacturing and construction);

(13) the highest rate of growth of real salaries; (14) the lowest national open unemployment rate; (15) the lowest adult illiteracy rate (highest literacy rate); (16) the highest school enrollment rate in secondary and higher education; (17) the lowest infant mortality rate; (18) the longest life expectancy; (19) the lowest reported rates of four communicable diseases; and (20) the highest number of new housing units built per 1,000 inhabitants.

The rankings were originally calculated by Mesa-Lago (2000) for four years: 1960, the first year for which statistical series were available for all three countries and the starting point for the Costa Rican and Cuban models; 1973, the start of the implementation of the Chilean neoliberal model; 1980, a year prior to the onset of the regional economic crisis; 1990, when Costa Rica and Chile had overcome their crises and Cuba's was about to begin; and 1993, when Cuba was at the worst point of its economic crisis. For this book we have extended the comparison to 2000 and concentrated our discussion on the years 1980, 1990, 1993, and 2000.

Comparison of the Indicators in 2000

In order to illustrate the performance of each country on the indicators, which we will use to calculate updated rankings of the countries, in table 23 we present data on the four clusters of 20 socioeconomic indicators for 2000. The information in table 23 is free from one of the most serious problems that affected our comparisons in earlier years, namely the lack of GDP statistics for Cuba, although there are some unanswered questions about the methodology behind the GDP estimates produced by Cuba. In the rest of this section, we summarize the results of the comparisons.

Table 23. Comparison of Economic and Social Indicators in Chile, Costa Rica, and Cuba, 2000

Economic and Social Indicators	Chile	Costa Rica	Cuba
Macroeconomic			
1. GDP growth rate, at constant prices (p/c, %, average, 1991–2000)	6.1	4.9	−1.5
2. Real GDP p/c, (PPP, $, 2000)	9,147	8,650	4,519[a]
3. Gross fixed capital formation (% of GDP, 2000)	21.2	18.4	13.2
4. Inflation rate (%, 2000)	3.8	11.0	−2.3
5. Fiscal balance (% of GDP, 2000)	0.1	−3.0	−2.5
6. Composition of GDP at constant prices (% of GDP, 2000)			
Agriculture, fishing, and forestry	6.5	11.6	6.8[b]
Manufacturing	17.4	23.0	17.9[b]

Economic and Social Indicators	Chile	Costa Rica	Cuba
External Sector			
7. Export concentration (% of total, 2000)	25.6	10.1	27.0
8. Import concentration (% of total, 1999)			
Foodstuffs	5	7	19
Machinery and transportation equipment	37	22	26
9. Concentration with main trade partner			
(% of total trade, 2000)	17.7	48.8	14.0
10. Merchandise trade ($ p/c, 2000)			
Volume	2,883	3,731	580
Balance	58	72	−281
11. External debt ($ p/c, 2000)	2,453	1,006	3,362[c]
Employment and Distribution			
12. Composition of the labor force (% of total, 2000)			
Primary sector (agriculture, fishing, forestry)	15.7	20.6	24.4
Secondary sector (manufacturing, construction, basic services)	22.0	22.0	22.9
13. Average real urban salary growth (% change in 2000 over 1990)	38.5	21.6	−36.7
14. Open unemployment (% of labor force, 2000)	9.2	5.3	5.5
Social Standards			
15. Illiteracy (% of population, 15+ years of age, 2000)	4.2	4.4	3.3
16. School enrollment (% of population of school age, 1999)			
Secondary school	87.5	56.0	81.9
Higher education	37.5	30.0[d]	20.8
17. Infant mortality (per 1,000 live births, 2000–5)	11.6	10.9	8.1
18. Life expectancy at birth (years, 2000–5)	76.0	77.3	76.7
19. Rates of contagious diseases (per 100,000 inhabitants, 2000)			
Hepatitis	38.1	45.5	136.7
Syphilis	24.2	17.2	82.2
Tuberculosis	19.8	22.5	10.1
Typhoid	5.8	0.2	0.3
20. Housing units built (per 1,000 inhabitants, 2000)	6.6	4.4	3.8

Sources: ECLAC 2000a; ECLAC, *Balance preliminar* 2001; *Statistical Yearbook* 2001, 2002c; UNESCO 1999; United Nations 2000; ILO 2001; IMF 2001b; UNDP 2002; PAHO 2004b. Also for Chile INE 2003; for Costa Rica INEC 2003; and for Cuba ONE 2001, BCC 2002.

a. Information from UNDP (2002); however, real GDP at the official dollar exchange rate in 2000 was $1,476, a third of the UNDP figure (ONE 2001).

b. The statistics for Cuba published by ECLAC, *Statistical Yearbook* 2000, do not agree with Cuban official statistics, and therefore, we have used the latter (BCC 2002).

c. Includes debt in nonconvertible currency with Russia and Eastern European nations.

d. UNESCO (1999) does not report statistics for Costa Rica and its most recent statistic in the table is for 1994.

Macroeconomic

The annual rate of GDP growth at constant prices for 1991–2000 averaged 6.1% for Chile, 4.9% for Costa Rica, and –1.5% for Cuba. Despite the recovery that started in 1994, in 2000 Cuban GDP was still 20% below its 1989 level. Chile's GDP p/c PPP US$ (see chapter 4) in 2000 was 8.9% higher than Costa Rica's, and Costa Rica's in turn was 91% higher than Cuba's. (Cuba's reported GDP p/c PPP US$ converted at the official exchange rate of 1 peso = 1 U.S. dollar was $1,476, one-third of the UNDP estimate we used in table 23.) With regard to gross capital formation as a percentage of GDP, in 2000 Chile's rate was 21.2%, Costa Rica's 18.4%, and Cuba's 13.2%. Cuba apparently experienced deflation in 2000 (–2.3%), whereas the other two countries experienced inflation: 3.8% in Chile and 11% in Costa Rica.[2] Recall that Cuba's inflation estimates are dubious: There is no information on the basket of commodities used to calculate the consumer price index and on the weights used to aggregate individual price changes, and reported deflation in 1999–2001 was contradicted by a 28% increase in the money supply. The fiscal balance as a percentage of GDP in 2000 ranged from a very small surplus in Chile (0.1%) to deficits in Cuba (–2.5%) and Costa Rica (–3.0%). The composition of GDP by economic sector in 2000–1 indicated that Costa Rica had become the most industrialized country (23% of GDP in manufacturing, followed by Cuba (17.9%) and Chile (17.4%), while Chile was the country with the lowest percentage of GDP generated by agriculture (6.5%), Cuba was second (6.8%), and Costa Rica (11.6%) had the largest share.

External Sector

Costa Rica had the lowest concentration of exports in a single commodity in 2000 (bananas, 10.1%; in fact, Costa Rica's principal export commodity in that year was office machinery parts).[3] Chile followed (copper, 25.6%), and Cuba was last (sugar, 27%, down from 65% in 1993). Chile was the country closest to food self-sufficiency (only 5% of food was imported in 1999), followed by Costa Rica (7%), and Cuba (19%). Chile was also the country that imported the largest share of machinery and transportation equipment (37% of total imports), followed by Cuba (26%, down from 33% in 1993), and Costa Rica (22%). The volume of merchandise trade per capita in US$ in 2000 was highest for Costa Rica ($3,731), followed by Chile ($2,883), and Cuba ($580). Costa Rica ($72) and Chile ($58) had sizeable surpluses per capita in the balance of merchandise trade in US$, while Cuba had a very large deficit (–$281). With regard to the foreign debt per capita in US$, Costa Rica had the lowest ($1,006), followed by Chile ($2,453), and Cuba ($3,362).[4]

Employment and Distribution

Cuba does not publish statistics on income distribution and incidence of poverty; therefore, data on these indicators are not included in table 23. In chapter 3, however, we provided evidence that both indicators deteriorated in Cuba in the 1990s, but these figures are not strictly comparable with those of Chile and Costa Rica. In 1999–2000, Costa Rica had a more even distribution of income than did Chile (Gini coefficients of 0.479 and 0.559, respectively). Meanwhile Chile reduced incidence of household poverty to levels below those of Costa Rica, 17.8% and 18.2% in 1998–99, respectively (ECLAC, *Statistical Yearbook* 2001). With regard to the composition of the labor force by sector, in 2000 Chile had the lowest share in the primary sector (15.7%), followed by Costa Rica (20.6%) and Cuba (24.4%). The shares of the labor force in the secondary sector were very similar for all three countries: 22.9% for Cuba and 22.0% for both Chile and Costa Rica. The highest increase in urban real salary during 1990–2000 was in Chile (38.5%) followed by Costa Rica (21.6%), whereas salaries fell by more than a third in Cuba (–36.7%). Costa Rica reported that open unemployment in 2000 was 5.3%, followed very closely by Cuba at 5.5%, while Chile had the highest open unemployment rate at 9.2%. But recall that Cuba's calculation of open unemployment considered as employed hundreds of thousands of persons who were studying or who worked part-time in backyard and urban vegetable gardens (see chapter 3).

Social Standards

In 2000, the difference in the adult illiteracy rate among the three countries was tiny, but Cuba's rate was the lowest at 3.3%, followed by Chile at 4.2% and Costa Rica at 4.4%. With respect to the percentage of the population enrolled in secondary education, Chile led in 1999 with 87.5%, followed by Cuba at 81.9%, and Costa Rica at 56.0%; meanwhile, with regard to enrollment in higher education, Chile also was first with 37.5%, followed by Costa Rica with 30.0%,[5] and Cuba with 20.8%. The infant mortality rate per 1,000 live births was fairly similar in the three countries, but Cuba remained in the lead (8.1), followed by Costa Rica (10.9) and Chile (11.6). Life expectancy figures were also very close: Costa Rica had the highest expectancy (77.3 years), followed by Cuba (76.7 years), and Chile (76.0 years). With regard to four contagious diseases, Costa Rica exhibited the lowest rates per 100,000 inhabitants in two (syphilis and typhoid), and Cuba had the highest rates in two (hepatitis and syphilis).[6] Some health indicators that have become available since the earlier work by Mesa-Lago indicate that malnutrition affected 4% of the population in Chile in 1998–2000, 5% in Costa Rica, and 13% in Cuba, while the average daily intake of calories was 2,950 in

Chile, 2,780 in Costa Rica, and 2,460 in Cuba (FAO 2002). Finally, with regard to the number of housing units built per 1,000 inhabitants, Chile was at the top with 6.6, followed by Costa Rica with 4.4 and Cuba with 3.8.

The Rankings of the Three Countries from 1980 through 2000

Four types of rankings were calculated: (1) absolute rankings; (2) relative improvement rankings; (3) individual index rankings; and (4) index of economic and social development rankings. Because of space limitations, we show the results of the rankings in several tables, but only briefly summarize the methodology of the rankings in the text (for details on methodology see Mesa-Lago 2000).

Absolute Rankings

We ranked the three countries from 1 to 3 (1 = best; 2 = middle; 3 = worst) with respect to their performance on each of the 20 indicators for the four comparison years (1980, 1990, 1993, 2000). The rankings for all indicators (1, 2, or 3) were totaled to derive estimated scores in each of the four clusters. For indicators with more than one variable (for example merchandise trade), the resulting scores were averaged. The subtotals in the economic area (macroeconomic and external-sector clusters) and in the social area (employment and distribution and social standards clusters) were also averaged. Finally, the total score was computed as the average of the four clusters and the 20 indicators. The lower the score, the better a country's performance and vice versa. For example, a country with a total score of 30 is best, a score of 35 ranks in the middle, and a score of 40 is worst.

Table 24 shows the absolute rankings of the three countries. Based on the total scores, Costa Rica ranked best in 1980 and 1990, while Chile was best in 1993 and 2000 (indicating the positive effect of policies under Chilean democracy). In those two years, Costa Rica ranked in the middle and relatively close to Chile; Cuba ranked worst in all years, and its gap with the other two countries, which was very small in 1980, increased over time. When we examine the clusters separately, Chile steadily led in the economic area (improving under democracy), followed by Costa Rica, with Cuba increasingly lagging behind as time went on. Meanwhile, in the social area, Costa Rica ranked best in all years except 1980, when it was very close behind Cuba; Cuba ranked best in 1980 (before the crisis), fell to middle position in 1990, and dropped to worst in 1993 and 2000 (due to the crisis and incomplete recovery). Finally, Chile ranked last in 1980 and 1990, but improved to middle ranking in 1993 and 2000, virtually tied with Costa Rica in the latter year, showing the beneficial effect of equity programs introduced by the democratic governments.

Table 24. Absolute Rankings of Chile, Costa Rica, and Cuba, 1980–2000[a]

Cluster of Indicators	Country	1980	1990	1993	2000
1. Macroeconomic	Chile	11.0	10.5	8.5	8.0
	Costa Rica	13.0	12.0	12.5	14.0
	Cuba	12.0	12.5	15.0	14.0
2. External sector	Chile	7.0	7.8	7.0	9.0
	Costa Rica	9.2	8.5	8.7	8.5
	Cuba	12.8	13.7	13.5	12.5
3. Distribution and employment	Chile	4.5	6.0	4.5	5.0
	Costa Rica	5.0	6.0	4.5	5.0
	Cuba	2.5	6.0	9.0	7.0
4. Social standards	Chile	15.5	13.7	13.2	12.5
	Costa Rica	9.2	11.6	10.6	12.3
	Cuba	11.3	10.7	11.2	11.7
Economic area (1 + 2)[b]	Chile	18.0	18.3	15.5	17.0
	Costa Rica	22.2	20.5	21.2	22.5
	Cuba	24.8	26.2	28.5	26.5
Social area (3 + 4)[b]	Chile	20.0	20.7	17.7	17.5
	Costa Rica	14.2	15.6	15.1	17.3
	Cuba	13.8	16.7	20.2	18.7
Total (1 + 2 + 3 + 4)[c]	Chile	38.0	39.0	33.2	34.5
	Costa Rica	36.4	36.1	36.3	39.8
	Cuba	38.6	42.9	48.7	45.2

Sources: 1980, 1990 and 1993 from Mesa-Lago 2000; 2000 are authors' calculations based on data from Table 23.

a. Scores are the sum of rankings (1, 2, or 3) for indicators in each cluster; the lower the score, the better the performance of the country.

b. Arithmetic average of the two clusters, equally weighted.

c. Arithmetic average of the four clusters, equally weighted.

Relative Improvement Rankings

In this exercise, we ranked the indicators with respect to magnitude of change over the period of observation: 1960–2000 for Costa Rica and Cuba, and 1974–2000 for Chile. As with the absolute indicators, we also used a scale of 1 to 3; the country with the greatest improvement on an indicator (for example, infant mortality) was ranked as 1, and the one with the least improvement as 3. Note that with respect to some of the social indicators, improvement is progressively harder to achieve after a very high level has already been achieved. This is the case, for instance, for infant mortality and, to a lesser extent, for life expectancy. To illustrate, in 2000, Cuba had the lowest infant mortality rate among the three countries (8.1 per 1,000 live births), followed by Costa Rica (10.9), and Chile (11.6). But the reduction in the infant mortality rate over the entire period was substantially higher for Costa Rica (63%) and Chile (54%) compared to Cuba (28%), in part because Cuba's rate was lower to start with. With regard to life expectancy, in 2000 Costa Ricans had the longest life span (77.3 years), followed by Cubans (76.7), and Chileans (76.0). Costa Rica's achievement in this area was particularly remarkable as it started out in 1960 with an average life expectancy 2.4 years lower than Cuba's.

One problem confronted in the relative improvement rankings is the different starting year of the Chilean model (1974) compared with the two other countries (1960), which means that Chilean changes are measured over a 14–year shorter time period. For instance, if life expectancy had been based in 1960 for all countries, the most significant increase would have been achieved by Chile (31%, rising from 58 to 76 years), but when life expectancy is based on 1974, Chile's improvement falls to second place (16%, from 65.7 to 76 years). To account for this problem, we computed Chilean scores starting in both 1974 and 1960, to test whether rankings changed depending on the starting year.

Table 25 shows the relative improvement rankings for the three countries. In the total scores, Costa Rica ranked best, closely followed by Chile, with

Table 25. Relative Improvement Rankings of Chile, Costa Rica, and Cuba, 1960–2000[a]

Clusters of Indicators	Chile	Costa Rica	Cuba
1. Macroeconomic	8	9	13
2. External sector	9	9	12
3. Employment and distribution	8	4	6
4. Social standards	11	11	14
Economic area $(1 + 2)$[b]	17	18	25
Social area $(3 + 4)$[b]	19	15	20
Total $(1 + 2 + 3 + 4)$[c]	36	33	45

Sources: Basic data for 1960 and 1974 from Mesa-Lago 2000; basic data for 2000 from table 23; authors' rankings based on data for 1960 and 2000.
a. Difference in indicators between 1960 and 2000 in Costa Rica and Cuba, and between 1974 and 2000 in Chile; if 1960 is used for Chile, the total score improves and Chile rises to the best ranking, Costa Rica falls in the middle, and Cuba does not change. Scores are the sum of rankings (1, 2, or 3) for each indicator; the lower the number the better the country's performance.
b. Arithmetic average of the two clusters, equally weighted.
c. Arithmetic average of the four clusters, equally weighted.

Cuba lagging by 12 points behind Costa Rica. When the clusters are disaggregated, however, Chile performed best in the economic area, Costa Rica ranked in the middle almost tied with Chile, and Cuba performed worst. In the social area, Costa Rica was markedly ahead of Chile, and Cuba was still worst but fairly close to Chile. When 1960 instead of 1974 is used as the starting year for Chile (not shown in table 25), Chile moves to top ranking (32.5) followed by Costa Rica (35.8), and Cuba continues to be last (42.7).

Index Rankings

In this exercise, we ranked the 20 indicators in each of the four years based on indices from 0 to 100. Unlike the previous two rankings, in this case 0 is the worst and 100 the best. This approach is better than absolute or relative improvement rankings for two reasons: (1) the measurement scale (1 to 3 in the absolute and relative improvement rankings) is expanded to 0 to 100, thereby showing more clearly gaps and differences in performance across countries; and (2) the method facilitates the use of different weighting schemes for each of the four clusters as well as adjustments to account for the smaller number of indicators in cluster 3.

Table 26 shows results of the index rankings for the three countries, which are basically the same as the absolute rankings in the economic and social areas, but they reveal more precisely the gaps among the countries. For instance, in the economic area, the distance in percentage points between Cuba and Chile expanded from 11.3 in 1980 to 38.1 in 1993 and, despite Cuba's partial recovery, it still was 34.4 points in 2000, three times the gap of 1980. Although Cuba's gap in the social area against the other two countries was reduced in 2000, Cuba still was 13.7 points behind Costa Rica and 13.3 points behind Chile, a notable difference that was not clearly shown in the absolute rankings. On the other hand, in the economic area, the gap between Costa Rica and Chile was cut from 19.6 points in 1980 to 9.9 in 2000, and in the social area the gap between the two countries decreased from 11.3 to 0.4 points in the same period.

Index of Economic and Social Development Rankings

Finally, an economic and social development index was calculated by averaging the index rankings of the 20 indicators (that is, the four clusters or the two areas). As with the index rankings, 0 is assigned to the worst performance and 100 to the best.

The bottom row of table 26 shows the index results based on equal weighting of all four clusters (25–25–25–25). In the four years of observation, Chile ranked best, Costa Rica in the middle, and Cuba the worst. Chile showed steady improvement, particularly since 1990 (with the return of de-

Table 26. Rankings of Chile, Costa Rica, and Cuba by Indices and by the Index of Economic and Social Development, 1980–2000[a]

Cluster of Indicators	Country	1980	1990	1993	2000
1. Macroeconomic	Chile	73.3	73.1	82.4	96.2
	Costa Rica	40.4	60.6	66.2	67.3
	Cuba	82.4	66.8	48.8	52.4
2. External sector	Chile	80.9	83.9	82.7	69.9
	Costa Rica	74.6	72.9	68.4	78.8
	Cuba	49.1	38.0	40.2	44.7
3. Distribution and employment	Chile	80.9	92.2	96.8	85.2
	Costa Rica	85.4	72.1	76.3	91.3
	Cuba	74.7	86.3	43.8	59.5
4. Social standards	Chile	72.7	77.9	82.3	83.8
	Costa Rica	90.9	82.7	80.3	78.4
	Cuba	82.0	84.7	79.5	80.9
Economic area $(1 + 2)$[b]	Chile	77.1	78.5	82.6	83.0
	Costa Rica	57.5	66.8	67.3	73.1
	Cuba	65.8	52.4	44.5	48.6
Social area $(3 + 4)$[b]	Chile	76.8	82.8	89.6	84.5
	Costa Rica	88.1	85.2	78.3	84.9
	Cuba	78.4	83.6	61.6	71.2
Index of economic and social development $(1 + 2 + 3 + 4)$[c]	Chile	77.0	80.6	86.0	83.8
	Costa Rica	72.8	76.0	72.8	79.0
	Cuba	72.0	68.0	53.1	59.4

Source: 1980, 1990 and 1993 from Mesa-Lago 2000 with a few revisions; 2000 authors' calculations based on table 23.
a. The higher the number, the better the country's performance: 100 = best; 0 = worst.
b. Average of the scores in the two clusters, equally weighted.
c. Average of the scores in the four clusters, equally weighted.

mocracy); Costa Rica's scores were stagnant between 1980 and 1993 but improved in 2000; and the gap between Cuba and the other two countries expanded. Despite some improvement in 2000, Cuba still lagged 24.4 percentage points behind Chile and 19.6 points behind Costa Rica.

We also computed three variations that reduce somewhat the weight of cluster 3 (employment and distribution): 25–25–20–30, 25–25–15–35, and 25–25–50 (the latter weight assigned to a merger of clusters 3 and 4). Although not shown in table 26, the three variant weighting schemes did not affect the ranking of the three countries. Finally, the exclusion of the two unreliable indicators (for Cuba)—GDP growth p/c and the inflation rate— did not change the rankings either, although it did expand the gap between Cuba and the other two countries.

Summary and Comparisons with International Rankings

The four methods of calculating the rankings among the three countries yield the following order in the total scores in all years, with very few exceptions: (1) in the absolute rankings, Chile and Costa Rica were either best or middle and Cuba worst; (2) in the relative improvement rankings, Costa Rica was best, Chile in the middle, and Cuba worst (if based on 1960 instead of 1974, Chile and Costa Rica's rankings reversed); and (3) in the index of economic and social development, regardless of the weighting scheme used, Chile ranked best, Costa Rica in the middle, and Cuba worst. In the economic area, Chile was the best performer, Costa Rica middle, and Cuba worst. The most diverse rankings were obtained in the social area: In absolute rankings, Costa Rica was best, Chile in the middle, and Cuba worst; in relative improvement, Costa Rica rose from middle to best, and Chile from worst to best (tying with Costa Rica), while Cuba deteriorated from best to worst. The index rankings were the most varied and most difficult to summarize for Chile and Costa Rica, but after 1990 Cuba deteriorated from best to worst. Trends between 1980 and 2000 were also quite diverse: The advent of democracy in Chile resulted in improved rankings in economic, social, and total scores, while Cuban trends were the opposite either throughout the entire period of observation or after 1990 with the crisis. Trends in Costa Rica were more complex; based on indices which show the gaps more precisely there was an economic improvement from worst to middle position over the entire period, including a reduction of the gap with Chile in 2000; but in the social area Costa Rica slipped to middle in 1993, then recovered best position in 2000.

These rankings did not place the three countries in the wider context of the world or the Latin American region. In chapter 4 we examined the Human Development Index (HDI), computed annually since the early 1990s and the only series that compares socioeconomic performance for a large number of countries around the world (up to 174 in some recent editions) and within Latin America. Recall that the HDI combines two social indicators (life expectancy and education) with one economic indicator (GDP p/c PPP US$). For the 1989–2000 period, the HDI order was always Costa Rica, then Chile, then Cuba. Chile's HDI ranking improved during the tenure of the democratic government, reaching first place in Latin America in 1994 and 1997, although it dropped to second place in 1998 and 2000. Costa Rica was in first place in the region in 1992 and 1993 but fell and remained in fourth place in the period 1995–2000. Cuba's ranking deteriorated until 1994–95, coinciding with the economic crisis on the island, but improved subsequently as a result of the economic recovery and a methodological change in the calculation of the HDI explained in chapter 4. In 2000, the HDI ranked the three countries as follows: Chile, 38th in the world and second within Latin America, Costa Rica, 43rd and 4th, and Cuba, 55th and 6th.[7]

At the start of this chapter we referred briefly to the economic freedom and political rights of the three countries, but did not explicitly include those dimensions in our comparisons. There are two international sources of comparisons in these areas:

- The Index of Economic Freedom, calculated by the Heritage Foundation, tracks many of the policies we have analyzed in this chapter (property rights, state intervention, degree of regulation, monetary policy, banking and finance, trade, foreign capital flows and investment, prices and salaries, and black markets). The Heritage Foundation assigns to each country a score ranging from 1 (best) to 10 (worst) for each of 10 indicators of economic freedom and aggregates the individual scores to obtain an overall score. The rankings for the three countries in 1995 (out of 101 countries) were Chile, 23rd, Costa Rica, 34th, and Cuba, 100th (Heritage Foundation 1995–96). In 2000, the rankings were (out of 161 countries) Chile, 11th, Costa Rica, 58th, and Cuba, 157th (Heritage Foundation 2001). Within Latin America, the rankings of the three countries in 1995 were Chile, 2nd, Costa Rica, 7th, and Cuba, 20th, while in 2000 they were Chile, 1st, Costa Rica, 10th, and Cuba, 20th.
- The Index of Political Rights and Civil Liberties, calculated annually by Freedom House, assigns scores from 1 (best) to 7 (worst) for 8 indicators of political rights and 14 of civil liberties and computes an overall freedom index score for each country. The ordering of the three countries (out of 191 countries) in 1993–94 was Costa Rica, 31st, Chile, 57th, and Cuba, 178th, while in 1999–2000 (out of 192 countries), the rankings were Costa Rica, 29th, Chile, 59th, and Cuba, 179th. The rankings within Latin America were the same in both years: Costa Rica, 1st, Chile, 2nd, and Cuba, 20th. With respect to the sub-index on economic freedom, the order is Chile, Costa Rica, and Cuba far behind, while with respect to political rights and civil liberties, the order is Costa Rica, Chile, and Cuba, again far behind.

Conclusions and Viability of the Models

In nearly all international comparisons—ours as well as those made by international organizations—the three countries rank as follows:

- Costa Rica is first with respect to social performance and second with respect to economic performance, first with respect to political freedom and civil liberties, but second with respect to economic freedom (reflecting some state intervention in the economy).

· Chile is first with respect to economic performance and economic freedom; it ranks third with respect to social performance during the military dictatorship but second or first during democratic governments to the point where it has tied Costa Rica. With respect to political freedom and civil liberties Chile ranks second behind Costa Rica, but its performance has improved under democratic governments.

· Cuba is third with respect to economic performance, well behind the other two. It falls from best or middle to worst on social performance after 1990, and is third with respect to political freedoms, civil liberties, and economic freedoms, ranking among the worst performers in the world with regard to the two latter areas.

In this chapter we have compared Chile, Costa Rica, and Cuba, three countries with diverse political and economic histories. We have shown that during the second half of the twentieth century and the start of the twenty-first, Cuba had the worst economic performance of the three countries, and its social performance shifted from best to worst during the economic crisis. Although its situation has improved somewhat since the mid-1990s, in 2000 Cuba still was well behind the other two countries. Furthermore, Cuba has paid the highest costs in terms of the suppression of political, civil, and economic liberties. Chile had the best economic performance and extreme economic freedom, but at the cost of a significant curtailment of political and civil liberties for a period of 17 years; Chile experienced substantial social costs during the transition to democracy, but social performance has improved substantially since democracy returned. Meanwhile, Costa Rica made significant socioeconomic gains without sacrificing political and civil liberties, albeit with some restraints on economic freedom (reversed in the 1980s and 1990s) that reduced the social costs of transition.

The Chilean model is highly viable in the mid-term. Its future success would be enhanced by pursuing the following policies: (1) continue efforts to reduce income inequality, open unemployment,[8] and poverty; (2) improve the efficiency and competitiveness of the agricultural sector; (3) develop new export lines and export markets; (4) reduce the foreign debt; (5) reform the social security pension system to expand its coverage, reduce gender discrimination, and improve the lack of solidarity;[9] and (6) reform the public health system by incorporating in it more equity and solidarity. (Two laws approved in 2004 and another being considered by the Parliament in 2005 have achieved that end.)

The mid-term viability of the Costa Rican model is also high. To continue its successful implementation would require the following policies: (1) control inflation; (2) expand the transportation infrastructure, particularly streets, roads, and highways; (3) reduce further the role of the state in the economy, particularly in the operations of unprofitable enterprises; (4) open to competition the finance and insurance sectors to enhance their efficiency; (5) improve credit allocation between the public and private sectors; (6) merge the several state institutions that combat poverty and focus assistance on vulnerable groups and those that most need help; (7) shift financial resources from urban to rural education; (8) increase school enrollment at the secondary level; (9) guarantee the freedom of workers to associate in unions (somewhat limited by the rise of *solidarismo*); (10) complete the implementation of the health-care reform enacted in the 1990s; (11) implement pending measures of the social security pension reform of 2000 and reinforce the financial stability of the public scheme; and (12) enhance governability, weakened in recent years as a result of divisions within the predominant party.

The Cuban model is the least viable of the three. To improve it would require the implementation of a broad program of reforms discussed in the following chapter.

6

Needed Economic and Social Reforms in Cuba

The Sixth Congress of the PCC, scheduled for October 2002, was cancelled. As of the spring of 2005, not only had the congress not been held, but a new date for it had not been announced. In chapter 2 we argued that the failure to fulfill the economic targets of the five-year plan for 1998–2002, approved by the Fifth Congress, may be one of the reasons contributing to the postponement. Another possible reason may be the desire to avoid a debate within the PCC about economic policies necessary to confront the prolonged economic crisis.

In 2002, the PCC organized several commissions to analyze economic policy initiatives that had surfaced in earlier debates but had not been acted upon since the reform process was halted in 1996. Among these were authorizing Cuban citizens to own and operate small- and medium-sized private businesses and liberalizing rules governing foreign investment. The depth of the economic problems was such that an open discussion of reform initiatives was deemed capable of generating a contentious debate and the risk of a political challenge to Castro's authority (Pérez-Stable 2003).

During a visit to China in 2003, his first visit to that country in seven years, President Castro was asked repeatedly by reporters about his impressions of China's economy and its development model in contrast to Cuba's. At a press conference prior to his departure from China, Castro commented that he was impressed by the economic changes that he observed in that country but foreclosed discussing potential changes in Cuba, pronouncing the island's economic situation "excellent." Shortly after his return to Cuba, Castro removed the minister of economics and planning from the Council of State and fired three of his vice-ministers. He later dismissed the minister of finance and prices. Both of these ministers were known to support economic reforms. Moreover, a group of academics that had been brought together to study the Chinese economy and its reforms was disbanded. Thus, the possibility of following the Chinese-Vietnamese model of reform within socialism—the model reportedly favored by many Cuban technicians and economists—was abandoned, despite the favorable effect such a model might have had on the economic and social welfare of the Cuban population.

The Cuban government deepened repression in 2003, jailing 75 peaceful dissidents and condemning them to long jail sentences, a violation of human rights that prompted criticism from the international community, sidetracked Cuba's accession to the EU's Cotonou Accord, and led to a UN Human Rights Commission resolution in April 2004 that criticized the crackdown on dissents and called on Cuba to accept a visit by an international human-rights monitor (Marx 2004). Castro reacted by insulting foreign leaders, accusing them of giving in to pressure from the United States, and increasing the island's international isolation. Notwithstanding Castro's abhorrence of reforms, there is no alternative to overcome the current economic crisis than for Cuba to carry out significant market-oriented reforms.

This chapter discusses conceptually the set of reforms that would be necessary for Cuba to improve the challenging socioeconomic situation it faces at the start of 2005. The chapter is divided into three parts. The first reviews some of the reform experiences of countries of central and eastern Europe, the Baltic States, and the Commonwealth of Independent States (CIS). It discusses transition strategies, assesses results, and identifies key issues related to the transition processes. The second section summarizes Cuban economists' suggestions regarding necessary changes *within* Cuba's socialist system. While we agree that many of these suggestions are sound, our view is that deeper and more comprehensive reform measures that would move Cuba faster toward a market economy are necessary. In the third section we examine reform measures that Cuba should take in order to overcome the ongoing economic crisis under two scenarios: (1) the continuation of the current political system, although presuming a return to the moderate reform path of 1993–96; and (2) political system change and faster transition toward a market economy.

International Transition Experiences

More than a decade has elapsed since the countries of central and eastern Europe and the Baltic States launched their transitions toward free markets and political pluralism and nearly as long since Russia and the members of the CIS did the same. These reforming countries have provided a living laboratory for economists and social scientists to analyze transition strategies and to assess the performance of different policy prescriptions.[1]

Although differences remain among economists regarding nuances of a transition strategy, there is a solid consensus on the critical issues that need to be addressed:

· macroeconomic stabilization, including reducing government expenditures and increasing government revenues and eliminating subsidies to state enterprises, while maintaining basic services to the population;

· microeconomic restructuring, including price and market reforms (reform of domestic prices, liberalization of foreign trade, creation or strengthening of factor markets) and enterprise reform (creation of a legal framework; creation of institutions that support legality such as property rights, commercial code, tax code, accounting and auditing functions, and economic information systems; allocation of property rights to prepare for privatization; preparation of enterprises for privatization and development of methods for valuing assets; and conduct of privatization); and

· institutional reform, including formalizing and deepening the legal environment and the institutions that support legality, creating a social safety net (which might include pensions, social security, basic health services, and unemployment insurance), and educating the public on market behavior.

Overall Economic Trends

All transition countries experienced significant GDP contractions that lasted for several years, typically until market-oriented reforms were able to exert a positive influence on growth. The depth and duration of the GDP decreases surprised most analysts. To be sure, some contraction was expected in connection with stabilization and price liberalization, as resources were reallocated across sectors. The GDP decrease was very dramatic, however, suggesting that other factors were at work.

Although there is no consensus on the cause of the sharp drop in GDP associated with the transitions, several explanations have been cited (Svejnar 2002), among them (1) tight macroeconomic policies; (2) a credit crunch stemming from the reduction of state subsidies to firms and rises in real interest rates; (3) disorganization among suppliers, producers, and consumers as a result of the collapse of central planning; (4) a switch from controlled to uncontrolled monopolistic structure in these economies; (5) difficulties in sectoral shifts in the presence of labor market imperfections; and (6) the dissolution in 1990 of the CMEA, which governed trade relations of Soviet bloc countries.

The time lag between the start of transition and the resumption of sustained growth resulting from the positive effects of market-oriented reforms on performance was about three years for the countries of eastern and central Europe and the Baltic States (see table 27). For the CIS countries, the response to reform took longer because of the more severe economic distortions in these countries at the outset of the transition and the greater obstacles to reallocating resources after liberalization (including physical size, distance to key external markets, and greater political and constitutional turmoil inhibiting investment). Overall, it took roughly a decade for the countries of eastern and central Europe and the Baltic States to return to the level of GDP they had reached in 1989, before the transition. By 2000, the GDP of the CIS countries was still less than 60% of its value in 1989.

For the sake of comparison, Cuban GDP contracted for four consecutive years in the early 1990s for a cumulative decline of 35%, substantially higher than the 19% decrease experienced by the countries of eastern and central Europe and the Baltic States and closer to the 44% decline experienced by the reforming CIS countries. Cuba's GDP in 2000 was 17% below its 1989 level. One very significant difference regarding economic performance and outlook between Cuba and the former socialist countries of eastern and central Europe, the Baltic States, and the CIS is that while Cuba suffered the pain of a severe output contraction, it did not undertake the reforms that have been shown to be necessary in other countries to achieve lasting gains through sustained economic growth. It is entirely possible that when Cuba does launch its transition to a market economy, it may suffer a second output contraction—this one associated with transition rather than external shock. Such a scenario would be disastrous for the Cuban people, who have already experienced a decade of very low living standards.

Explanations of Differences in Economic Performance

A large literature has emerged seeking to explain the differences in economic performance among the transition economies, focusing on the following variables: (1) the characteristics of countries at the start of the transition, that is, their initial conditions;[2] (2) external shocks to the economy that resulted from the disappearance of the socialist community, the dissolution of the Soviet Union, wars, and civil strife; and (3) policies to facilitate the transition.

The World Bank (2002a) found that initial conditions alone explained 51 percent of the variation in average rate of GDP growth across transition countries during 1990–94. Another set of studies (cited by Aslund 2002) showed that over-industrialization and trade with socialist countries explained 60–75 percent of the output contraction. Empirical studies suggest that the influence of initial conditions on performance is strongest early in the

Table 27. GDP Change in Transition Countries of Eastern and Central Europe and the Baltic States, the CIS, and Cuba, circa 2000

Country	Consecutive Years of GDP Contraction	Cumulative GDP Decrease	Estimated Level of GDP in 2000 (1989 = 100)
Albania	3	−39.9	95
Bulgaria	4	−26.7	67
Croatia	4	−41.4	78
Czech Republic	5	−13.1	95
Estonia	5	−38.2	77
Hungary	4	−18.1	99
Latvia	3	−50.4	60
Lithuania	5	−46.7	62
Macedonia	6	−28.3	74
Poland	2	−17.8	122
Romania	3	−29.4	76
Slovak Republic	4	−25.0	100
Slovenia	3	−19.4	109
Total: Eastern and Central Europe and Baltic States	**3**	**−19.3**	**97**
Armenia	4	−56.6	42
Azerbaijan	6	−64.7	47
Belarus	6	−37.3	80
Georgia	5	−75.6	34
Kazakhstan	6	−38.9	63
Kyrgystan	5	−51.1	63
Moldova	7	−64.7	31
Russia	7	−42.5	57
Tajikistan	7	−61.9	44
Turkmenistan	7	−52.0	64
Ukraine	10	−63.5	36
Uzbekistan	5	−18.0	94
Total: CIS	**7**	**−44.4**	**55**
Cuba	4	−34.9	83

Source: EBRD 2000; Cuba, from chapter 2.

transition and tends to weaken over time. Moreover, the adverse effects of initial conditions on GDP growth are not immutable and can be offset by greater reform efforts. Once the GDP contraction has commenced, the intensity of external economic shocks is critical in affecting—typically delaying—the onset of the recovery.

The empirical studies also found that the extent of economic policy reform[3] makes a difference in output performance, with respect to both levels of GDP and annual growth rates. Better policies were significantly associated with higher annual GDP growth in central and eastern Europe after controlling for the effects of initial conditions and external economic shocks.

Speed of Reforms

One of the most heated controversies in the early days of the reforms of the former socialist countries was the speed of reforms. Radical reformers argued for reforms in all areas as soon as possible (the "Big Bang" or "shock therapy" approach, incorporated in the reform plan pursued by Poland).[4] Other reformers meanwhile argued for a more gradual approach that might start with localized reforms and expand to other areas as apparent successes emerged.

The controversy over speed of reforms was implicitly about the sequencing of reform measures: In shock therapy simultaneous action was taken on many fronts, whereas in gradualism the timing of specific actions depended on the introduction and success of others. The classic gradualist position was that market institutions had to be created *before* macroeconomic stabilization, liberalization, and privatization could occur.

In practice, the debate over the speed of reforms turned out to have been overblown. Most transition countries actually undertook macroeconomic stabilization measures—to control fiscal deficits, inflation and, in some instances, exchange rates—and microeconomic restructuring (such as liberalizing prices on food and other consumer goods and deregulating imports) shortly after the launch of reforms. In fact, one of the consensus findings of the literature on transition is that macroeconomic stabilization is a necessary condition for the recovery of output. Distilling away the numerous arguments and counterarguments from economists of different stripes, the main practical distinction between so-called radical and gradual reforms seems to have been in how and when they tackled enterprise and institutional reform, and more specifically about the role they gave to institution building within the overall reform strategy.[5]

Transition Findings and Issues

Several findings and issues from the transition experiences of the former socialist countries may be relevant to the design of a transition strategy for Cuba. Among these are the significance of institutions in shaping the transition, the relatively long time it takes to build (or rebuild) institutions to support the market, the potential for corruption to derail transition processes, and the pitfalls associated with privatization.

Institutions

A key finding from the transition experiences is the central role of institutions in promoting the return to positive economic growth and the long time needed to build—or rebuild, as the case may be—institutions that support the market. Since markets depend on institutions in order to function, it stands to reason that their operation cannot be improved unless there is an institutional framework that supports them. Not only are institutions critical to the reform process, but they matter increasingly over time: Whereas macroeconomic stabilization and liberalization can stimulate growth early in a transition process even in the absence of institutional development, longer-term, sustainable economic growth requires continuous institutional improvement.

Corruption

An unexpected finding is the eruption of corruption in reforming countries and its pernicious potential to derail economic reform processes. During the transition, not only did administrative corruption[6] grow significantly in many countries (in large part because of the elimination of socialist institutions coupled with the lack of a market-oriented legal structure) but the short-term winners of reform—the so-called oligarchs—managed to "capture" the state for their own benefit, promoting decisions that favored their narrow interests and preventing others from challenging their monopoly on power by becoming competitors. The conventional wisdom at the onset of the transitions (that with the scaling back of state control over the economy, elimination of privileged elites, and increased transparency associated with a vibrant civil society, corruption would wither in transition economies) did not prove to be the case in reality. Policymakers believed too readily that free markets would deter corruption and were slow to include anti-corruption measures into their transition strategies

Privatization

Privatization, broadly defined as the process whereby private individuals and firms increasingly control the economic resources of a nation and generate larger shares of the nation's output, has been an integral component of all transition strategies. Privatization of *existing* state-owned enterprises early in the transition has received a great deal of attention in the literature.[7] Not as thoroughly treated—although perhaps more important in the longer run—has been the creation of *new* private enterprises that have the potential to create a private sector that generates jobs and promotes economic efficiency through linkages with other enterprises in the economy.

Factors that have affected the privatization of existing state-owned enterprises include the speed with which privatization has been carried out (which affects the state's ability to properly value the asset being privatized in order to maximize the revenue to the state from privatization), what type of individuals can own the assets (for example, in some cases, ownership is limited to the enterprise's workers or managers), and whether ownership is limited to nationals or available to foreigners.

Promoting the establishment of new firms does not typically require overt government action but does require, among other factors, (1) a stable macroeconomic environment; (2) freedom for owners/managers to set prices for their output and to purchase the goods and services they require in operating factor markets for labor and intermediate goods; (3) access to operating capital markets; and (4) well-established rules of the game, that is, a legal and regulatory framework that is conducive to the protection of property rights, including intellectual property rights, and the enforcement of contracts.

Broader Socioeconomic Developments

Table 28 presents data on a variety of socioeconomic variables for the transition countries of eastern and central Europe, the Baltic States, and the CIS around 2000. They are listed on the basis of their ranking in the HDI of 2002. In addition to the HDI ranking, we provide information on the average annual rate of growth of GDP over the 1990–2001 period; GDP p/c PPP US$; literacy; combined educational enrollment in primary, secondary, and higher education; infant mortality; access to water and sanitation; and life expectancy.

Generally speaking, the faster-reforming countries in eastern and central Europe and the Baltic States have performed much better than the slower-paced CIS nations with respect to the HDI rankings, with the top five tightly grouped from the 29th to the 37th positions in HDI rankings among 173 countries. These five top performers also had relatively high per-capita incomes (ranging from $9,051 for Poland to $17,367 for Slovenia), low infant mortality, and high levels with respect to adult literacy, school enrollment, access to water and sanitation services, and life expectancy.

In the HDI for 2002, Cuba ranked 55th among 173 countries and 10th among the 26 countries of eastern and central Europe, the Baltic States, and the CIS (table 28). Cuba's economic performance (an average GDP growth rate over the 1990–2001 period of −1.2%) trailed behind the countries with strong market-oriented reforms, as did its GDP p/c PPP US$ (the estimated $4,519 per annum ranked Cuba 16th out of the 26 countries, placing it behind all of the nations of central and eastern Europe and the Baltic States

Table 28. Economic and Social Indicators of Transition Countries of Eastern and Central Europe, the Baltic States, the CIS, and Cuba, circa 2000 (by HDI Rank)

Country[a]	HDI Rank	% GDP growth rate 1990–2001	GDP p/c PPP$	Adult Literacy (%)	Enrollment (3 levels) (%)	Infant Mortality (1,000 births)	Access Water (%)	Access Sanitation (%)	Life Exp. (years)
Slovenia	29	2.9	17,367	99.6	83	4	100	98	75.5
Czech Republic	33	1.1	12,289	99.0	70	5	n/a	n/a	74.9
Hungary	35	1.9	12,416	99.3	81	8	99	99	71.3
Slovakia	36	2.3	11,243	100.0	76	8	100	100	73.3
Poland	37	4.5	9,051	99.7	84	8	n/a	100	73.3
Estonia	42	0.2	10,066	99.8	86	17	n/a	n/a	70.6
Croatia	48	1.1	8,091	98.3	68	8	n/a	n/a	73.8
Lithuania	49	−2.3	7,106	99.6	80	17	n/a	n/a	72.1
Latvia	53	−2.2	7,045	99.8	82	17	n/a	n/a	70.4
Cuba[b]	55	−1.2	4,519	96.7	76	7	95	95	76.0
Belarus	56	−0.8	7,544	99.6	77	17	100	n/a	68.5
Russian Federation	60	−3.7	8,377	99.6	78	18	99	n/a	66.1
Bulgaria	62	−1.5	5,710	98.4	72	14	100	99	70.8
Romania	63	−0.3	6,423	98.1	69	19	58	53	69.8
Macedonia	65	−0.2	5,086	94.0	70	22	n/a	n/a	70.5
Armenia	76	−0.7	2,559	98.4	80	25	n/a	n/a	72.9
Kazakhstan	79	−2.8	5,871	98.0	77	60	91	99	64.6
Ukraine	80	−7.9	3,816	99.6	77	17	n/a	n/a	68.1
Georgia	81	−5.6	2,664	100.0	70	24	n/a	n/a	73.2
Turkmenistan	87	−2.8	3,956	98.0	81	52	n/a	n/a	66.2
Azerbaijan	88	2.7	2,916	97.0	71	74	n/a	n/a	71.6
Albania	92	3.7	3,506	84.7	71	27	n/a	n/a	73.2
Uzbekistan	95	0.0	2,441	99.2	76	51	85	100	69.0
Kyrgyzstan	102	−2.9	2,711	97.0	68	53	77	100	67.8
Moldova	105	−8.4	2,109	98.9	72	27	100	n/a	66.6
Tajikistan	112	−8.7	1,152	99.2	67	54	n/a	n/a	67.6

Sources: GDP rates from World Bank 2003 (except Cuba from ECLAC, *Balance preliminar* 2000); rest from UNDP 2002.

a. Countries are ranked based on the HDI; the first nine countries as "high human development" and the rest as "middle"; the World Bank ranks countries by GNP p/c PPP$, into high, middle, and low.

b. GDP rate 1990–2000 from ECLAC (the series was discontinued; our estimate for 1990–2001 is −0.9%); GDP per capita PPP$ is an HDI rough estimate.

and behind Kazakhstan, Belarus and the Russian Federation within the CIS nations).

Cuba's performance with regard to social indicators was stronger: On education and basic infrastructure (water and sewage), Cuba ranked below most of the other countries in table 28, but the opposite was true with regard to infant mortality (third lowest) and life expectancy (highest). Basic infrastructure did not match those public health achievements, however: In access to potable water, Cuba ranked eighth among the 12 nations for which data were available; and in access to sanitation, Cuba ranked ninth among 10 countries for which data were available (three countries poorer than Cuba in terms of GDP p/c provided better access). Cuba ranked behind all nations in table 28 (except Albania and Macedonia) with regard to adult literacy, with nine countries with lower GDP p/c than Cuba having higher literacy rates; on combined educational enrollment, Cuba ranked 13th (tied with two other countries) and four poorer countries in terms of GDP p/c in the CIS had higher rates.

Reform Measures Suggested by Cuban Economists

In chapter 2, we summarized the views of five prominent Cuban academic economists regarding the economic situation on the island. In this section we summarize their recommendations, as well as those of other Cuban economists, regarding changes that Cuba could make within the framework of a socialist system to mitigate current problems (Carranza 2001; González Gutiérrez 2001, 2003; Marquetti 2000; Monreal 2001; García Alvarez 2003; Pérez Villanueva 2003; Togores and García 2003a; Triana 2003).[8] Our reading of the work of these economists suggests that most concur in the view that it is essential to restructure the economy, restart the reform process, change property relations, decentralize economic decision making, and promote domestic competition. Others focus on specific, short-term sectoral measures and do not make broader suggestions about overall restructuring or changes to property relations. In what follows we summarize their views, taking full responsibility for any inadvertent distortion of their views.

· Physical central planning is not a viable model, but there is no consensus regarding the future role of planning or about a long-term development strategy. The partial reforms of the early 1990s were insufficient to transform the economy to the degree required to promote development within the current international context. The economy cannot grow, as it did prior to 1990, based on an extensive accumulation model that resulted in low efficiency, which was viable then only because of economic support from the Soviet Union and the socialist countries. It is essential, then, to have a rigorous debate on alternatives to cope with the effects of the crisis and to address economic problems through a more logical and viable development strategy (Carranza).

· The centralization measures introduced in 2002–3 distribute the economic pie differently, but they must be supplemented with other policies to increase the size of the pie, as was done during the economic reforms of the 1990s; otherwise such centralization could adversely affect some economic activities (González Gutiérrez).

· To overcome the current crisis, it is essential to adopt a model that promotes higher investment and higher efficiency. This is feasible only through a fundamental restructuring of the economy and the adoption of a coherent economic reform blueprint during the first decade of the twenty-first century (Carranza, Monreal).

· Property relations and economic institutions must be transformed. Enterprises organized under different forms of ownership must find ways to work together. The state sector should be stimulated through more competition (González Gutiérrez, Carranza). Ministries should exert regulatory rather than management functions (Marquetti).

· The new development strategy should be based on activities with high technological complexity produced by sectors that use skilled labor intensively. This would reinforce positive labor market incentives and address the contradiction between high individual expectations based on high investment in human capital and low remuneration levels (Carranza).

· Low agricultural yields result in production costs that are noncompetitive with imports, particularly those from the United States. Introducing financially sustainable technologies in agriculture is therefore necessary to cut imports. For that purpose, workers should be paid higher wages and farmers higher procurement prices. The creation of the UBPCs has been insufficient to increase competition. Producers should decide for themselves what inputs to buy, within a financial regulatory framework, because it is impossible to make those decisions centrally; the state's physical allocation system leads to waste, and produces shortages and lack of agricultural diversity (García Alvarez 2003).

· The main source of future growth is an expanding domestic market, spurred by increased competition. Prices should be liberalized (Marquetti). There should be socialist competition to impede the development of monopolies (González Gutiérrez).

· To increase sales at dollar stores and maximize government revenue, the prices of mass-consumption consumer goods in these stores should be lowered and the range of products available for sale expanded. This would stimulate domestic production by the state sector for sale in these markets and would generate revenue that the state could use to make goods available to those without access to dollars (Triana).

· The priority should be to create buyers' markets rather than sellers' markets, in order to promote competition, reduce prices, and improve quality. Managerial decision making must be decentralized. The domestic economy must adjust to changes in the external sector and move progressively toward convertibility of the peso through establishing a realistic exchange rate (González Gutiérrez).

· The structure of exports should be radically transformed. The focus should be on increasing exports of manufactured products as well as services with significant added value and high technological complexity. These efforts would support an export-oriented strategy rather than the import-substitution strategy geared to the domestic market that has been the priority in the past. Ways for Cuba to insert its economy into the world market must be redefined (Monreal).

· Sectors such as real estate should be made more attractive to foreign investment through legislation that balances the interests of the nation and those of the real-estate sector. Further opening of the real-estate sector would attract fresh investment that, through a multiplier effect, would stimulate construction and generate jobs (Triana).

· Foreign debt problems are critical because it is impossible to generate sufficient domestic savings to finance growth and development. Collaboration between the state and foreign investors has eased the domestic investment and technology bottlenecks. But it is important to broaden the scope of foreign investment and connect it more closely to technology transfer. The experience of the last five years has demonstrated that attracting foreign investment requires not only getting the macroeconomics right, but also having coherent policies in other areas and undertaking profound internal reforms of the economy and the financial sector. The process of opening to foreign direct investment should continue by fine tuning the system of incentives to attract foreign investment without compromising control over the nation's patrimony (Pérez Villanueva).

· The growth in the number of tourists will eventually slow. Thus, it is important to develop a network of tourism services beyond hotels that will capture tourist expenditures, permit lower lodging prices, and enhance Cuba's competitiveness vis-à-vis other tourist destinations in the region (Triana).

· During the current crisis, social policies have been adversely affected by a lack of resources, economic reforms, and the adjustment process. The preservation of social benefits should be based on their financial sustainability and the performance of the economy. Social policy decisions should be made on the basis not only of social objectives, but also on macroeconomic principles. Social security expenditures contribute significantly to the budget deficit; hence, it is essential to lighten the government's load by expanding the number of contributors to social security, raising the retirement age, and promoting productivity growth (Togores and García).

· The growth in the number of self-employed workers has been curtailed in recent years by restrictions on the number and types of services that they can legally perform and by the creation of near-monopolistic niches. An alternative might be the promotion of services cooperatives and cooperatives related to the production of goods that complement the activities of the state sector, thereby improving overall efficiency, increasing competition, and expanding employment and the supply of goods and services (Triana).

The Need for Broader and Deeper Reforms

Although we agree with many of the Cuban economists' policy suggestions for reforming Cuba's socialist system, in our opinion additional and deeper reforms are necessary to promote a strong and sustained economic recovery, create productive employment, reduce extreme inequalities, increase real levels of population income and consumption, and protect the most vulnerable groups within the population. In designing policies to correct current economic problems and promote sustainable economic growth and the welfare of the population, it is essential to distinguish two different scenarios: (1) in the short and medium term, the continuation of the current political regime, albeit with resumption of market-oriented reforms; and (2) in the longer term, regime change and a more rapid transition to the market. In both scenarios, therefore, we assume movement toward the market, but such movement is significantly more modest and slower paced in the first scenario than in the second. If the first scenario does not materialize in the very near future, prospects are that economic stagnation will continue and the population's social welfare will deteriorate further.

The following measures discussed in 1995–96 had not been implemented by the spring of 2005:

· creation of a fully convertible peso;
· dismissal of 500,000 to 800,000 redundant workers from the state sector;
· levying of contributions from all workers to the social security pension system;

- authorization for university-level graduates to practice self-employment in their field of study; and
- approval for Cubans to own and operate their own businesses.

As discussed in chapter 1, the reason for the postponing, halting, and reversing of some reforms was the Cuban hard-liners' fears that progressive movement toward the market would imply loss of economic power and political weakening of the regime. Political logic, therefore, took precedence over economic logic and the welfare of the Cuban people. And yet, as several Cuban pro-reform scholars and technocrats have argued, without a return to the reform path, the island's economy will not be able to sustain its recovery, which slowed in 2001–2 and grew only modestly in 2003. Most Cuban economists' proposals mentioned in this chapter, as well as those discussed during 1995–96 but never implemented, should be amenable to implementation under the first scenario; that is, under the continuation of the current political regime with resumption of market-oriented reforms.

In the long run, the current leadership will disappear (the "biological" solution), and the regime will be transformed, we hope in a peaceful manner toward a pluralistic democracy. At that time, there could be a bolder move toward the market that would allow implementation of stronger policies to generate economic growth and overcome socioeconomic disparities. The experience of the countries of eastern and central Europe, the Baltic States, and the CIS suggests that, unless appropriate policies are explicitly designed and implemented, income inequality, unemployment, poverty, corruption, and deterioration in social services will increase during such a transition. It is important, therefore, to adopt an adequate set of policies to confront the challenges of the market transition.

A successful reform strategy is essential to promote economic growth, stimulate production, generate employment, increase real wages, increase government revenue, more fully satisfy basic needs, reduce poverty, and improve the quality of social services. Although many of these issues go beyond the scope of this volume, we nevertheless offer some general guidelines.[9]

Macroeconomic Stabilization

A transition strategy for Cuba would have to recognize the very difficult economic situation of the country after the economic crisis that began in the early 1990s. As we have documented in chapter 2, the economy continues to operate below the level of GDP in 1989, monetary liquidity has risen, and the budget and trade deficits have expanded in recent years. The external-sector imbalances are particularly severe. Stabilization of the economy is a prerequisite for successful economic reforms.

The following stabilization actions would be appropriate to address internal- and external-sector imbalances:

1. Put in place a hard budget constraint to avoid unlimited extensions of government credit to unprofitable enterprises.
2. Cut government expenditures, particularly by reducing subsidies to unprofitable state enterprises, while maintaining basic services to the poor and the needy.
3. Reduce the size of the government bureaucracy and eliminate overstaffing in state enterprises.
4. Strengthen tax revenue collection and conduct public education programs to encourage individuals to pay taxes.
5. Seek expedited membership in international financial institutions (see "The Need for Foreign Aid").
6. Seek to renegotiate the foreign debt.

In addition, under the full transition to market economy scenario, the following actions in the area of stabilization might be undertaken:

7. Eliminate costly special health and social security programs for members of the armed forces and the internal security services.
8. Encourage the Cuban community abroad to increase remittances and financial flows to the island.
9. Appeal to the international community, particularly the United States, for emergency assistance, including food and balance of payments assistance, to overcome the initial economic hardships (see "The Need for Foreign Aid").

Irrespective of the scenario that occurs, there is a serious and urgent need to fill the enormous vacuum of data on Cuban economic and social statistics in the following crucial areas: a consistent series on GDP at constant prices, reliable and transparent estimates of inflation (including the effect of prices in dollar shops), the value of goods and services generated by the informal economy and its accounting in GDP statistics, accurate figures on open unemployment and the magnitude of disguised unemployment, measurements of income distribution and poverty incidence, and so on. Another information vacuum relates to socioeconomic inequalities (analyzed in chapter 3); filling this void will require the inclusion of questions about economic status in future population and housing censuses, the taking of periodic household surveys, and the publication of the corresponding data series. Many of these statistics are necessary to identify the most vulnerable groups within the population, design adequate corrective policies, and estimate their costs. In addition, there must be informed public discussions on ways to deal with such inequalities. Public participation in this process will be an important step toward democracy and national consensus building.

Price and Market Reform

Although physical rationing is still in place after more than 40 years and prices of most rationed goods at the consumer level remain fixed, in the 1990s Cuba permitted the establishment of agricultural free markets, where prices are largely set by supply and demand, and of government-run stores that sell consumer goods—including imported goods—for hard currency although at very high prices in comparison with the earning capacity of the average Cuban worker. In the 1990s, Cuba allowed joint ventures with foreign investors and semi-autonomous enterprises (*sociedades anónimas*) to engage directly in international trade, although in 2004 there is some evidence that the Cuban government is limiting the ability of these entities to trade independent of the central authorities. Despite these developments, retail and wholesale prices in Cuba continue to be controlled by the state, except for those that prevail at farmers' and artisans' markets; foreign trade remains largely under state control; and there are no operating markets on the island for intermediate goods, labor, and credit.

A transition strategy under either of the two scenarios might contain the following policy actions regarding price and market reform:

1. Eliminate the government's monopoly over foreign trade.
2. Eliminate price controls on traded goods and services, and allow domestic prices of such goods to adjust to international market prices.
3. Abolish the artificial official parity of the peso with the U.S. dollar and set an exchange rate that approximates the market-clearing exchange rate.
4. Relax rules regarding self-employment.

In addition, under the full transition scenario, the following actions might be taken:

5. Eliminate domestic price controls and allow intermediate and consumer prices to be determined by the interplay of supply and demand.
6. Lift restrictions on employment and on worker mobility.
7. Establish a truly convertible peso tradable in international markets, an action that would gradually eliminate the current dual monetary system.
8. Eliminate restrictions that prevent foreign investors from directly hiring Cuban workers, allow these employers to set wages for their employees, and ensure that all earned income is reported to the state for tax purposes.

Enterprise Reform

In order for markets to operate in Cuba, a foundation of legal, economic, and financial institutions that support them must be in place. Notwithstanding the enactment of a tax code in 1994 and the recent creation of some financial control and audit entities (primarily to try to stem a wave of corruption associated with joint ventures with foreign investors, mainly in the tourism sector), when the transition comes, Cuba will need to develop a legal framework to establish private property rights and nurture establishment of a private sector, support market behavior, and pursue policies that promote competition. The following policies might be implemented:

1. Transform UBPCs into truly autonomous cooperatives by transferring ownership title to cooperative owners, and empower these cooperatives to decide freely what to produce, to whom to sell their output, and at prices set by demand and supply, thereby providing economic incentives to increase production and delivery of goods to agricultural markets.
2. Grant more land parcels to individuals and families to increase production for self-consumption and delivery of produce to agricultural free markets.
3. Expand goods- and service-producing activities by private, cooperative, and mixed enterprises, and introduce competition against the state sector.
4. Authorize Cuban citizens and groups of workers to manage small businesses, eliminate current restrictions on self-employment and permit university graduates to practice in their field as self-employed professionals, thereby creating sufficient jobs in the non-state sector to absorb redundant state-sector workers who are dismissed.
5. Establish a much stronger link between the domestic economy and the tourism sector, in order to increase the extent to which domestic producers supply the tourism industry, thereby stimulating domestic employment and reducing imports by the tourism sector.

Under the second scenario, Cuba would move toward a market economy at a faster pace, and more profound changes in property rights and market relations would be introduced, allowing additional policies:

6. Establish clear rules on property rights, including some special rules regarding residential property that would protect residents; begin the selective privatization of state enterprises, breakup of state monopolies, and incentives for the creation of private enterprises.
7. Make rules regarding foreign investment more flexible.
8. Overhaul the tax code (see "Overhaul of the Tax System") and issue

a new commercial code, banking and financing rules, clear rules for firms entering and exiting the market (that is, bankruptcy laws), transparency rules, accounting and auditing standards and regulations (including setting accounting, disclosure, and reporting standards), and regulations for labor and capital markets.

9. Establish capital markets and create specialized credit institutions to support small and medium-sized enterprises (for example, commercial banks, savings and loans institutions, credit unions) and specific economic needs (such as agricultural credit, home loans).

10. Adopt an anti-corruption transparency/accountability framework and incorporate it into the transition strategy.

Overhaul of the Tax System

In either of the two scenarios, economic incentives to promote growth and development are essential, which means accepting some level of income and wealth inequality. To reject such inequalities would be tantamount to returning to the excessive egalitarianism practiced during the idealist stages of Cuban socialism and to its negative results. Ignoring or allowing such inequalities to exist without taking any corrective action runs the risk of worsening economic and social disparities during the transition, particularly in the second scenario. The question is how to reach an optimal balance between economic inequalities that are necessary and acceptable and the adverse social effects they would cause. This problem is likely to be aggravated during the transition—as was the experience of many reforming eastern and central European nations, Baltic States, and CIS nations—because of rapid declines in tax revenue associated with the disappearance from the budget of revenue formerly contributed by profits of state enterprises and by turnover tax revenue, coupled with lack of institutional capacity to collect taxes in the new market economy (Gallagher 1999). The proper approach is to completely overhaul the tax system in order to generate the needed resources to underwrite market reforms, including the costs of implementing a social safety net and other social programs. This section discusses changes to the tax system, while later sections address changes to social services, approaches to racial inequality, the components of a social safety net, and the need for foreign assistance.

The 1994 tax code did not create a general income tax, although it did create specific taxes such as inheritance taxes and taxes on income earned abroad in hard currency. Because of restrictions on wealth accumulation, sizeable inheritances are virtually impossible in Cuba today and therefore tax revenue from that source is very limited. Hard currency earnings from abroad are essentially limited to famous artists and musicians, and their taxation is not a very significant source of fiscal revenue either. (Professionals working abroad pay as much as 50% on income beyond a certain level, a very high rate of taxation, in order to retain the right to return to Cuba.) Heavy taxes and other charges levied on self-employed workers, owners of *paladares*, and individuals renting rooms to tourists have contributed to the decline of these enterprises, thereby reducing government revenue. All these private activities, and others still not authorized today (such as self-employment by university graduates, Cuban ownership of small- and medium-sized businesses, and in the second scenario, ownership of large enterprises), should be promoted rather than discouraged, and their income taxed properly. Currently, only 2.4% of government revenue is generated by direct taxes on personal income.

Indirect taxes contribute 60% of government revenue; we have already discussed in chapter 3 the general regressive effect of indirect taxes on distribution. Taxes on sales of alcohol and tobacco should be maintained because of their positive health effects. General sales taxes are a heavy burden on the lowest income groups and broaden consumption inequalities. The value-added tax (VAT) to date has not been a major revenue generator during the transitions of former socialist countries, but it could become significant after economic reforms are successfully implemented. Sales taxes should be limited to the essential minimum and replaced by a combination of a progressive personal income tax and a corporate tax. All residents of Cuba as well as Cubans who earn income abroad should be obligated to pay income taxes; the tax system should have few exemptions (only those who receive below some minimum income threshold), and taxes should be withheld on earned income, interest, and dividends.

The 1994 tax code also includes levies on natural resource extraction, such as mining, forestry, and fishing. However, these taxes apparently generate very little revenue despite the vigorous growth of the nickel and oil extraction industries. Other revenue-enhancing taxes that could be considered are import duties (which need to be handled very carefully so that they do not close the market to competition from abroad and do not result in violations of international trade commitments), excise taxes on consumption of luxury goods and hydrocarbons, and taxes on tourism, levied either as special taxes or as part of the VAT. Technical assistance will be needed to create or strengthen the government's institutional capacity to collect taxes (Gallagher 1999).

In 1995, Carranza, Gutiérrez, and Monreal (1995) recommended a change in currency as a measure to eliminate excessive concentration of savings in banking accounts; in practice this would have resulted in confiscation of savings above a given level.[10] An income tax should be able to limit savings concentration without the need to resort to confiscation by taxing interest income. Taxing remittances is more problematic, however, because of its potential to create a disincentive and because of the several informal channels through which most remittances are transmitted. Currently, remittances are effectively taxed by the hard currency shops through huge markups and sales taxes, as well as a 10% charge for sales in dollars. In the second scenario, as more consumer goods become available and privately owned stores are established, the sales tax rates may be lowered because increased sales volume will more than compensate for lower tax rates in generating revenue.

Institutional Reform

The experience of the reforming countries in eastern and central Europe, the Baltic States, and the CIS strongly suggests that creating an institutional framework to support the market in Cuba will be difficult and time-consuming. The breadth of formal and informal institutions necessary for a market economy to work efficiently is daunting. By definition, the institutions that Cuba will require to create and nurture the market and thereby foster economic development and improve the standard of living of its citizens in the medium and long term are not compatible with the limited reforms of the first scenario.

Among the specific policy actions in this regard are the following:

1. Formalize and deepen the legal framework that recognizes and protects private ownership, including a commercial code and trade, investment, banking, and tax policies that promote competition and economic growth.
2. Formalize and deepen institutions (such as accounting and auditing rules, information management systems) that create the legal framework for and permit the valuation of assets prior to their privatization, and develop transparent bidding rules.
3. Strengthen the social safety net, which in addition to pensions and programs to assist the poor and elderly might include temporary income support and employment services to assist dislocated workers and their families until they are able to regain productive employment (see "Changes in Social Services").
4. Carry out the privatization of large state enterprises.

Changes in Social Services

Perhaps the most important accomplishment of the revolution, generally praised at home and abroad, is universal free access to health care, education, and social security pensions. In chapter 3 we analyzed the severe problems that these social service programs currently face, including deterioration of health care and education, reduction in pension coverage and in the real value of pensions, and escalating costs of pensions and of state subsidies to finance the pension system. Moreover, we have documented a steady increase in the housing deficit throughout the revolutionary period. Last but not least, we have also discussed the increasing disparities in social services. In this section we suggest policies to address these problems.

Health Care

In a 1999 survey of recent Cuban émigrés to the United States, 53 percent of all respondents and 73 percent of blacks credited the revolution for improving health care. Ninety percent considered the health-care system a great accomplishment, and 89 percent favored its preservation under a new government (Roberts et al. 1999; see also Betancourt and Grenier 1999). The national health system (NHS) should be preserved, but with some changes to make it financially viable, improve the quality of its services, increase its efficiency, incorporate private activities by health professionals, and eliminate current disparities. (For various approaches see Alonso, Lago, and Donate Armada 1994 and Mesa-Lago 2003b.)

Currently all health-care services are free for the entire population, regardless of their income or ability to pay, which increases costs, reduces the quality of the services provided, and makes the NHS financially untenable. To make the NHS affordable, improve its efficiency, and enhance the quality of its services, it is essential to take the users' income (ability to pay) into account, particularly with regard to curative care. The following measures are recommended to reduce NHS costs (these changes would be more feasible under the second scenario):

1. Place more emphasis on prevention, particularly by improving the infrastructure of potable water distribution and sanitation, instead of focusing on more expensive curative medicine.
2. Cut the overhead expenditures of the Ministry of Public Health, which are between two and three times the international average.
3. Halt the construction of new hospitals, given the low occupancy rate of existing ones and the long hospital stays, and shift resources to maintenance of facilities and equipment.
4. Convert underutilized hospitals (particularly the most underutilized, that is, those specializing in gynecology and pediatrics) into facilities to care for senior citizens in need.
5. Shift scarce resources currently targeted at further reducing the already low infant mortality rate and at the extremely expensive and rela-

tively low-effective family doctor program to other areas such as improving potable water and sanitation infrastructure, preventing and treating contagious diseases, and importing essential medicines and prophylactics.

6. Limit medical school admissions until the current glut of physicians is eliminated, at the same time encouraging the training of nurses and other medical support personnel; reduce the number of physicians in the state sector by facilitating their shift to private practice (discussed later).

7. End the free overseas medical assistance program and the scholarship program for foreign students to study medicine in Cuba, as the nation lacks the resources for these expensive programs and its available resources can be better spent at home.

8. Maintain the pharmaceutical and biotechnological industries but impose an economic framework that will spur them to become profitable.

The following changes would be needed to raise revenues to finance the health-care system; as with the preceding changes, they are more compatible with the second scenario. (The first two measures would be very difficult to implement under the first scenario).

1. Introduce user fees and co-payment arrangements in hospitals and medical laboratories (except in prevention and primary care) scaled to the financial means of users, exempting those in the lowest income groups.

2. Charge the full cost of nonessential, extra hospital services (such as private rooms, better food, more personalized attention, TV sets, and other amenities) to high-income patients who want and can afford better quality service.

3. Maintain and expand contracts of medical personnel who are working and being paid abroad, and collect taxes on their income.

4. Attract Cubans living abroad, particularly retirees, to receive health care in the island on a fee-for-service basis, and negotiate health insurance reimbursement mechanisms with foreign governments. (This would only be possible in the second scenario.)

The promotion of a private health-care system not only would reduce state-sector costs, but would also create competition and allow high-income groups to get more personalized attention by paying for those services. The NHS would then be able to concentrate on providing services to low-income groups and improve the quality of the care they provide. To achieve these objectives, the following steps should be taken:

1. Authorize private practice by physicians, dentists, and other health-care personnel, either through self-employment or through cooperatives

(first scenario) or in private clinics and hospitals (second scenario), and tax their income through the general income tax.

2. Encourage large enterprises to pay for their employees' health care by allowing them to deduct those expenses from their corporate taxes (both scenarios).

3. Allow the private sector to provide health-care services to foreigners for a fee (unfeasible under the first scenario).

To address current disparities in health care, the privileged and costly special scheme benefiting the armed forces, internal security personnel, and top political leaders should be integrated with the NHS, an action that would reduce overall costs and promote more equitable treatment. Members of these groups who have the ability to pay and want to have more personalized care could pay for it, either from the NHS or from new private-sector health-care providers. This change would be politically difficult to implement under either scenario, but more so under the first scenario. Should the armed forces play a key role in the transition, they no doubt would strongly oppose the loss of the special health-care system they enjoy. Those provinces that face the lowest health standards—Las Tunas, Granma and Guantánamo—should be targeted to receive additional resources, initially for primary and secondary health care, and later also for specialized health care.

Education

In Roberts and colleagues' 1999 survey of recent Cuban émigrés to the United States 67 percent of respondents believed that the revolution had improved education, 93 percent praised its being free, and 72 percent its availability for all regardless of race. Although 88 percent favored the reintroduction of private schools, 60 percent supported public education under a new government. At the same time, 84 percent considered that current education emphasizes ideology over knowledge, while 50 percent noted the drawbacks of limited classroom resources and poor job prospects after graduation.

A strong public education system should be a top priority: one that is knowledge-centered, free of political bias, efficient, competitive with private schools, affordable, solvent, and attuned to the economy's labor needs. Cuba has an abundance of teachers and the decline in population growth and the aging of the population will demand fewer resources for elementary schools in the future. Cuba has been praised for its very high teacher-to-student ratio in elementary school, a ratio that will rise further with the decrease in the elementary-school population due to population aging, but this is a very expensive luxury in view of the lack of school materials and other crucial shortages. It is important, therefore, to have an adequate number of teachers, properly motivated, with adequate wages, to meet the demand for teachers at both the elementary and secondary levels.

Educational services (particularly at the secondary and higher education levels) should be geared to meet the requirements of a competitive world market (including shifts from formal to vocational education), and resources should be reassigned accordingly. Internal efficiency of the educational system should be improved to reduce dropout and grade retention rates. Rigorous quality standards for the evaluation of educational attainment should be established. Proper incentives should be created to promote the training of university-level technicians, agronomists, business managers, bankers, and other professionals who will be critical for the development process. The higher education "explosion" in enrollment of 2003–4 must be reevaluated to ensure that it serves the needs of the nation and that its cost is balanced with its results. As with all other higher education graduates, teachers should be allowed to practice their profession either as self-employment or as employees in public or private schools. Private education, subject to a framework of rules set by the state and under general state supervision, should be allowed. Those who are able to afford it should have to pay for higher education (which would not be compatible with the first scenario). Educational resources should be targeted on the segments of the population that need it the most, on the poorest provinces, and on the occupations in highest demand (Castañeda and Montalván 1997).

Social Security Pensions

Cuba's unified and relatively universal pension system is an important achievement that should be maintained. Currently, the system is challenged by very low pensions in real terms, virtual disappearance of the supplementary social safety net, declining coverage of the labor force as the non-state sector expands, and skyrocketing costs that require huge state subsidies. The situation is likely to be aggravated by the rapid aging of the population (for different views see Alonso, Lago, and Donate Armada 1994; Peñate and Gutiérrez 2000; Mesa-Lago 2003b; Togores and García 2003a).

To address these problems it is essential first to reduce costs and increase revenue of the pension system in order to reduce and eventually eliminate the deficit and generate resources to permit raising the level of pensions. On the expenditure side, the most important measure that needs to be taken—under either transition scenario—is a gradual rise in the retirement age, from the current 55 for females and 60 for males, to 65 years for both genders, to be accomplished over a period of perhaps twenty years for females and ten years for males; if this step is politically unfeasible, then the retirement age should be increased to 60/65 over a period of ten years. While this action would substantially reduce costs, it would be insufficient by itself to bring solvency to the system in the long run because of the aging population. There would be an urgent need, therefore, also to implement the clause of the 1994 tax code —suspended for political and economic reasons—mandating that workers contribute to the social security system. Worker contributions would range from 3% to 8% of salaries (based on two different estimates; see Mesa-Lago 2003b), and would have to continue to increase over time.

An alternative might be to close or terminate the current pension system, make the state responsible for existing pension obligations, and create a new mandatory pension system for new hires that would have a younger insured population and lower costs, at least for a considerable period of time. The state would be financially responsible for the pensions under the old system, while the pension system for new hires would be financed by contributions by employers and workers as well as by the returns from a reserve fund that would be created and would be permitted to invest its assets. A supplementary voluntary pension program could be created for high-income groups financed with their own contributions. The very low pension amounts could be gradually increased by a combination of these measures and by the potential economic expansion resulting from the implementation of the policy measures recommended in this chapter. The expanding non-state sector, both formal and informal (self-employed workers, owners of *paladares* and small businesses, private farmers, and their potential salaried employees) would be mandated to contribute to the new system, and special conditions and benefits would need to be designed to incorporate informal-sector workers (Mesa-Lago 2003b).

The special pension schemes that benefit members of the armed forces, internal security personnel, and the political leadership are unaffordable. They cost roughly the same amount as the deficit of the general social security system and create unjustifiable inequalities, as entitlement requirements are less demanding and benefits more generous than under the general system. These special schemes should be integrated with the general system and, if this were not politically feasible, members of these pension systems should be required to make adequate contributions to support their privileges.

Housing

We estimated in chapter 3 that in 2003, Cuba's housing deficit had surpassed the one million mark, more than one-third of the existing stock; moreover, half of the existing stock was not in good condition. Adequate housing, therefore, is one of the worst needs faced by Cubans. The very low rate of housing construction over the last four decades, combined with the deterioration of the existing stock due to lack of maintenance, have preserved prerevolutionary patterns of housing distribution, with particularly adverse effects on blacks. Also significant are disparities regarding the quality of housing across provinces and within Havana neighborhoods. The government's failure to alleviate, let alone solve, the housing problem has been compounded by excessive regulations and restrictions on housing construction, repair, exchange, and lease.

According to the 1970 census, 86% of Cuban families either owned the dwelling where they lived or were making monthly payments to the state (in the form of rent paid to the government) to buy it, while 8% paid rent for public housing (fixed at 6% of monthly household income), and 6% were exempted from paying any rent because their monthly income was below 25 pesos. The 1981 census did not update this information, and results of the 2002 census had not been published by the spring of 2005. The 1984 housing law allows tenants to convert their leases with the state into purchase contracts, with monthly installments equal to the rent they were paying. In 1988, between 200,000 and 500,000 such contracts had been signed (Mesa-Lago 1993). Available information indicates that in 2002, the overwhelming majority of the Cuban population owned their homes, but citizens endured significant overcrowding and severe deterioration of the housing stock, which often affected basic sanitation and water services, and sometimes even placed them in danger of building collapses. The four hurricanes that struck the island in 2001–4 aggravated those problems.

It is obvious that the state has been unwilling or unable to solve the current housing problems, and therefore the population needs more flexibility to repair their own homes, build new ones, exchange them (swap), or rent them as they see fit. The degree of flexibility consistent with the first scenario would be considerably less than under the second scenario. In either case, the poorest segments of the population, who currently occupy public dwellings rent-free, should either be allowed to continue that arrangement or receive a means-tested housing allowance that could be used to rent a housing unit.

The level of resources the government allocates for the housing sector must be increased and its distribution changed. A portion of the government resources available for direct housing construction should be redirected to improve the dwellings in worst condition (which tend to be populated by the poor or blacks, or located in the least developed provinces). Preferably, dwellers will repair the units where they live with minimal government involvement. Another portion of the resources should be used for small loans for repair and construction of modest dwellings. The Popular Savings Bank (Banco Popular de Ahorro) reportedly provides personal loans to buy new housing units, as well as for construction and maintenance, but no data are available on the number of such loans or their amounts. Furthermore, the bank does not extend credit to buy existing houses, to buy land to build new units, or to exchange homes. The creation of a specialized bank for housing that could provide loans for all those purposes would be the preferred approach.

Addressing Racial Inequalities

In spite of the significant advances that blacks have made in Cuba (in education, health care, employment, access to recreational facilities), important disparities remain. Blacks are still heavily concentrated in poor-quality housing, are underrepresented in top managerial and political positions, and are overrepresented in the prison population.

The economic crisis of the 1990s through the present has reversed some of the previous gains made by blacks and created new inequalities; for example, blacks are underrepresented in receipts of foreign remittances and in jobs in tourist facilities. The government claims disingenuously that the racial problem has been solved and bans public discussion of racial discrimination issues, thereby blocking the development of approaches to address them.

It is crucial that a public discussion on racial discrimination and ways to address it be held in Cuban schools, workplaces, and mass media. Blacks—like all Cuban citizens—should have the right to form and join organizations to defend their rights and promote their advancement, as blacks did in South Africa and elsewhere. Particular attention should be given to providing blacks with adequate housing and to ensuring that they are not discriminated against in hiring, retention, and promotions, especially in foreign enterprises. Current laws barring all Cubans—including blacks—from tourist facilities should be terminated at once under both scenarios.

Creating a Social Safety Net

The current policy of providing free social services and subsidies to the entire population, including those who are well off, receive bonuses in hard currency or in kind at their jobs, or receive foreign remittances, not only wastes scarce resources but is also an obstacle to targeting aid to those in desperate need.

Social assistance expenditures in real terms shrank 29% from 1989 to 1998; the share of the state budget spent on social welfare in 2002 was 2.3% of total expenditures, or 1.3% of GDP. In the 2002 budget, social assistance expenditures were 29% the size of those for defense and internal security and were equal to those for the arts (ONE 2003). Only 1.7% of the population received social assistance in 2002. The policies we have suggested in this chapter would shift from universal provision of social services to a means-tested system. The resources freed up by the changes we propose could be targeted at the population with the greatest need, particularly the extremely poor whose income is insufficient even to satisfy food needs. The shift from universal to targeted aid would ease current inequalities, progressively improve income distribution, and eliminate or reduce the need for price subsidies for consumer goods subject to the rationing system. Since Cuban academic reformers advocated such a policy shift in the early 1990s (Carranza, Gutiérrez, and Monreal 1995), it should be feasible to implement it under the first scenario. Under the second scenario, in which market forces would operate much more freely, prices of consumer goods, services, and housing would rise significantly and there would be an even greater need for a social safety net.

The social safety net should provide temporary income support, preferably in the form of flat payments targeted to the poor (means-tested) that would guarantee a subsistence minimum (of food, housing, and energy). It should be simple to administer and monitored closely to ensure it is received only by those in need. Cash payments would be supplemented with free health care and education for the needy, as discussed previously. The social safety net can be a key instrument in facilitating the other reforms suggested in this chapter by mitigating their potentially harmful effects. It should be accompanied by a public information and awareness campaign explaining the rationale of the social safety net and of the other reforms (Mesa-Lago 1993; Alonso, Lago, and Donate Armada 1994).

The Need for Foreign Aid

Most of the reforms recommended in this chapter would require substantial financial and technical assistance from the international community. Although Cuba is a member of the United Nations and collaborates with its specialized agencies, it is not a member of the international financial institutions (IFIs), such as the International Monetary Fund (IMF), the World Bank, and the Inter-American Development Bank (IDB). The Cuban government withdrew from the IMF and the World Bank in the early 1960s and never signed the founding agreement of the IDB. The possibility of becoming a member of the IFIs under the first scenario is slim because of the prominent role that the United States plays in these institutions and the stipulations of the Helms-Burton Act. Joining the IFIs would be more propitious under the second scenario.

In any event, Cuba would have to apply for membership in the IFIs, and it would take time to be admitted and to obtain the full benefits of membership. Although Cuba has a significant foreign debt (an estimated $13.8 billion to western countries and an additional $22.0 billion to the former USSR and the socialist countries at the close of 2003), in its relations with the IFIs, it would have the advantage of entering with a clean slate and having no debt with them. Thus, once it has crossed the membership threshold, a Cuban government committed to the reforms suggested here could receive support from the IFIs in a relatively short period of time. Moreover, because of its dire economic situation, Cuba could also become a member of the International Development Association (IDA), the agency within the World Bank Group that provides interest-free credits to the world's poorest countries, and perhaps could also benefit from the Highly Indebted Poor Countries (HIPC) Program, which seeks to assist poor countries in managing their foreign debt (Castañeda and Montalván 1997).

In view of Cuba's widespread economic hardship and the enormous difficulties it will face in reforming its economy and launching a program of sustained development, the Paris Club and other creditors might consider restructuring the Cuban debt and forgiving a portion of it, provided the island carries out needed reforms. A record of respect for human rights would facilitate accession to the EU Cotonou Accord and the flow of other assistance from the international community.

Conclusions

In this chapter we have described the obstacles that in 2004–5 have prevented Cuba from undertaking the reforms necessary to break out of its socioeconomic stagnation. We also summarized 15 suggestions by prominent Cuban academic economists for reforming the economy within the socialist system. Some of the economists appear to favor a reform path similar to China's and Vietnam's, while others recommend specific changes at the sectoral level and are silent on the larger restructuring issues. In any event, there seems to be consensus among the economists whose work we analyzed that unless some structural reforms are implemented, the economy will not be able to achieve sustained growth, which will have an adverse effect on the social welfare of the population.

Although we agree with many of the Cuban economists' proposals, we believe that more comprehensive, deeper, and faster paced reforms are needed, under either of two scenarios: (1) in the short and medium term, modest changes within the current political system, along the lines of those implemented in 1993–96; and (2) in the longer term, after the disappearance of the current political regime, a bolder transition toward the market. We recommended a coherent set of policies under each scenario aimed at promoting economic growth and social equality while being mindful of resource limitations.

· Economic reforms: Cuba should move toward the market, but it is highly unlikely that the current regime would be willing to undertake reforms along the lines of China or Vietnam in the short and medium term (first scenario); in the longer term (second scenario), Cuba should move expeditiously toward a market economy.

· Macroeconomic stabilization: The Cuban economy is afflicted by serious internal and external imbalances. An economic stabilization program that reduces government expenditures and increases revenues; seeks expedited Cuban membership in the international financial institutions and renegotiation of the foreign debt; and attracts remittances, foreign aid, and foreign investment would be an essential foundation for a broad transition program.

· Price and market reform: Policy actions in this area under both scenarios might include eliminating the government's monopoly over foreign trade, eliminating price controls on traded goods and services and allowing domestic prices of such goods to adjust to international market prices, abolishing the artificial official parity of the peso with the U.S. dollar, and relaxing rules regarding self-employment. Deeper reforms such as eliminating domestic price controls, allowing intermediate and consumer prices to be determined by the interplay of supply and demand, and lifting restrictions on employment and on worker mobility are only compatible with the second scenario.

· Enterprise reform: Many of the policy actions in this area would be geared at establishing property rights on the island, such as transforming UBPCs into true cooperatives, granting more land parcels to individual farmers, expanding private-sector economic activity and creating competition for the state, eliminating restrictions on self-employment and encouraging the formation of small businesses, and relaxing foreign investment rules. They would also include establishing clear rules on property rights and issuing a new commercial code, banking and financial rules, accounting and auditing standards, transparency rules, and regulations for labor and capital markets. Most of the meaningful changes in this area are only compatible with the second scenario.

· Tax reform: The following policies may be adopted under either scenario, but they are more likely to be implemented in the second scenario: a progressive income tax; a careful evaluation of a VAT prior to its implementation; increasing taxes on alcohol and tobacco products; and levying taxes on consumption of hydrocarbons, on interest earned in savings accounts, and on the tourism sector.

· Institutional reform: A wide range of formal and informal institutions are necessary for the market to function and thrive. The changes necessary in order to build institutions to support the market by definition are not compatible with the first scenario. They include formalizing and strengthening the legal framework that recognizes and protects private ownership, strengthening institutions that implement this legal framework, strengthening the social safety net, and starting the privatization of large state enterprises.

· Changes in social services: With regard to health care, preserve the NHS but modify it to make it financially affordable for the nation; improve the efficiency and quality of health-care services; permit the private sector to provide health-care services for a fee; eliminate geographical disparities in health care; and target free health-care services on those segments of the population without the ability to pay. With regard to education, maintain a universal, free educational system but modified to make it more efficient and affordable to the nation; adjust educational services to the demands of a global market; allow for a private education system subject to quality standards set by the state; provide incentives to attract students into high-demand fields of study and training; and create disincentives to limit enrollment in fields where there are already surpluses of trained personnel or where the anticipated demand is weak. With regard to social security pensions, raise the retirement age to 65 years of age for men and women; reintroduce worker contributions; conduct a financial feasibility study to determine the level of the minimum pension; expand the coverage of the system to the private sector; and provide an optional supplementary pension system with individual retirement accounts for those who are able to afford contributions to this system. With regard to housing, eliminate restrictions and provide incentives for individuals to repair and maintain their dwellings, exchange them, and build new housing units; allow low-income families to remain in the houses they occupy and provide them with a means-tested rent subsidy and with small loans to build or purchase new housing units.

· Eliminating remaining racial discrimination: Launch a national public debate in schools and workplaces and through the mass media on racial discrimination and ways to eliminate it, and give all citizens (including blacks) the right to form and join organizations to promote their advancement.

· Creation of a social safety net: Transform the current system of universal subsidies and free services (subsidized prices for consumer goods, free health care and education) into a system that targets the segments of the population in greatest need, through a means-testing system.

· Need for foreign assistance: The reforms we have recommended will require technical and financial support from regional and international organizations. The likelihood of assistance from these organizations is very low in the first scenario but higher in the second. Creditor countries, through the Paris Club, may consider restructuring the Cuban debt and forgiving a portion of it subject to the island's implementation of appropriate socioeconomic reforms and the upholding of human and civil rights.

As the Cuban revolutionary government enters its 47th year in power, it is essential that economic logic and the welfare of the Cuban people prevail over Castro and the hard-liners' absurd political logic of maintaining the regime at any cost and blocking the necessary reforms. If the reform paralysis continues, so will the economic and social crisis and the deteriorating condition of the Cuban people. In the longer term, reforms will come to Cuba, but they may be held off until the death of Fidel Castro, hindering the socioeconomic recovery of a nation that has suffered hardships for several decades and deserves peace, prosperity, and social equality.

Notes

Chapter 1. Half a Century of Economic and Social Policies in Socialist Cuba, 1959–2004

1. It should be noted that by the time the Helms-Burton Act was adopted (1996), Cuba was already into its third year of economic recovery. In addition, negotiations to liberalize or eliminate the U.S. trade embargo were derailed three times by Cuban actions: (1) during the Ford presidency, by Cuba's military intervention in Angola; (2) during the Carter presidency, by Cuban military intervention in the war between Somalia and Ethiopia and by the Mariel boatlift that brought 125,000 Cuban citizens to the United States; and (3) during the Clinton presidency, by the downing in international waters of two unarmed airplanes that had dropped leaflets on the island. These events galvanized U.S. congressional support for the Helms-Burton Act. Note the similarity of these events with the aborted entrance of Cuba into the Cotonou Accord following the jailing of 75 peaceful dissidents in 2003.

2. Extensive information on the dissidents, the charges against them, the sentences they received, and the prisons where they are serving their sentences is available at http://www.ruleoflawandcuba.fsu.edu.

Chapter 2. The Economic Crisis, Partial Recovery, and Stagnation

1. The ECLAC series (*Cuba* 2002) for the same period based on 1997 prices (not shown in table 3) is 11% higher than the corresponding Cuban series and 18% higher than the Cuban series based on 1981 prices.

2. The new GDP series based on 1997 prices resulted in an unexplained jump of 66% in the gross capital formation rate in 1996 over the previous estimate based on 1981 prices (ONE 2001, 2003). ECLAC (*Balance preliminar* 2003) estimates considerably lower fixed gross capital formation rates.

3. ONE did not publish balance of payments data for 2002, and the BCC did not publish its 2003 report at all. ECLAC (*Balance preliminar* 2003, and *Cuba* 2004) gives a schematic summary of the balance of payments for 2002–3, but we preferred not to use those data because they are likely to be unreliable and we are unable to cross-check them.

4. A Cuban economist has shown that since 1998, the fall in the value of merchandise exports has been more than offset by an increase in the value of services exports (mostly tourism); nevertheless, the combined value of goods and services exports in 2001 was only about two-thirds of the value for 1985–89 (Marquetti 2003).

5. Spain is second among Cuba's trading partners and the largest foreign investor in the island (with 29% of the total number of international economic associations). Italy is sixth among trading partners and an important source of foreign investment (with 15% of total international economic associations). After the crackdown on dissidents, Italy cancelled its bilateral foreign aid program amounting to about 40 million euros and Spain was considering doing the same with respect to its assistance valued at 7 million euros (Vicent 2003).

6. U.S. official trade statistics show different values of agricultural exports to Cuba than are reported by Cuban officials. According to U.S. Census Bureau statistics, total U.S. exports to Cuba of food and live animals amounted to $4.0 million in 2001, $95.5 million in 2002, $160.1 million in 2003, and $400.0 million in 2004. See www.census. gov/foreign-trade/statistics/product/site1index.html. Although lower than Cuban statistics, U.S. statistics show that the United States has become a significant source of Cuban food imports, displacing exports from Canada, Europe, and Latin America in the Cuban market.

7. In May 2004, the Commission for Assistance to a Free Cuba 2004, convened by President Bush, proposed several measures to limit the flow of foreign currencies into Cuba (Luxner 2004): (1) sending of remittances would be limited to immediate family members and prohibited to members of the PCC; (2) family visits would be restricted to one visit to immediate relatives every three years for a maximum of 14 days, no more than 44 pounds of baggage could be carried, the daily allowance for food and lodging would be cut from $164 to $50, and the previously allowed imports of $100 worth of Cuban goods would be abolished; and (3) the contents and frequency of gift parcels from Cuban Americans would be limited. The U.S. government issued interim regulations to implement these measures in mid-June 2004, and the new rules became effective on June 30, 2004 (U.S. Department of the Treasury 2004; Alfonso 2004b; U.S. Department of Commerce 2004; Cancio Isla 2004c). The Cuban government criticized the proposals when they were first announced but did not take direct action against the United States; instead it raised prices of nonfood items sold in dollar shops (see chapter 3).

8. The change in sugarcane lands under irrigation is for 1990 to 2000; the most recent Cuban statistical yearbook (ONE 2003) does not contain statistics on sugarcane lands under irrigation for 2001 or 2002.

9. However, per-capita electricity output in 2003 was 1.41 Gw/h compared with 1.44 Gw/h in 1989 (based on CEE 1991; ECLAC, *Cuba*, 2004).

10. An article published in Cuba noted that whereas Vietnam has become a "rice-exporter power," Cuba has to import 58% of its rice consumption needs (Pagés 2004a).

11. The two more conventional types of cooperatives are Cooperativas de Producción Agropecuaria (CPA), in which members are collective owners, and the Cooperativas de Crédito y Servicios (CCS), in which owners remain as individual owners but share agricultural machinery and services and credit.

12. The open unemployment rate in 2000 was reported as 5.5% but a former vice-president of Cuba's central planning board estimated (based on employment and unemployment data from ECLAC) that it was actually 9% (García Díaz 2004). Mesa-Lago (2005) has estimated a rate of 21% in the same year based on data from Cuba, ECLAC, and the ILO. According to a Cuban independent economist, the real unemployment rate could be on the order of 25% (Ramos Lauzurique 2003).

13. The results of the 2002 population census had not been released by mid-2004, but ONE (2003) published the total population as 11.18 million, 0.7% lower than its own population estimate of 11.25 million in June 2002.

14. In 2004 Cuba broke relations with Sweden in reaction to that country's vote in favor of the UN resolution condemning human-rights violations in Cuba. Mexico recalled its ambassador to Havana and expelled the Cuban ambassador; ambassadors were reestablished subsequently as Cuba and Mexico attempted to patch up their relations. Peru also withdrew its ambassador from Havana, and Cuba quarreled with Chile over the issue of human rights. For details about the UN resolution see Malamud (2004).

Chapter 3. Social Welfare and Growing Inequalities

1. During visits to Havana in 1980 and 1990, Mesa-Lago asked Cuban statisticians why they did not produce income distribution statistics that would support Cuba's claims of having an egalitarian society, and they responded that this was not a topic of interest.

2. When transfers related to health and education, food subsidies, and imputed value of housing were taken into account, the Gini coefficient was reduced by 0.08 to 0.30, comparable to that of South Korea and higher than those of Taiwan and Japan (Ferriol 2001a, 2001b).

3. In the 51 tables and figures of the ECLAC study, many related to equity, Cuba appears in only three, two on demography and one on coverage of services.

4. Recall that the official exchange rate is one peso for one U.S. dollar. As shown in table 4, in 1989 the unofficial (black market) rate was seven pesos per dollar. CADECA exchanges pesos for dollars at rates considerably higher than the official one. In 1998, the average exchange rate at CADECA outlets was 21 pesos for US$1.

5. ECLAC (2004a) reports an increase of 17.4% in the real average wage between 1998 and 2002, which is doubtful in view of all the other available estimates.

6. Mesa-Lago asked a dozen interviewees for the lowest and highest salaries or incomes for various occupations in pesos or dollars. Although the answers were fairly consistent, we do not consider this a formal survey.

7. The "convertible" peso was introduced in the mid-1990s as an alternative domestic currency, officially valued at par with the U.S. dollar. Despite the peso's comparabil-

ity to dollars in terms of purchasing power, the population prefers dollars because of the latter's generalized acceptance. Strictly speaking, the convertible peso is not actually so because its value is not set by supply and demand in the world market.

8. Labor productivity declined by 30% from 1989 through 1993, and despite the economic recovery was still 20% below the 1989 level in 1998 (ECLAC 2000a: 253). Based on annual productivity rates published for 1999–2002 (ECLAC 2004a: 216), productivity in 2002 was still 12.6% below 1989 levels (Mesa-Lago 2005).

9. In November 2004, the use of the U.S. dollar was banned and only convertible pesos are now accepted by all state entities. Those who need to convert dollars to convertible pesos are charged a 10% fee but Canadian dollars, euros, British pounds, and Swiss francs can be converted without charge. No new deposits or transfers may be made into existing dollar bank accounts, although opening new accounts is allowed (Resolución 80 of the BCC, October 23, 2004).

10. Based on the 1990 U.S. census data on the number of Cuban Americans, their average income, and year of arrival in the United States, and considering that the largest concentration of Cuban exiles lives in the United States, Díaz-Briquets (1994) estimated that only if all Cuban-American households remitted 10% of their income could the upper limit of $1 billion in remittances be accurate, which he considered impossible. He estimated a more reasonable figure of $400 million. A survey of Cuban American households in south Florida conducted in 2004 estimated that 269,868 households sent an average annual remittance to Cuba of $387 each in 2003, for a total of only $104 million (Grenier and Gladwin 2004). The authors caution that their figures may be low because some of the interviewees declined to answer the questions about remittances, the survey was taken during a recession, and Cuban Americans visiting the island might have carried cash with them. Even so, their estimate is only 11% of the ECLAC figure. Beginning in 2000–1, ECLAC began omitting remittance estimates in its annual report on Cuba, stopping the series after 1999 (ECLAC, *Cuba* 2003, 2004). Recently the Inter-American Development Bank estimated $1 billion in remittances to Cuba without explaining how it arrived at that estimate.

11. Calculated on the basis of an average monthly salary of 261 pesos, annualized to 3,132 pesos, converted to dollars at the 2002 CADECA exchange rate of 26 pesos per US$1.

12. The idea for this estimate comes from de la Fuente (2001).

13. An analysis of the composition of population income between 1989 and 2000 reveals that the share of salaries within total population income fell considerably, while the shares of bank withdrawals and remittances rose considerably, and the shares accounted for by social security, social welfare, and payments by the state to the non-state sector remained largely unchanged (Togores and García 2003a).

14. In 2003, the profit tax was increased to 35% and could range up to 50% in case of exploitation of national resources (Resolución 379 of the Ministerio de Finanzas y Precios, June 20, 2003). Only 45% of those subject to that tax had paid it by March 2004 (*Granma*, March 16, 2004).

15. Cuba paid only the equivalent of $500 million in debt service to the USSR during the entire 1960–90 period.

16. On the other hand, 50% of children between 6 and 11 months of age are anemic (INHA 2002).

17. In 2001 Cuba changed the maternal mortality series by eliminating deaths from "other causes"; hence the rate was artificially reduced by between 8.5 and 15.3 per 100,000 live births in the new series for 1996–2000 (Mesa-Lago 2005).

18. Chicken pox rates peaked at 1,138 in 1995 but reportedly shrank to 149 cases in 2002, a decrease of 87% and the lowest rate since the late 1970s, another probable statistical manipulation.

19. In 1988, Cuba's statistical yearbook stopped publishing statistics on housing units built by individuals without an occupancy permit. These units accounted for 46% of total housing units built in 1981–87. (ECLAC, *Cuba* 2002, 2003, does not include these units in its series either.)

20. Between 1993 and 1996, there were 5,381 total or partial building collapses in Havana city; 100,000 Havana residents currently live in unsafe housing, and 80% of residents in central Havana live in housing that has deteriorated or is in need of maintenance (Driggs 2004b).

21. According to ECLAC (2004a) the housing stock rose from 1.26 to 3.13 million units from 1970 to 2002, and the ratio of dwellers per unit decreased from 4.51 to 3.13, but this was not entirely the result of new construction but also of divisions, extensions and room additions.

22. The gap apparently expanded in 2002, as investment in Havana was reported as seven to ten times higher than in Granma, Guantánamo, and three other provinces (Iñiguez and Pérez Villanueva 2004).

23. According to Decree 217 of May 1997, prospective migrants to Havana must receive prior approval from the municipal authorities of the locality (neighborhood) within the city where they intend to reside. Those found in violation of this decree could be fined from 200 to 1,000 pesos and deported to their city of origin.

24. A comparison of the cost of purchasing the same quantity of 14 goods at rationed and non-rationed prices in 1995–2001 showed that the total cost of the products at rationed prices was 9 pesos versus 109 pesos at non-rationed prices. Virtually all prices in agricultural markets declined through 2000, but some rose in 2001 (Pérez Villanueva 2000a). In 2002 the average increase was 23% and new increases occurred in 2003–4. Prices in dollar shops rose by between 10% and 30% in 2004 (ECLAC 2004a; Resolución 54 of the Ministerio de Finanzas y Precios, March 15, 2004).

25. Togores and García (2003a) show a sharp decline between 1989 and 1993 in consumption of clothing, footwear, toiletries and personal hygiene products, and durable goods (refrigerators, TV sets, radios). Furthermore, the consumption of these products stagnated between 1994 and 2001.

26. Fernández (2003) notes that the agricultural markets, and even more so the dollar shops, are inaccessible to low-income groups; therefore, the inclusion of those sources of supply in the basic basket quantity overestimates food security of a very high percentage of the population.

27. The first version of this report was prepared by a team led by Angela Ferriol, director of social studies, Institute of Economic Studies, Ministry of Economics and Planning, and was released in June 1997. The final version referenced in this chapter was published in October without crediting any authorship.

28. However, in another study she compared Cuba's population at risk in 1999 with poverty incidence in four other Latin American countries in 2000–1, and ranked Cuba

lowest after Uruguay (ECLAC 2004a: 79). Not only was the comparison inaccurate, but it excluded Costa Rica, which had a lower poverty incidence than Cuba, and Chile, which was tied with Cuba (Mesa-Lago 2005).

29. The equation for calculating the severity of poverty index (SPI) is $SPI = H [I + (1 - I) G]$, where H is poverty incidence (poor population/total population), I is the percentage gap between the average income of the poor and the poverty line based on the value of a basket of essential goods, and G is the Gini coefficient of the distribution of average income among the poor population.

Chapter 4. Cuba and the Human Development Index

1. Nevertheless, ECLAC for many years published Cuban GSP in tables containing GDP for the rest of the region. A footnote in fine print was the only warning that the Cuban figure actually referred to GSP, and there was no explanation of the implications of using one methodology versus the other.

2. The first edition of the *Report*, published in 1990 with figures for 1985–88, ranked the countries from lowest to highest level of human development, while the second edition, published in 1991 with figures for 1980–90, inverted the ranking from highest to lowest level of human development and made other changes. The third and subsequent editions have followed the latter approach. As our main interest is to analyze the Cuban situation around the 1990 crisis, we start with the third edition of the *Report*.

3. Until 1998 there was a gap of three years between the year of publication of the HDI and the reference year for the data used. Starting with the 1999 edition, that gap was reduced to two years, which led to 1996 being skipped.

4. A study of the HDI conducted in Cuba gives a life expectancy of 74.7 years in 1998 (CIEM 2000: 146), compared with 75.8 years reported by the HDI (UNDP 2000).

5. In fact, for 1970–85 the enrollment rate exceeded 100% because of mismatches between enrollment and the school-age population at the primary level (UNESCO 2001).

6. A study of the HDI done in Cuba acknowledges that "the secondary level is the most problematic within the Cuban educational system" and that there was "a slight enrollment decline in the 1993–94 and 1994–95 school years, but it recovered in the following two years" (CIEM 2000: 82). However, the 1989 level had not been regained by 1997.

7. The HDI *Report* publishes only combined gross enrollment rates, so it is not possible to compare the HDI figures with those reported by Cuba and UNESCO. The HDI study done in Cuba does not present separate series for the three enrollment rates either (CIEM 2000).

8. As we discussed in chapter 2, the base year for the GDP series was shifted in 2001 from 1981 to 1997, and the new series only goes back to 1996; therefore, we lack a consistent GDP series for 1985–2003.

9. This is the highest estimate available. The study on urban population at risk in 1997, discussed in chapter 3, estimated that the value of state social transfers was equal to 40% of average income. It should be noted that the 2003 GDP, calculated according

to the revised methodology that includes the value of state transfers for social services, price subsidies, and so on (Rodríguez 2003), is only 16 percent higher than the corresponding figure based on the conventional SNA methodology.

10. On February 7, 1996, during a seminar on poverty eradication held by UNDP in New York, Mesa-Lago was introduced to the analyst responsible for estimating Cuba's economic indicator. When he attempted to engage her in a discussion of the methodology for making the estimates, the analyst avoided the issue and slipped away.

11. The referenced Penn World Tables are found in Summers and Heston 1991.

12. The World Bank, *World Bank Atlas 1996* (Washington, D.C., 1996: 19) placed Cuban GDP p/c PPP US$ in the range between $726 and $2,895 in 1994, and the HDI again estimated it at $3,000. The *World Bank Atlas 1997* (Washington, D.C., 1997: 36–37) placed GDP in the range between $766 and $3,035 in 1995, and the HDI estimated it at $3,100. In both cases the HDI estimate was outside of the range estimated by the World Bank.

13. The high-income Caribbean countries tend to have very small populations (from 38,000 to 307,000 inhabitants). The three largest countries in the region in terms of population are the Dominican Republic (8.5 million), Haiti (8.4 million), and Jamaica (2.6 million). These larger countries have lower incomes relative to the smaller countries, and therefore would bring down a regional income average weighted by population.

14. For example, in 1989–95, when the HDI high group was enlarged, but not in 1997–99, when that group was reduced.

15. For example, in 1989–90, when that group was enlarged.

16. This is a technical and complex issue that cannot be analyzed thoroughly in this chapter. Briefly, according to the 1994–98 formula, if the GDP p/c PPP US$ of a country was below the threshold, it was not adjusted; if it was above the threshold, it was adjusted by a factor that reduced GDP p/c PPP US$ in proportion to the difference between the income value and the threshold. As income rose, the adjustment factor increased. Beginning with the 1999 edition (data from 1997 on), the method was changed to use a logarithmic adjustment factor. For the differences between the two formulas, see UNDP (1998: 107; 1999: 127–30).

17. Surprisingly, life expectancy at birth in 1995–97 declined slightly in Chile and somewhat more in Costa Rica, apparently due to a revision of previous estimates. All available information for both countries confirms that their life expectancy increased between 1980 and 2000 (ECLAC, *Balance preliminar* 2001: 12–13).

18. It should be noted that the CIEM study defends Cuba's advances, criticizes the HDI methodology, and proposes to replace it with a new Index of Human Development and Equity, in which Cuba would rank second among 23 countries of Latin America and the Caribbean.

19. Around the time we completed the manuscript for this book, the 2003 edition of the *Report,* with data for 2001, raised Cuba in the HDI to 52nd place in the world and 5th in Latin America, surpassing Mexico and falling below only Argentina, Uruguay, Chile, and Costa Rica.

20. This would appear to be the component accounted for by the PPP calculation that was first made in 2002.

Chapter 5. The Performance of Cuba's Economic and Social Model Compared with Those of Chile and Costa Rica

1. Our intention was to use in the comparison five additional indicators, but we were unable to do so because of lack of data or comparability problems: incidence of poverty and income distribution (because they are not available for Cuba); female labor force participation and percentage of the population with access to running water and sewage services (because no recent reliable statistics for Cuba are available); and social security coverage (because the statistics for the three countries are not comparable).

2. We ranked Cuba best in this indicator, but it is questionable to assume that deflation is a positive factor. Some macroeconomists argue that deflation could be a destabilizing factor as it could induce or aggravate a recession or be a reflection of one. If we accept that argument, a low rate of inflation would be preferable, as was experienced by Chile.

3. In 2000, Costa Rica was the Latin American and Caribbean country with the second lowest percentage of primary products exports within total exports, and the second highest percentage of manufactured products exports (ECLAC, *Statistical Yearbook*, 2002).

4. This figure is based on Cuba's overall foreign debt, including debt to Russia and eastern European nations. If debt with these countries is excluded, Cuba's debt per capita becomes $977 (based on ONE 2001), the lowest for the three countries.

5. Costa Rica's figure refers to 1994; more recent statistics are not available, but by 2000 the situation should have improved.

6. In his book, Mesa-Lago (2000) focused on five diseases for which there were significant differences in the three countries (as there was no point in comparing those eradicated or with negligible rates) and taking into account that some diseases (such as malaria) were not endemic in all countries. In table 23, we did not include measles because it appeared to be virtually eradicated in the three countries by 2000.

7. About the time we finished this book, the UNDP 2003 *Report* had the following HDI rankings: Chile 39th in the world and 3rd in Latin America, Costa Rica 43rd and 4th, and Cuba 52nd and 5th, respectively.

8. Chile started a very innovative unemployment insurance program in 2002.

9. The pension and health-care reforms eliminated all solidarity elements within the private system. For example, there are no transfers from high- to low-income covered groups; the employer contribution was terminated and only the worker contributes; and the non-covered population indirectly contributes to the benefits of those covered through regressive taxes.

Chapter 6. Needed Economic and Social Reforms in Cuba

1. This chapter draws heavily from several important recent studies that assess transition strategies and their outcomes, including World Bank (2002a), Aslund (2002), International Monetary Fund (2001c), and Svejnar (2002). These studies do not address the socialist market transitions in China and Vietnam, and neither do we.

2. The variables that analysts have used as indicators of initial conditions relate to

economic structure (share of GDP in industry, degree of urbanization, the share of trade with the Soviet bloc, per-capita income prior to reforms, natural resource endowment, and proximity to western markets); distortions associated with the socialist nature of the economy (degree of repressed inflation, spread between the official exchange rate and black market exchange rates, prior history of economic reforms); and institutions (years under central planning, degree of exposure to western markets, degree of maturity of the state).

3. In the empirical studies, the extent of economic policy reform was measured by an economic liberalization index that considered reforms needed (1) to make markets the main mechanism for allocating resources; and (2) to ensure the efficient functioning of markets.

4. Of course, the ultimate "instant" transition was the unification of West and East Germany in 1990. As a result of unification, East Germany adopted by the stroke of a pen all of the policies and institutions of West Germany.

5. To paraphrase Nobel Laureate Douglass North (1994: 359), radical reformers, dominated by neoclassical theory, focused narrowly on how markets operate, while gradual reformers were also concerned with how markets develop.

6. Administrative corruption is defined as "the use of public office for private gain, where an official (the agent) entrusted with carrying out a task by the public (the principal) engages in some sort of malfeasance for private enrichment which is difficult to monitor for the principal" (Bardhan 1997: 1321).

7. Eastern and central European nations, the Baltic states, and CIS nations have employed many methods for privatizing state-owned enterprises, often combining more than one technique. They include assets sales (Hungary, East Germany), voucher privatization (Czech Republic, early Polish divestitures, Russia), share offerings (later Polish sales), insider privatization (Russia), and spontaneous privatization (Slovenia).

8. See also the recommendations of Espinosa Chepe (2004). The latter's recommendations are predicated on systemic changes and therefore are not included here.

9. For analyses of Cuba's economic and social transition, see, for example, Mesa-Lago 1993; numerous articles published in *Cuba in Transition* 1–14 (1990–2004); and monographs published by the Cuba Transition Project of the University of Miami, 2002–4.

10. In 2000, the Cuban government decreed that old peso bills had to be exchanged for new currency issued by the BCC. Some people perceived this measure as a way for the government to demonetize individual holdings not deposited with the banking system.

Bibliography

"Adoptan más medidas para el ahorro de electricidad." 2004. *Nuevo Herald*, August 6.

Alemann, Juan. 2004. "La deuda de Cuba con Argentina por casi US $2,000 millones." *Razón* (Buenos Aires), February 28.

Alfonso, Pablo. 2003. "Escándalo sacude a la cúpula del turismo cubano." *Nuevo Herald*, December 5.

———. 2004a. "¿Petróleo a la vista?" *Nuevo Herald*, July 21.

———. 2004b. "Restringen viajes y envíos a Cuba." *Nuevo Herald*, June 17.

Alonso, José, Armando Lago, and Ricardo Donate Armada. 1994. "A First Approximation Design of the Social Safety Net for a Democratic Cuba." *Cuba in Transition* 4: 88–154.

Alonso Tejada, Aurelio. 2003. "Lidiar con la pobreza en el Caribe hispano: en busca de claves efectivas." Paper presented at the XXIV LASA Congress, Dallas, March.

Añé, Lía. 2000. "Cuba: reformas, recuperación y equidad." Paper presented at the Simposio sobre Reforma Económica y Cambio Social en América Latina y el Caribe, Cali, Colombia.

"Aplazan la zafra hasta enero." 2004. *Nuevo Herald*, November 4.

Aslund, Anders. 2002. *Building Capitalism: The Transformation of the Former Soviet Bloc*. New York: Cambridge University Press.

"Balance del MINCEX." 2002. *Granma*, March 25.

Banco Central de Cuba (BCC). 1999–2002. *Informe Económico, 1998, 1999, 2000, 2001*. Havana: BCC.

Bardhan, Pranap. 1997. "Corruption and Development: A Review." *Journal of Economic Literature* 35: 1320–46.

Barreiro, Georgina. 2003. "Presentación del presupuesto." *Granma*, December 26.

Barrionuevo, Alexei, and José de Córdoba. 2004. "For Aging Castro, Chávez Emerges as a Crucial Crutch." *Wall Street Journal*, February 2.

Bauzá, Vanessa. 2001. "Cuba's Entrepreneurs Find It Tough." *Sun Sentinel*, June 11.

Bauzá, Vanessa, and Tim Collie. 2002. "Housing Crisis on Island Literally Killing Some Cubans." *Sun Sentinel*, January 18.

Benítez Pérez, María Elena. 2001. "La política social y la vejez en Cuba: algunas reflexiones." Paper presented at the CISS VI Conferencia de Actuarios y Financistas a Nivel Internacional, Mexico City, September 3–5.

Betancourt, Ernesto, and Guillermo Grenier. 1999. "Measuring Cuban Public Opinion: Economic, Social and Political Issues." *Cuba in Transition* 9: 251–69.

Boadle, Anthony. 2003. "Cuba frena incipiente iniciativa privada." Reuters (Havana), June 16.

"Brasil tras el petróleo en Cuba." 2004. *Nuevo Herald*, July 24.

Brundenius, Claes. 1979. "Measuring Income Distribution in Pre- and Post-Revolutionary Cuba." *Cuban Studies* 9 (July): 29–44.

———. 1984. *Revolutionary Cuba: The Challenge of Economic Growth with Equity.* Boulder: Westview Press.

———. 2002. "El turismo como 'locomotora' de crecimiento: reflexiones sobre la nueva estrategia de desarrollo de Cuba." In *Cuba: reestructuración económica y globalización*, edited by Mauricio de Miranda, 265–94. Bogotá: Centro Editorial Javeriano.

Brundenius, Claes, and Pedro Monreal. 2001. "The Future of the Cuban Model: A Longer View." In *Globalization and Third World Socialism: Cuba and Vietnam*, edited by Claes Brundenius and John Weeks, 129–50. Houndmills, England: Palgrave.

Bussey, Jane. 2004. "Is the U.S. Becoming Cuba's Bread Basket?" *Miami Herald*, Monday Business Supplement, January 19.

Cancio Isla, Wilfredo. 2003. "Cuba exige apoyo contra embargo a empresas de EEUU." *Nuevo Herald*, December 24.

———. 2004a. "Castro se atrinchera en el pasado." *Nuevo Herald*, May 24.

———. 2004b. "Corrupción en la cúpula empresarial cubana" and "Un chivo expiatorio para la corrupción en Cuba." *Nuevo Herald*, February 16 and 22.

———. 2004c. "Restringen el envío de paquetes a Cuba." *Nuevo Herald*, June 23.

Carbone, Maurizio. 2003. "EU-Cuban Relations Taking Further Steps towards Cotonou Membership." *The Courier ACP-EU* 196 (January–February): 6–7.

Carranza Valdés, Julio. 2001. "La economía cubana: un balance breve de una década crítica." Presented at the Facing the Challenges of the Global Economy workshop, University of London Institute of Latin American Studies, January 25–26.

Carranza Valdés, Julio, Luis Gutiérrez, and Pedro Monreal. 1995. *Cuba: la reestructuración de la economía—una propuesta para el debate.* Havana: Editorial de Ciencias Sociales.

Castañeda, Rolando. 2000. "Cuba y América Latina: consideraciones sobre el nivel y la evolución del Índice de Desarrollo Humano y el gasto social en la década de los noventa." *Cuba in Transition* 10: 234–53.

Castañeda, Rolando, and George Plinio Montalván. 1997. "Cuba: cooperación internacional de emergencia y para la recuperación." *Cuba in Transition* 7: 269–94.

Castro, Fidel. 1993a. "Discurso en la clausura del 40 aniversario del asalto al Cuartel Moncada." *Granma*, July 28.

———. 1993b. "Discurso en el 5to congreso de la UNEAC." *Granma*, December 8.

———. 2003. "Discurso en el acto de inauguración del curso escolar 2003–2004." *Granma*, September 10.

———. 2004. "Estamos en guardia ante los peligros que nos amenazan." *Granma*, February 14.

Centro de Investigaciones de la Economía Mundial (CIEM). 1997. *Investigación sobre desarrollo humano en Cuba 1996*. Havana: PNUD.

———. 2000. *Investigación sobre el desarrollo y la equidad en Cuba 1999*. Havana, CIEM and UNDP.

Céspedes, Dorka. 2004. "Pescando en tierra firme." *Cubanet Independiente*, April 7.

"Ciclones causaron pérdidas millonarias." 2002. France Press (Havana), December 16.

Comité Estatal de Estadísticas (CEE). 1991. *Anuario estadístico de Cuba, 1989*. Havana: CEE.

Commission for Assistance to a Free Cuba. 2004. *Report to the President*, May. Washington, D.C.: GPO.

Cosano, Reinaldo. 2004. "Agricultura e intermediarios en Cuba." *Cubanet Independiente*, April 7.

"Crecimiento del PIB evidencia recuperación de economía cubana." 2003. *Granma*, December 23.

"Cuba adeuda al país $266 millones." 2003. *El Universal* (Caracas), March 7.

"Cuba espera recibir 1.7 millones de turistas." 2002. *EFE* (Havana), December 16.

"Cuba Is the 25th Largest Agricultural Export Market to U.S." 2005. Reuters (Havana), February 16.

"Cuba's Hard Currency and Non-Convertible Currency Debt." 2004. In *Cuba Facts*. Coral Gables: University of Miami, Institute for Cuban and Cuban-American Studies, Cuba Transition Project.

De Jesús, Ventura. 2002. "Prevén crecimiento en la producción de crudo para el actual año." *Granma*, January 31.

De la Fuente, Alejandro. 2001. *A Nation for All: Race, Inequality and Politics in Twentieth-Century Cuba*. Chapel Hill: University of North Carolina Press.

De la Osa, José. 2003. "Mortalidad infantil en 2002 ¡6,5%!" *Granma*, January 8.

De Miranda, Mauricio, ed. 2003. *Cuba: reestructuración económica y globalización*. Bogotá: Centro Editorial Javeriano.

"Declaración del MINREX sobre las mentiras de la oposición golpista de Venezuela." 2003. *Granma*, June 9.

Delgado, Angel. 2004a. "Se incumple plan de siembra de caña." *Cubanet Independiente*, September 6.

———. 2004b. "Y de la próxima zafra, ¿qué?" *Cubanet Independiente*, November 2.

"Destituyen a un ministro por crisis eléctrica." 2004. *Nuevo Herald*, October 15.

Díaz-Briquets, Sergio. 1994. "Emigrant Remittances in the Cuban Economy: Their Significance during and after the Castro Regime." *Cuba in Transition* 4: 218–27.

Díaz-Briquets, Sergio, and Jorge Pérez-López. 2000. *Conquering Nature: The Environmental Legacy of Socialism in Cuba*. Pittsburgh: University of Pittsburgh Press.

———. 2002. *A Transparency/Accountability Approach for Combating Corruption in Post-Castro Cuba*. Coral Gables: University of Miami, Institute for Cuban and Cuban-American Studies, Cuba Transition Project.

"Disposición gubernamental afecta abastecimiento de productos agrícolas." 2003. *Cubanet Independiente*, September 10.

Domínguez, Jorge I. 1997. "Comienza una transición hacia el autoritarismo en Cuba." *Encuentro* 6–7 (Fall-Winter): 7–23.

———. 2000. "The Cuban Political System in the 1990s." Paper presented at LASA Congress, March 16–18.

Donate, Ricardo. 1995. "Preliminary Analysis of Retirement Programs for Personnel of the Ministry of the Armed Forces and of the Ministry of the Interior of the Republic of Cuba." *Cuba in Transition* 5: 448–58.

Driggs, Eric. 2004a. "Aiding a Cuba in Transition: Humanitarian Challenges and Practical Considerations on Both Sides of the Florida Straits." *Cuba in Transition* 14: 325–36.

———. 2004b.*Deteriorating Living Conditions in Cuba.* Cuba Transition Project publication 59, October 14. Coral Gables: University of Miami, Institute for Cuban and Cuban-American Studies.

Economic Commission for Latin America and the Caribbean (ECLAC). 1998, 2000a. *La economía cubana: reformas estructurales y desempeño en los noventa.* 1st and 2nd eds. Mexico City: Fondo de Cultura Económica.

———. 2000b. *Equidad, desarrollo y ciudadanía.* Versión definitiva. Santiago de Chile: ECLAC.

———. 2000–3. *Balance preliminar de las economías de América Latina y el Caribe, 2000, 2001, 2002, 2003.* Santiago de Chile: ECLAC.

———. 2000–4. *Cuba: evolución económica durante 1999, 2000, 2001, 2002, y 2003.* Mexico City: ECLAC.

———. 2001b. *Panorama social de América Latina 2000/2001.* Santiago de Chile: ECLAC.

———. 2001–2. *Statistical Yearbook for Latin America and the Caribbean, 2000, 2001.* Santiago de Chile: ECLAC.

———. 2001–3. *Estudio económico de América Latina y el Caribe, 2000/2001, 2001/02, 2002/03.* Santiago de Chile: ECLAC.

Economic Commission for Latin America and the Caribbean (ECLAC), Instituto Nacional de Investigaciones Económicas y Programa de Naciones Unidas para el Desarrollo. 2004a. *Política social y reformas estructurales en Cuba a principios del siglo XXI.* Coordinadores Elena Álvarez y Jorge Máttar. Mexico City: ECLAC.

———. 2004b. *Política social y reformas estructurales en Cuba a principios del siglo XXI: Anexo Estadístico.* http://www.eclac.cl/mexico.

The Economist Intelligence Unit (EIU). 2002. *Cuba: Country Profile 2002.* London: EIU.

"Esperan producción récord de níquel en el 2001." 2001. *Nuevo Herald*, June 17.

Espina Prieto, Mayra. 2003. "Efectos sociales del reajuste económico: igualdad, desigualdad y procesos de complejización en la sociedad cubana." Paper presented at the XXIV LASA Congress, Dallas, March.

Espino, María Dolores. 2001. "Cuban Tourism: A Critique of the CEPAL 2000 Report." *Cuba in Transition* 11: 379–83.

Espinosa Chepe, Oscar. 2001a. "El cuentapropista continúa reduciéndose." *Cubanet Independiente*, March 18.

———. 2001b. "Suben los precios en los mercados agropecuarios estatales en La Habana." *Cubanet Independiente*, December 19.

———. 2002a. "Crisis alimentaria en provincias orientales de Cuba." *Cubanet Independiente*, October 16.

———. 2002b. "La economía cubana evolucionó negativamente en 2001." *Cubanet Independiente*, January 9.

———. 2002c. "Huevos sólo para diplomáticos." *Cubanet Independiente*, February 26.

———. 2002d. "Panorama económico complicado." *Cubanet Independiente*, December 31.

———. 2003a. "Anuario estadístico 2001: una inexplicable modificación." *Encuentro en la Red* (Madrid), no. 536, January 17.

———. 2003b. "Inversiones disminuyen en Cuba." *Cubanet Independiente*, April 1.

———. 2003c. "Miseria planificada." *Encuentro en la Red* (Madrid), no. 540, January 23.

———. 2004. *Crónicas de un desastre: apuntes sobre la economía cubana 1998–2002*. Madrid: Fundación Hispano Cubana.

European Bank for Reconstruction and Development (EBRD). 2000. *Transition Report 2000*. London: EBRD.

Fabienke, Rikke. 2001. "Labour Markets and Income Distribution During Crisis and Reform." In *Globalization and Third World Socialism: Cuba and Vietnam*, edited by Claes Brundenius and John Weeks, 102–28. Houndmills, England: Palgrave.

Fernández Mayo, María A. 2003. "La disponibilidad de alimentos." Paper presented at the XXIV LASA Congress, Dallas, March.

Ferradaz, Ibrahim. 2002. "Noticiero estelar nocturno" (Havana), January 31.

Ferriol Muruaga, Angela. 2001a. "Apertura externa, mercado laboral y política social." *Siglo XXI* 3 (March), *http://www.nodo50.org/cubasigloXXI/economia2.htm*.

———. 2001b. "Reforma económica cubana e impactos sociales." Paper presented at the Congreso de Latinoamericanistas y Caribólogos, June 25–29.

———. 2003. "Acercamiento al estudio de la pobreza en Cuba." Paper presented at the XXIV LASA Congress, Dallas, March.

Figueras, Miguel A. 2002. "El turismo internacional y la formación de clusters productivos en la economía cubana." In *Cuba: Reflexiones sobre su economía*. Havana: Universidad de La Habana.

Food and Agricultural Organization (FAO). 2002. *The State of Food Insecurity in the World, 2002*, http://www.fao.sof/sofi/index_es.htm.

"Foreign Investment in Cuba Falls." 2002. Reuters (Havana), July 8.

Fornasis, José. 2004. "Reaparecen vendedores privados en mercados agropecuarios." *Cubanet Independiente*, April 7.

Frank, Marc. 2001. "Destituyen al ministro de la pesca." *Nuevo Herald*, March 25.

———. 2002a. "Caída en ingresos obliga a renegociar la deuda" and "Cuba incumplirá su deuda con Japón y México." Reuters, February 22 and October 26.

———. 2002b. "Cuban Peso under Increasing Pressure." *Forbes*, July 10.

———. 2004a. "Communist Cuba Reins in Capitalist Enterprises." Reuters (Havana), April 14.

———. 2004b. "Cuba's Businesses Feel Pinch as Dollar is Squeezed from Economy." *The Financial Times*, April 14

———. 2004c. "Cuba's Communists Launched Crackdown." *Financial Times*, July 5.

———. 2004d. "Cuba's Sugar Harvest Plagued with Mill Problems." *Nueva Cuba*, March 3.

Freedom House. 2001. *Freedom in the World, 1999–2000*. http://www.freedomhouse. org/ratings/index.htm.

Gallagher, Mark. 1999. "Some Ideas for Taxation during Cuba's Transition." *Cuba in Transition* 9: 36–46.

García Alvarez, Anicia. 2003. "Sustitución de importaciones de alimentos en Cuba: necesidad vs. posibilidad." Paper presented at the XXIV LASA Congress, Dallas, March.

———. 2004. "El sector agropecuario cubano: Cambios en su paradigma de desarrollo." In *15 años del Centro de Estudios de la Economía Cubana*, 79–111. Havana: Editorial Félix Varela.

García Díaz, Manuel. 2004. *La economía cubana: estructuras, instituciones y tránsito al mercado*. Granada: Universidad de Granada.

García-Zarza, Isabel. 2004. "Crisis energética agrava aún más las dificultades en la isla." *Nuevo Herald*, October 1.

González, Edward. 2002. *After Castro: Alternative Regimes and U.S. Policy*. Coral Gables: University of Miami, Institute for Cuban and Cuban-American Studies, Cuba Transition Project.

González Gutiérrez, Alfredo. 2001. "Aspectos estratégicos en el perfeccionamiento del modelo de planificación." *El Economista de Cuba*, June 20.

———. 2003. "El sistema de planificación y circulación monetaria dual en la etapa actual." *Economía y Desarrollo*, special edition (December): 11–21.

"Gran expectación por el resultado de la exploración petrolera." 2004. *Nuevo Herald*, July 28.

Grenier, Guillermo, and Hugh Gladwin. 2004. *2004 Cuba Poll*. Miami: Florida International University, Cuban Research Institute–Institute for Public Opinion Research. http://lacc.fiu.edu/cri. Also authors' correspondence with Grenier, May 27, 2004.

Grogg, Patricia. 2004. "Economía Cuba: panorama hostil." *Nueva Cuba* (Havana), June 19.

Grupo Cubano de Investigaciones Económicas. 1963. *Un estudio sobre Cuba*. Coral Gables: University of Miami Press.

Henken, Ted. 2002. "Condemned to Informality: The Self-employed Operators of Cuba's New Bed and Breakfast." *Cuban Studies* 33: 1–29.

Heritage Foundation. 1995–96, 2001. *Index of Economic Freedom 1996, 2001*. Washington and New York: Heritage Foundation and the *Wall Street Journal*, http://www.heritage.org/reasearch/features/index.

Hoag, Christina. 2002. "Venezuela to Cuba: Oil Isn't Free." *Miami Herald*, May 25.

"Información del Ministerio de Trabajo y Seguridad Social." 2004. *Granma*, October 4.

Informe de Cuba. 1997. "Proyecto: efecto de políticas macroeconómicas y sociales sobre niveles de pobreza." Second version. October, unpublished paper, Havana.

Iñiguez, Luisa, and others. 2001. "La exploración de las desigualdades espacio-familias en la ciudad de La Habana." Havana: Universidad de La Habana, CESBH.

Iñiguez, Luisa, and Omar Everleny Pérez Villanueva. 2004. "Territorio y espacio en las desigualdades sociales de la provincia de La Habana." In *15 años del Centro de Estudios de la Economía Cubana*, 21–50. Havana: Editorial Félix Varela.

Institute for Cuban and Cuban-American Studies (ICCAS). 2003. "Cuba's Economy in Doldrums." ICCAS publication, no. 43, June 18. Coral Gables: University of Miami.

———. 2004. "Castro's Venezuelan Bonanza." ICCAS publication, no. 54, April 20. Coral Gables: University of Miami.

Instituto Nacional de Estadísticas (INE). 2003. *www.ine.cl/08–edifica/11218–serie.xls*.

Instituto Nacional de Estadísticas y Censos (INEC). 2003. *Estadísticas de construcción*. San José: INEC.

Instituto de Nutrición e Higiene de los Alimentos (INHA). 2002. "Anemia nutricional en el grupo de niños aparentemente sanos de 2 a 4 años de edad." *Revista Cubana de Alimentos y Nutrición* (Havana) 6(1):31–34.

International Labor Organization (ILO). 2001. *Anuario estadístico del trabajo 2001*. Geneva: ILO.

———. 2004. *Quinto punto del día: 344 informe del Comité de Libertad Sindical*. Geneva: ILO.

International Monetary Fund (IMF). 2001–3. *International Financial Statistics Yearbook*. Washington D.C.: IMF.

———. 2001b. *Direction of Trade Yearbook 2001*. Washington D.C.: IMF.

———. 2001c. "Transition Economies: How Much Progress?" Special issue, *IMF Staff Papers* 48.

"Investigan actividades de cuentapropistas." 2004. *Cubanet Independiente*, January 8.

Jiménez, Eduardo. 2002. "Creciendo a pesar de. . . ." *Economista de Cuba*, February.

Kornai, János. 1992. *The Socialist System: The Political Economy of Socialism*. Princeton: Princeton University Press.

Lage, Carlos. 2002. "Intervención en la Asamblea Nacional." *Granma*, March 4.

———. 2003a. "Conclusiones del balance de la gestión del MINCEX en 2002." *Granma*, February 24.

———. 2003b. "Disciplina y control, absolutas prioridades para el turismo." *Granma*, March 8.

Lee, Susana. 2002. "Incrementar los ingresos y reducir los costos en el turismo." *Granma*, March 5.

León, Francisco. 2002. "Cuba: las reformas económicas en las negociaciones internacionales: La coyuntura actual." In *Cuba: reestructuración económica y globalización*, edited by Mauricio de Miranda, 221–64. Bogotá: Centro Editorial Javeriano.

López Oliva, Enrique. 2002. "¿Qué le espera al pueblo en 2003?" Havana, mimeo, December 30.

Luxner, Larry. 2004. "Remittances, Travel Privileges Curbed under Bush Proposals Unveiled May 6." *Cuba News*, May.

Madruga, Aldo. 2003. "En recuperación producción citrícola." *Granma*, May 15.

Malamud, Carlos. 2004. "América Latina y los derechos humanos en Cuba." Real Instituto Elcano, Madrid, April 26.

"Marcha atrás a la dolarización." 2003. *Cubanet Independiente*, August.

Marquetti Nodarse, Hiram. 2000. "Cuba: Reanimación del sector industrial." *Revista Bimestre Cubana* 13 (July–December): 5–30.

———. 2002. "Cuba: importancia actual del incremento de las exportaciones." In *La economía cubana en 2001*, 168–71. Havana: Centro de Estudios de la Economía Cubana/Fundación Friedrich Ebert.

———. 2003. "Cuba: situación actual y perspectivas de las exportaciones de servicios." In *Seminario anual de la economía cubana*, 1–27. Havana: Centro de Estudios de la Economía Cubana/Fundación Friedrich Ebert.

Martínez, Osvaldo. 2002. "Intervención sobre el plan de la economía nacional y el presupuesto del Estado." *Granma*, December 24.

———. 2003. "Intervención sobre el plan de la economía nacional y el presupuesto del Estado." *Granma*, December 24.

Marx, Gary. 2004. "UN Panel Criticizes Cuba's Crackdown on Dissidents." *Chicago Tribune*, April 16.

Maseda, Héctor. 2002a. "El misterio de los televisores Panda." *Cubanet Independiente*, February 25.

———. 2002b. "Muchos son los alertados, pocos los cumplidores." *Cubanet Independiente*, October 24.

Mayoral, María. 2002. "Una ley para estimular las producciones agropecuarias." *Granma*, October 31, and *Juventud Rebelde*, November 3.

Mayoral, María, and Ventura de Jesús. 2004. "Nada ni nadie nos puede intimidar ni amenazar." *Granma*, October 26.

"Menos empresas con capital foráneo." 2004. *Nuevo Herald*, February 4.

Mesa-Lago, Carmelo. 1993. "The Social Safety Net in the Two Cuban Transitions." In "Transition in Cuba: New Challenges for U.S. Policy." FIU, Cuban Research Institute, Miami, unpublished document.

———. 1994. *Breve historia económica de la Cuba socialista*. Madrid: Alianza Editorial.

———. 1998. "Assessing Economic and Social Performance in the Cuban Transition of the 1990s." *World Development* 26(5):857–76.

———. 2000. *Market, Socialist and Mixed Economies: Comparative Policy and Performance—Chile, Cuba, and Costa Rica*. Baltimore: Johns Hopkins University Press.

———. 2001a. "The Cuban Economy in 1999–2000: Evaluation of Performance and Debate on the Future." *Cuba in Transition* 11: 1–17.

———. 2001b. "The Resurrection of Cuban Statistics." *Cuban Studies* 31: 139–50.

———. 2002a. "Cuba in the Human Development Index in the 1990s: Decline, Rebound and Exclusion." *Cuba in Transition* 12: 450–63.

———. 2002b. *Growing Economic and Social Disparities in Cuba: Impact and Recommendations for Change*. Coral Gables: University of Miami, Institute for Cuban and Cuban-American Studies, Cuba Transition Project.

———. 2003a. *La economía y el bienestar social en Cuba a comienzos del siglo XXI*. Madrid: Editorial Colibrí.

———. 2003b. "La seguridad social en Cuba en el Período Especial: diagnóstico y sugerencias de políticas en pensiones, salud y empleo." In *La seguridad social en Cuba*, edited by Lothar Witte, 32–115. Caracas: Nueva Sociedad.

———. 2003c. *The Slowdown of the Cuban Economy in 2001–2003: External Factors or Internal Malaise?* Coral Gables: University of Miami, Institute for Cuban and Cuban-American Studies, Cuba Transition Project.

———. 2005. "Problemas y políticas sociales en Cuba durante la crisis y la recuperación," forthcoming.

Mesa-Lago, Carmelo, and Jorge Pérez-López. 1985. *A Study of Cuba's National Product System, Its Conversion to the System of National Accounts, and Estimation of GDP Per Capita and Growth Rates.* Staff Working Papers, no. 770. Washington D.C.: World Bank.

Ministerio de Economía y Planificación (MINEP). 2000. *Plan económico y social 2001.* Havana: MINEP.

Ministerio de Finanzas y Precios (MINFP). 2001. *Presupuesto del estado proyecto 2002.* Havana: MINFP.

Ministerio de Salud Pública (MINSAP). 2000–1. *Anuario estadístico 1999, 2000.* Havana: MINSAP.

Mogollón, Henry. 2003. "Deuda petrolera." *Nacional* (Caracas), March 25.

Monreal, Pedro. 1999. "Las remesas familiares en la economía cubana." *Encuentro* (Fall): 49–62.

———. 2001. "Export Substitution Industrialization in Cuba." Paper presented at the Facing the Challenges of the Global Economy workshop, University of London Institute of Latin American Studies, January 25–26.

———. 2003. "Migraciones y remesas familiares: veinte hipótesis sobre el caso de Cuba." *Economía y Desarrollo,* special edition (December): 89–121.

Montiel Ortega, Leonardo. 2001. *Convenio petrolero cubano-venezolano. Una rectificación indispensable.* Caracas.

Mujal-León, Eusebio, and Joshua W. Busby. 2001–2. "¿Mucho ruido y pocas nueces? El cambio de régimen político cubano." *Encuentro* 23 (Winter): 105–24.

Muñoz, Mario Jorge. 2001. "El complejo mundo de la locomotora." *Granma,* January 11.

North, Douglass. 1994. "Economic Performance through Time." *American Economic Review* 84: 359–68.

"Nota del Comité Permanente de la Conferencia de Obispos Católicos de Cuba." 2004. Havana, May 26.

"Nota oficial." 2003. *Granma,* November 24.

———. 2004. *Granma,* October 14.

Nova González, Armando. 2001. "Las Unidades Básicas de Producción Cooperativa y las granjas cañeras entre 1993 y el 2000." In *La economía cubana en el 2000: desempeño macroeconómico y transformación empresarial,* 59–72. Havana: Centro de Estudios de la Economía Cubana/Fundación Friedrich Ebert.

Núñez Betancourt, Alberto. 2002. "Vital incrementar la productividad para alcanzar mayor competencia." *Granma,* February 18.

Oficina Nacional de Estadísticas (ONE). 1998–2003. *Anuario estadístico de Cuba 1996, 1997, 1999, 2000, 2001, 2002.* Havana: ONE.

"Ofrecen en Cuba reportes sobre las operaciones de cambio de dólares." 2004. *Notimex* (Havana), November 8.

Orrio, Manuel David. 2001. "Mitos de la educación superior." *Cubanet Independiente*, June 19.

Ortega Alamino, Cardenal Jaime. 2003. "Carta pastoral en el 150 aniversario de la muerte del Padre Félix Varela." Havana, February.

Pagés, Raisa. 2004a. "Año internacional del arroz." *Granma Internacional*, July 20.

———. 2004b. "Charley no aplacó la sequía." *Granma Digital Internacional*, August 27.

———. 2004c. "Entrevista con Orlando Lugo, presidente de la ANAP." *Granma Internacional*, April 26.

Pan American Health Organization (PAHO). 1998. "Country Profile of Cuba." In *Health in the Americas*. Washington D.C.: PAHO.

———. 2004a. *Indicadores básicos: situación de la salud en las Américas*. Washington D.C.: PAHO.

———. 2004b. Regional Core Health Data System. *http://www.paho.org*.

Peláez, Orfilio. 2004. "Sequía se agravó en septiembre." *Granma Digital Internacional*, October 15.

Peñate, Orlando, and Luis Gutiérrez. 2000. *La reforma de los sistemas de pensiones en América Latina: la alternativa cubana*. Havana: Editorial de Ciencias Sociales.

Pérez-López, Jorge. 2002. "The Cuban Economy in an Unending Special Period." *Cuba in Transition* 12: 507–21.

———. 2003. "The Cuban Economy in 2002–2003." *Cuba in Transition* 13: 1–13.

Pérez-López, Jorge, and Matías Travieso-Díaz. 2000. "The Helms-Burton Law and Its Antidotes: A Classic Standoff." *Southwestern Journal of Law and Trade in the Americas* 7 (1): 95–155.

Pérez Soto, Carlos, et al. 2003. "Aproximación al estudio de los mecanismos de transmisión de la política monetaria en Cuba." *Economía y Desarrollo*, special edition (December): 22–58.

Pérez-Stable, Marifeli. 1999. "Caught in a Contradiction: Cuban Socialism between Mobilization and Normalization." *Comparative Politics* (October): 63–82.

———. 2003. "Cuba: mito y realidad." Análisis del Real Instituto Elcano (Madrid), May 8, *www.realinstitutoelcano.org*.

Pérez Villanueva, Omar Everleny. 2000. "Estabilidad macroeconómica y financiamiento externo: la inversión extranjera directa en Cuba." In *La economía cubana: coyuntura, reflexiones y oportunidades*, 17–41. Havana: Centro de Estudios de la Economía Cubana/Fundación Friedrich Ebert.

———. 2001. "Ciudad de La Habana, desempeño económico y situación social." In *La economía cubana en el 2000: desempeño macroeconómico y transformación empresarial*, 35–58. Havana: Centro de Estudios de la Economía Cubana/Fundación Friedrich Ebert.

———. 2002a. "La evolución de la economía cubana en los 90s: una valoración." In *Cuba: reestructuración económica y globalización*, edited by Mauricio de Miranda, 65–115. Bogotá: Centro Editorial Javeriano.

———. 2002b. "La inversión extranjera directa en Cuba: evolución y perspectivas." In *Cuba: reflexiones sobre su economía*, 65–98. Havana: Universidad de La Habana.

———. 2003. "El papel de la inversión extranjera en el desarrollo económico: la experiencia cubana." In *Seminario anual de la economía cubana*, 1–33. Havana: Centro de Estudios de la Economía Cubana/Fundación Friedrich Ebert.

"Plataforma petrolera prepara inicio de exploración en aguas cubanas." 2004. *Encuentro en la Red*, July 19.

"La presencia social de la iglesia: instrucción teológico-pastoral." 2003. Havana, September 9.

"La primera exploración en Cuba no dio los resultados esperados." 2004. *Encuentro en la Red*, August 3.

"Quiet Deal Funds Cuba with Venezuelan Oil." 2002. *Strafor*, February 6.

Quintana Mendoza, D., et al. 1995. "Mercado agropecuario, ¿apertura o limitación?" *Cuba Investigación Económica* 4 (December): 21–54.

Ramos Lauzurique, Arnaldo. 2003. "Cuba está muy bien." Holguín, unpublished report on the Cuban economy sent from prison, December 27.

"Repsol reanudará el año próximo las exploraciones petroleras en aguas cubanas." 2004. *Encuentro en la Red*, August 3.

"Resolución económica del V Congreso del Partido Comunista de Cuba." 1998. *Granma Internacional*, February 22.

Ritter, Archibald R. M. 2002. "Cuba: la unificación de los sistemas monetarios duales y los sistemas de tasa de cambio en Cuba." In *Cuba: Reestructuración económica y globalización*, edited by Mauricio de Miranda, 65–115. Bogotá: Centro Editorial Javeriano.

———. 2005. *Cuba's Underground Economy*. Ottawa: Carleton University, forthcoming.

———, ed. 2004. *The Cuban Economy*. Pittsburgh: University of Pittsburgh Press.

Roberts, Churchill, Ernesto Betancourt, Guillermo Grenier, and Richard Schaeffer. 1999. "Measuring Cuban Public Opinion: Project Report." Report prepared for the U.S. Agency for International Development under contract LAG-G-00–98–00021–01. Gainesville: University of Florida.

Roca, Vladimiro. 2004. "¿Se puede vivir decorosamente con el salario promedio en Cuba?" Miami: Instituto de Estudios Cubanos, http://www.iecubanos.org/decorosamente.htm.

Rodríguez, Andrea. 2004. "Se agrava la crisis por falta de energía." *Nuevo Herald*, October 3.

Rodríguez, José Luis. 2000. "Informe sobre la economía cubana." *Granma*, December 23.

———. 2001. "Intervención en la Asamblea Nacional." *Granma*, December 22.

———. 2002. "Informe sobre los resultados económicos del 2002 y el Plan Económico Social de 2003." *Granma*, December 26.

———. 2003. "Informe sobre los resultados económicos del 2003 y el Plan Económico Social de 2004." *Granma*, December 25.

Rodríguez Castellón, Santiago. 2001. "Consideraciones sobre el sector energético cubano." In *La economía cubana en el 2000*, 18–34. Havana: Centro de Estudios de la Economía Cubana/Fundación Friedrich Ebert.

Rosales del Toro, Ulises. 2003. "Marcha de la zafra." *Granma*, March 13.

"La salud pública." 2004. Editorial in *Revista Vitral* (Pinar del Río), 11 (May–June): 61.

San Martin, Nancy. 2004. "Cuba's Tourism Chief Replaced by Army Colonel." *Miami Herald*, February 12.

Sandó, Dora. 2003. "Modificaciones en el sistema de pensiones de Cuba y su incidencia en los servicios sociales." Paper presented at the Conferencia Interamericana de Seguridad Social, Montevideo, June 10–12.

"Sesión de la Asamblea Nacional que aprobó los lineamientos del plan económico y social y la ley de presupuesto del estado, el 23 de diciembre de 2003." 2003. *Granma*, December 24.

"Sherritt Eyes Cuba Nickel Expansion as Price Rises." 2003. Reuters (Toronto), June 4.

Sixto, Felipe. 2003. "Una evaluación de cuatro décadas de atención de salud en Cuba." In *Seguridad social en Cuba*, edited by Lothar Witte, 143–173. Caracas: Nueva Sociedad.

Spadoni, Paolo. 2003. "The Role of the United States in the Cuban Economy." *Cuba in Transition* 13: 410–29.

Suchlicki, Jaime. 2001–2. "La Cuba de Castro: más continuidad que cambio." *Encuentro* 23 (Winter): 125–41.

Summers, Robert, and Alan Heston. 1991. "Penn World Tables (Mark 5): An Expanded Set of International Comparisons, 1950–1988." *Quarterly Journal of Economics* 106: 327–68.

Svejnar, Jan. 2002. "Transition Economies: Performance and Challenges." *Journal of Economic Perspectives* 16: 3–28.

Togores González, Viviana. 1999. "Cuba: Efectos sociales de la crisis y el ajuste económico de los 90s." In *Balance de la economía cubana a finales de los 90s*, 82–112. Havana: Centro de Estudios de la Economía Cubana.

———. 2004. "Ingresos monetarios de la población, cambios en la distribución y efectos sobre el nivel de vida." In *15 años del Centro de Estudios de la Economía Cubana*, 112–35. Havana: Editorial Félix Varela.

Togores González, Viviana, and Anicia García Álvarez. 2003a. "Algunas consideraciones acerca del acceso al consumo en los noventa, factores que lo determinan." In *Seminario anual de la economía cubana*, 1–55. Havana: Centro de Estudios de la Economía Cubana/Fundación Friedrich Ebert.

———. 2003b. "Consumo, mercados y dualidad monetaria en Cuba." *Economía y Desarrollo*, special edition (December): 165–223.

Triana Cordoví, Juan. 2000. "La economía cubana en 1999." In *La economía cubana: coyuntura, reflexiones y oportunidades*, 1–16. Havana: Centro de Estudios de la Economía Cubana/Fundación Friedrich Ebert.

———. 2001. "La economía cubana en el año 2000." Introduction to *La economía cubana en el 2000*. Havana: Centro de Estudios de la Economía Cubana/Fundación Friedrich Ebert.

———. 2002. "La economía cubana en 2001, una perspectiva global." In *La economía cubana en 2001*, 3–18. Havana: Centro de Estudios de la Economía Cubana/Fundación Friedrich Ebert.

———. 2003. "El desempeño económico en el 2002." In *Seminario anual de la economía cubana*, 1–14. Havana: Centro de Estudios de la Economía Cubana/Fundación Friedrich Ebert.

———. 2004. "Cuba 2003." In *15 años del Centro de Estudios de la Economía Cubana*, 1–20. Havana: Editorial Félix Varela.

Trumbull, Charles. 2000. "Economic Reforms and Social Contradictions in Cuba." *Cuba in Transition* 10: 305–20.

"La UBPC y la fantasía de la recuperación agropecuaria." 2004. *Cubanet Independiente*, January 13–14.

"La UE reorienta su apoyo financiero, pero no lo incrementa." 2002. *CN Cuba en Negocios* (Madrid), February 6.

United Nations. 2000. *International Trade Statistics Yearbook, 1999*. New York: United Nations.

United Nations Development Programme (UNDP). 1990– 2003. *Human Development Report, 1990–2003*. New York: Oxford University Press.

———. 2001. *Human Development Report, 2001*. Addendum (online version). http://www.undp.org/hdr2001/Addendum4.pdf.

United Nations Educational, Scientific, and Cultural Organization (UNESCO). 1999. *Anuario estadístico 1999*. Paris: UNESCO.

———. 2001. Available at http://unescotat.unesco.org/en/stas/stats.htm.

United Nations World Food Program (WFP). 2001. *Food Aid to Women and Children in Eastern Cuba*. New York: United Nations.

Uribe, Juan. 2002. "Se agudiza la escasez de petróleo." *Carta de Cuba* (Havana), March 12.

U.S. Department of Commerce. 2004. "Cuban Assets Control Regulations: Interim Final Rule." *Federal Register* 69, no. 115 (June 16): 33768–33774.

U.S. Department of the Treasury. 2004. "Revision of Export and Reexport Restrictions on Cuba." *Federal Register* 69, no. 119 (June 23): 34565–34567.

Varela Pérez, Juan. 2003. "Validez y vigencia de las UBPC." *Granma*, November 3.

———. 2004a. "El futuro azucarero está en la aulas universitarias." *Granma*, March 22.

———. 2004b. "Se aviva el rendimiento del azúcar." *Granma*, February 17.

———. 2004c. "Terminó la zafra azucarera." *El Economista de Cuba*, June 20.

Vicent, Mauricio. 2003. "Castro arremete contra la UE por las sanciones en Cuba" and "La ofensiva de Castro contra la UE somete a Cuba a un completo aislamiento internacional." *El País* (Madrid), June 8 and 10.

Vidal, Pavel, and Yaima Doimeadios. 2003. "Inflación vs. deflación en la economía cubana." *Economía y Desarrollo*, special edition (December): 59–72.

World Bank. 2002a. *Transition: The First Ten Years—Analysis and Lessons for Eastern Europe and the Former Soviet Union*. Washington D.C.: World Bank.

———. 2002b, 2003. *World Development Report 2002, 2003*. New York: Oxford University Press.

Zimbalist, Andrew, and Claes Brundenius. 1989. *The Cuban Economy: Measurement and Analysis of Socialist Performance*. Baltimore: Johns Hopkins University Press.

Index

in, 8; MPS in, 112–13, 122; in 1990–
2004, 26, 27–53; physical output in, 42–
49; post-Soviet, xi, xiv; private sector in,
xi–xii, 50, 52, 74, 81, 82; recentralization
in, 70; slowdown (2001–02), 64–65; in
Soviet era, 1; Soviet model for, 6, 7–9,
133, 139; structural problems of, 64–65,
68–69; terms of trade in, 35–36; of
twenty-first century, xii; viability of, 152–
54. *See also* Socioeconomic development,
Cuban
Economy, Soviet: command, 132; as model
for Cuba, 6,7–9, 133, 139
Ecuador: GDP of, 126
Education: Costa Rican, 154, 194n5; in HDI
calculation, 114, 116, 126, 151; as socioeconomic indicator, 141
Education, Cuban, xii; deterioration in, 87–
90, 109; for elites, 87; enrollment in, 87–
88, 192nn5,7; in HDI rankings, 117–18,
128; incentives in, 178; long-distance, 90;
primary, 118, 128; reform of, 174–75,
177–78, 185; secondary, 117, 128, 192n6
—higher, 87–90; Castro on, 89; economists
on, 90; enrollment in, 87–89, 109, 117; in
HDI rankings, 118, 128; in humanities,
89; in social sciences, 89; statistical measurement of, xvi
Egalitarianism, Cuban, 132; Castro on, 71;
during idealistic cycles, 8, 71; in 1971–85,
12; during Rectification of Errors and
Negative Tendencies, 12, 13–15,17; in
Special Period, 20; in tax system, 172
Eggs, price of, 102–3
Electric energy, Cuban, 45; crisis in, 46–47;
disruptions in, 86; per-capita output,
188n9
El Salvador, HDI ranking of, 125
Émigrés, Cuban, 177; family visits by,
188n7; medical personnel, 176; race of,
79, 98; remittances by, 77–79. *See also*
Cuban Americans
Employment: Chilean, 145; Costa Rican, 145
Employment, Cuban: illegal, 50, 52; in so-
cioeconomic development ranking, 145;
socioeconomic policies on, 141. *See also*
Self-employment; Unemployment

Energy conservation, targets for, 55
Equality: during Special Period, xiii. *See also*
Inequality
Ernesto "Che" Guevara nickel plant (Cuba),
44, 45
Espinosa Chepe, Oscar, 195n8
Europe, central/eastern: GDP of, 158;
privatization in, 195n7; reform in, xiv,
156, 168, 174; socioeconomic develop-
ment in, 162–63; tax revenue in, 172;
transition to market economy, 156–57
European Union: Cuba in, 37; and Helms-
Burton Act, 16; on investment in Cuba,
41; sanctions on Cuba, 37
Exchange rate, Chilean, 132
Exchange rate, Cuban: at CADECAS, 41,
73–74; dollar-peso, 41–42, 63, 113, 170,
189n4; in GDP calculation, 112, 119–20;
in HDI calculation, 119; official *versus*
PPP, 121
Exports: Chilean, 144, 153; Costa Rican,
136, 144, 194n3
Exports, Cuban, 144; decrease in, 67; in
1971–85, 12; in 1989–93, 33; recovery
of, 62–63; service, 188n4; targets for, 56.
See also Merchandise trade, Cuban

Family doctor program, 176
Farmers, private, 48; Afro-Cuban, 98; in-
come of, 73; payments to, 49; in social se-
curity system, 90
Fat consumption: decrease in, 104, 110
Ferriol, Angela, 191nn27–28
Fertilizers: manufacturing of, 46
Fishing industry, 47
Food: cost of, 104–6; rationing of, 100–103,
108; unrationed, 101
Food basket, monthly: value of, 104–5
Food imports: dependency on, 63; reduc-
tion in, 68; from United States, 38,
188n6
Food self-sufficiency, 2, 14, 139; in develop-
ment strategies, 134; failure of, 15
Ford administration: relations with Cuba,
11; trade embargo under, 6
Foreign aid, Cuban, 169, 188n5; need for,
182–83, 185–86; from Italy, 188n5

Carmelo Mesa-Lago is distinguished service professor emeritus of economics and Latin American studies at the University of Pittsburgh. The author of 60 books and more than 200 articles or chapters published in eight languages, half of them on the Cuban economy, he was founder and editor for 20 years of *Cuban Studies*. He has been a visiting professor/researcher in eight countries and a lecturer in 36 countries, and has worked throughout Latin America. He has also been a consultant for many international organizations, president of the Latin American Studies Association, and the recipient of many prizes and awards for his work on Cuba.

Jorge F. Pérez-López is an international economist. His work on different aspects of the Cuban economy has been published in professional journals and edited volumes. He is the author of *Cuba's Second Economy: From Behind the Scenes to Center Stage* (1995), coeditor, with Matías Travieso-Díaz, of *Perspectives on Cuban Economic Reforms* (1998), and coauthor, with Sergio Díaz-Briquets, of *Conquering Nature: The Environmental Legacy of Socialism in Cuba* (2000).